ENGAGING WITH DIFFERENCE

Engaging with Difference:
The 'Other' in Adult Education

Edited by
Mary Stuart and Alistair Thomson

niace
promoting adult learning

Published by the National Institute of Adult Continuing Education
(England and Wales)
21 De Montfort Street, Leicester LE1 7GE

Company registration no. 2603322
Charity registration no. 1002775

First published 1995
Reprinted 1997, 2000, 2001 (twice), 2002, 2004

Cataloguing in Publication Data
A CIP record for this title is available from the British Library

ISBN 1 872941 59 1

Typeset by Bookcraft, Stroud, Gloucestershire

Printed & bound by Antony Rowe Ltd, Eastbourne

Contents

Introduction

Engaging with Difference: Education and 'Other' Adults

Mary Stuart and Alistair Thomson

Our Aims

Engaging With Difference focuses on attempts in adult education to engage with the learning needs of individuals and groups who have been marginalised or excluded by the education system. It is a book about education practice, drawing on theories from education, sociology, anthropology and social psychology. Each chapter reflects on specific adult education projects and draws together common concerns for adult education practitioners in the 1990s.

Our work is based upon the belief that society and education – including adult education – differentiates and limits who can be a learner and what and how she or he can learn, and that this process prescribes our potential and status in society. Certain individuals and groups are thus constructed as 'other' to the educational norm and, perhaps inevitably, many people internalise this definition, articulating their negative learning experiences and identities through phrases such as 'education is for other people'.

Of course this is not a static or unchallengeable process. Throughout history individuals have questioned and subverted their educational status and have struggled for learning which has been deemed inappropriate or unattainable. Acting in concert, communities and groups which have been denied educational opportunities – by virtue of their class background, or because of their gender, ethnicity, age or disability – have asserted their rights for learning. The contexts for these individual and collective struggles have shifted over time, and contributors to this book refer to the specific histories of different groups of marginalised adult learners. Our primary focus is on the particular historical context of the 1990s, and on the constraints and possibilities for adult education which genuinely

engages with the motivations, hopes and needs of groups of
adult learners who have been constructed as 'other' by the education system.

To explore these issues we draw upon examples from a variety of different projects which developed in partnership with a
diverse range of local statutory, voluntary and community organisations with a concern for adult education. The majority of
the projects, though not all of them, grew out of the New Opportunities Work programme (NOW) which was established in
1992 and is based at the Centre for Continuing Education at the
University of Sussex. The NOW programme aims to generate
new and appropriate educational opportunities for groups who
are either under-represented in adult education, or for whom
such educational provision has often been inappropriate or in-
accessible: adults with learning difficulties; the elderly and
housebound learners; members of refugee and ethnic minority
communities; women and working class people who missed
out on initial educational opportunities.

In developing the NOW programme and reflecting on our
practice as a team of tutors, students and organisers, we felt
that a number of issues needed to be explored: about 'new'
ways of offering learning in response to different adult needs;
about the implications of developments in accreditation, recognition of prior learning, open and distance learning and com-
puter-assisted learning; about the respective roles of adult
learners and educators and about who has autonomy and
power in the learning process; and about the relationships between adult education and pressing social issues such as community care, refugees and an ageing population. We decided to
write up our explorations and share our practices and reflections through this book.

We hope that these writings about the issues and dilemmas
posed by our practice will speak to the concerns of both adult
learners and professionals – not only adult education practitioners and managers in further and community education and
university continuing education, but also community groups
who make demands on the adult education system and those in
connected fields outside of education, such as community
workers and social care providers. *Engaging With Difference* is
intended to challenge some of the boundaries and assumptions
of adult education in the 1990s. We argue that while there are
many difficulties in enabling adults with different experiences
to participate in adult education, the potentials for all concerned are far greater when groups of 'other' students are enabled to participate. We hope to chart some of the changes in
structures, language and perception which such an engage-

ment requires, and to open out a debate which will help to reshape the changing map of adult education.

Engaging With Difference also introduces new and diverse voices, of learners, tutors and organisers, and highlights our personal experiences of engagement with educational institutions and 'other' adult learners. Our practice and writing has often opened up our own experiences of difference (suggesting that adult education practitioners are often drawn to their vocation through empathy with common histories of marginalisation or failure), and has posed painful dilemmas about our own educational roles and relationships. Writing and publishing has highlighted feelings of inadequacy – that we are not 'real' researchers and that we are incompetent at 'academic' writing. Throughout the book we each explore what those feelings suggest about the social definitions and control of academic knowledge and writing, and we discuss the ways in which we have worked together to try to overcome our feelings of inadequacy and to make our voices heard.

The book focuses on how education as an idea, as a series of social structures and as a set of professional practices has, in contradictory ways, both deliberately and unknowingly discriminated against specific groups who participate in learning. The work of the NOW programme set out, like many other forms of adult education, to challenge this discrimination. The process of reflecting on our practice has further highlighted the complexity of offering educational equality. The book does not set out to provide solutions. It does ask some uncomfortable questions, questions which we continue to struggle to answer.

Education, Difference and 'Othering'

The concepts of the 'other' and 'othering' describe the ways in which, as individuals and communities, we make sense of and construct the identities of people who are different. Cultural historians initially applied these concepts to the ideological practices of Europeans in the 'other' lands of the 'Orient' and the 'New World' (Said, 1978). Explorers, missionaries, imperialists and colonists responded to the peoples (and to the environments) of these unfamiliar worlds by understanding and constructing them as different from and inferior to the prevailing norms of Western European culture and society, as 'other'. Anthropologists entrenched these attitudes by studying 'other' cultures from Euro-centric perspectives and by explaining their differences in derogatory or romantic terms (see Evans Pritchard, 1937). Through the cultural and psychological processes of 'othering', Europeans denigrated or dismissed the oth-

ers' ways of knowing the world and being human; they released themselves from blame for imperial conquest and behaviour (the white man's burden was to civilise the native);
they dealt with disconcerting and threatening difference by defining it as inferior (often as an earlier, less civilised stage of human development); and they displaced or denied the
contradictions in their own identities, their own difference and
'savageness'.

These processes of 'othering' did not only happen on the
frontiers of exploitation and empire. Within the new European
nation states cultural and political elites established their own
ways of being in and knowing the world as the norm, as 'Scientific' or 'Enlightenment' truths, and constructed the different
peoples of their own countries as inferior and ignorant, as the
undifferentiated 'masses' or 'the lower orders'. This ideological
construction of 'others' was part of the process of subjugation,
just as the attempts by other groups to define themselves in
their own terms – as Azandi, as the working class, as suffragists
– was a rebellious assertion of rights, and of different experiences and ways of knowing the world (Berger, 1972).

Education has been a central part of these processes and
struggles. It has been used by cultural and political elites to define and institutionalise what knowledge is appropriate
(through intellectual disciplines and educational curricula) and
who should have access to the institutions of learning and to
which types of knowledge. These themes can be explored
through the histories of English schooling and initial education.

For example, prior to the mid-nineteenth century institution-
alisation of schooling, the time, resources and opportunities for
working class children to learn to read and write were scarce
and hard won, and they were less readily available for girls
(even enlightened thinkers like Jean Jacques Rousseau prescribed a specific gendered learning in their ideals for raising
boys and girls: *Emile and Sophie*, 1762). Yet the family and community based sites of informal literacy learning provided some
spaces for a broad and creative learning which was linked to local knowledge and the experiences and desires of everyday life.
As governments and manufacturers sought a workforce which
could undertake the necessary skills of industrialisation – and
were thus motivated to ask how education could be extended
'to the people' (Commons Select Committee, 1835 – see Pugh,
1990) – formal state schooling reduced and controlled such
spaces, despite the efforts of children, parents and radical
movements to create opportunities for 'really useful knowledge' (Johnson, 1979). With the development of popular state
education after the Elementary Schools Act of 1870 and 1876,

and the development of structured curricula for literacy and other learning (Pugh, 1990), the forms of literacy learning available to working class children were carefully limited according to prevailing notions about what was useful and appropriate: reading but not writing; technical writing skills rather than creative expression; rote learning rather than critical thinking; the needs of industry, nation and empire rather than ideas about class and change. Within this system certain groups – girls and children of colour or with disabilities – were often deemed to have even less need for education, or as requiring only an education appropriate to their narrowly perceived status and role (Howard, 1994; Pinchbeck and Hewitt, 1973).

These patterns of differentiation and control have been defining features of English schooling in the twentieth century. The 11-plus system determined that all but the brightest or luckiest working class children were destined to 'learn to labour' in secondary modern schools, while academic education and professional futures were preserved for selective grammar school entrants (Willis, 1977). Indeed, technical education itself was defined as inferior to academic learning. Girls were often denied parental or institutional support for educational opportunities made available to brothers and other boys, and at school were generally afforded less teaching time and resources than boys, and directed to subjects deemed appropiate to future roles as mothers, housewives or secretaries (Purvis, 1991). Studies of black school children confirm that they too were often stereotyped and undervalued in these ways (Brah, 1986). Young people with disabilities or learning difficulties – or the feeble-minded as they were termed in the early part of this century – were perceived to be threatening to the moral fibre of the nation (Jones, 1989). Often they were placed in religious or state institutions and certified as unfit for any but the most limited education (see the Mental Deficiency Act of 1913, and the Mental Health Act of 1957).

Attempts in the 1960s and 1970s to redress some of these inequities through comprehensive education, equal opportunity policies and child-centred learning are now blamed by Tory educationalists for Britain's social and economic malaise (neatly diverting blame from deeper structural forces and divisions within British economy and society). Though clothed in a language of opportunity and choice, current education policies are reasserting structures and values which will perpetuate inequality and marginalisation. Opting-out and parental choice of schools may re-establish a streamed system of 'good' and 'bad' schools, and reduce opportunities for children perceived to be a problem or more expensive to teach. The national curriculum is defining appropriate learning and knowledge within particular normative terms (history and literature, for example, are framed by the limiting discourse of a British heritage or tradition). The transfer of responsibility for training teachers from higher education to schools is intended to reduce the impact of theories which challenge such approaches and policies, and to encourage a pedagogical practice which is about classroom management and information delivery, rather than active, interactive and challenging learning.

The education policy of the last decade has not been entirely consistent or coherent. It is riven by internal contradictions: between a bureaucratic and prescriptive national curriculum and student-centred learning; between parent power and equality of opportunity; or between an education in British traditions and an education in transferable skills for the marketplace. There have also been significant challenges and changes to that policy over the last decade, not least within the classroom itself. Yet the changing face of British school education in the 1980s and 1990s has highlighted patterns and issues which are central to the arguments of this book.

Recent educational developments remind us that the structures and curricula of education police and reproduce particular forms of knowledge, and naturalise ways of knowing the world which are, in fact, class-biased, Euro-centric and gendered. In the preface to *S/Z*, Roland Barthes' exploration of how readers read, Richard Howard argues that, 'We require an education in literature … in order to discover that what we have assumed – with the complicity of our teachers – was nature is in fact culture, that what was given is no more than a way of taking' (Barthes, 1975: ix). The culture children learn in their upbringing and schooling comprises and reproduces particular ways of taking meaning from, and making meaning of, the world around them. The means of making sense from books and relating their contents to knowledge about the real world is but one 'way of taking' that is often interpreted as 'natural' rather than 'learned' (Brice Heath, 1982).

From a related perspective, Richard Edwards and Robin Usher show how Foucault's notion of 'power-knowledge' can be applied to learning and education:

> For Foucault, power and knowledge rather than being counterposed are inseparable from one another. He refers to power and knowledge as being correlative, always found together in 'regimes of truth', the knowledge practices and discourses through which power is manifested and exercised. Knowledge does not represent the truth of

what is but rather constructs what is taken to be true. Individuals are regulated and governance secured through power-knowledge formations constituted by networks of discursive and material practice (Edwards and Usher, 1994: 2).

From Foucault's perspective learning and knowledge is, paradoxically, both 'empowering' in that it generates active subjects who 'better understand' the world and themselves, and yet is also controlling because regimes of knowledge limit and prescribe that understanding. This paradox is particularly apt for current educational practices, which are characterised in terms of student-centred, empowering and humanistic forms of learning and teaching, but through which the exercise of power has taken on more subtle and invidious forms. Though Foucault focused on the operations of power-knowledge in prisons and asylums, and in sexuality, he also showed how education institutions are 'important sites of regulation in modern social formations'. Education prescribes normative knowledge and tests the success of pupils in terms of how well they take on that knowledge and how well they measure up to the normative standards:

> The significance of a norm is that it works by excluding; it defines a standard and criteria of judgement thus identifying all those who do not meet the standard. In this way, a picture is provided of what a person is 'good at' and correspondingly where s/he is lacking or deficient (Edwards and Usher, 1994: 5).

By not acknowledging the nature and effects of power-knowledge formation, we too easily perceive educational under-achievement as the responsibility of the individual. The under-valuing of girls and black children within classroom situations has more to do with different learning patterns and different cultural knowledges than it has to do with different individual abilities. Yet these tensions between different ways of knowing, and the difficulties students have in engaging with ideas which do not easily connect to, or make sense of, their own particular social experiences, are part of the process which identifies people who don't 'fit' within the accepted knowledge base as different. In so doing education begins a process which makes people seem 'other' to dominant cultural norms, and to those of us who live more comfortably with those ways of knowing.

The work of Foucault and other theorists shows how educational institutions and policies tend to reflect and reproduce the

structure and inequalities of the wider society. Indeed, education which is institution and teacher-centred is likely to perpetuate inequalities precisely because of the bureaucratic and
normative requirements of an institutional structure. For example, the limited success of anti-sexist and anti-racist equal opportunities training for educators in the 1980s demonstrates
that changing individual understandings and practices is not
enough if institutional systems and social structures are not
themselves changed (Brah, 1986; Gilroy, 1987; Leicester, 1993).
The features of educational systems – entry and progression
rules, assessment and evaluation, processes of group and time
management, financial pressures which limit resources to support different learners – are central to the process of educational marginalisation and exclusion. Professional educators
are themselves constrained and shaped by these institutional
requirements and the frames of mind which underpin them;
though they may be critical of these institutional and discursive
practices, to survive they must accept and even internalise them.

Through the definitions of knowledge and learning, and
through the institutional processes of assessment and differentiation which determine and define success in schooling, initial
education thus reinforces some children's sense of 'otherness'
and sets them up for failure and marginalisation. People who
have been socialised within the framework of white, male, middle class knowledge are more likely to succeed and their identity will be affirmed. Those who have not received that cultural
socialisation, and who cannot come to terms with it, will be
identified as failures. As Scheff (1990) argues, the educational
system offers success or esteem to those who fit the system and
failure and shame to those who don't. Education as an identity
forming process is further discussed in the conclusion.

One result of this process of marginalisation and exclusion is
disillusionment with education and an internalisation by many
adults (not to mention school students) of the perception that
'education is for other people'; it is not about us and is not for
us. That perception, and the consequent non-participation in
education by significant sectors of the adult population, is both
the challenge and starting point for much adult education theory and practice (McGivney, 1992; Ward and Taylor, 1986).

Adult Education's Engagements with Difference

Adult education has sometimes been seen as somehow outside
of the power-knowledge formation, and valorised for meeting

the needs of those 'others', individuals and groups who have been failed by the initial education system, for 'picking up the pieces' and providing alternative or even oppositional learning. Certainly spaces have been allowed and made for doing work which does engage with the material situations and perspectives of diverse individuals and social groups. A significant proportion of adult education activities have always existed outside the formal structures and prescriptions of state education, and self-organised groups of adults have made their own learning opportunities. Within the state-funded system, adult education has always been marginal and underfunded, and despite the lack of resources has therefore had opportunities to be more flexible and responsive, even quietly subversive.

Yet British adult education's mission of extension and opportunity has also been riven by internal contradictions and limited by financial constraint and political control. The growth of adult education institutions in the early twentieth century highlights these patterns. In 1920 the 'Master' [sic] of the London City Lit., T. G. Williams, argued, 'It seems to me that a system of adult education was good if it took the adult as it found him and started from there ... That means adult education has to adjust its methods and its standards to a wide variety of types and conditions of men!' (Pugh, 1990: 19). Such institutions attempted to extend educational provision to working class adults and to offer forms of provision which met their interests and needs.

Yet that gendered language suggests that such provision was framed by perceptions of the adult learner as working man, and the histories of such institutions are lined with tensions about what learning was 'really useful' and who it was 'really useful' for. In 1926 Her Majesty's Inspectors for Education summarised the achievements of the working men's institutes in these terms:

> Some thousands of men have been taught how to use their leisure to better advantage; they have discovered new interests and new powers in themselves. Their recognition of the benefits they have derived, and their attitudes towards the teachers and others with whom they have been brought into contact, are in themselves a testimony to the civilising influence of the institutes (Pugh, 1990: 21).

This ideal of a 'civilising influence' has been one of the central ideological tensions within British adult education – both providing access to windows of knowledge and learning, and yet also prescribing that knowledge in socially acceptable forms. This tension might be most obvious in the liberal tradition of classical education, but you only need to see the reactions to dress-making classes in adult education to see how even so-called radical adult education privileges certain types of knowledge and does not challenge the definitions of appropriate or 'civilised' knowledge. Even liberatory discourses, such as feminism, have sometimes created a sense of 'false consciousness' which values some women's experiences over others and ignores 'other' feminine knowledge (Opie, 1990).

Other aspects of the language and practice of adult education have been equally fraught with contradictions. Adult education has often been perceived and created to have a remedial role, signified by the language of 'second chance' and of 'the returner'. For example, in 1970 the Russell Committee recognised that, 'For the rest of the century the vast majority of the adult population will have ended their formal education at fourteen, fifteen or sixteen and all but the determined few will have found their career horizons set by their period of schooling'. The Committee charged adult education with the responsibility to give adults 'another opportunity' to 'complete secondary, further and higher education' (Pugh, 1990: 12). While this aim was worthy, it was contained within, and perpetuated, a discourse of individual failure. The very concept of 'returner' ignores the continuum of learning and can create a sense of otherness and inadequacy in people who decide to take up formal learning opportunities later in life.

The concept of 'outreach' poses similar dilemmas. Many of the innovative adult education projects which were developed from the 1960s onwards recognised that significant sectors of the population perceived the institutions, approaches and subjects of formal adult education as alien to their life situations and identities. For example, radical university adult education – including work initiated by Jane Thompson in Southampton or Tom Lovett and Keith Jackson in Liverpool, and more recently Pioneer Work in Leeds and the development of a community university of the Valleys in South Wales – was intended to engage with the learning needs of particular communities in familar settings, focusing on subjects and issues of local and immediate concern, making learning in mutual and appropriate ways (Thompson, 1983; Lovett, 1975; Ward and Taylor, 1986; Alheit and Francis, 1989).

Yet there were tensions implicit in this outreach work, tensions that we recognise in our own practice. The very notion of 'outreach' implies a reaching out from the centre of learning and power, and that the institutional centre is the necessary and appropriate starting point. At worst this might reinforce a deficit model of education, in which education-impoverished communities are nourished by learning handouts. Even when outreach work values the existing experiences and knowledges of particular communities and responds to stated needs, the assumed direction of the knowledge transfer, and the comparative power of the centre, will privilege and reproduce the prevailing forms of knowledge from the centre. By contrast, the centre's own educational assumptions may be relatively unaffected by the relationship. Engaging with different experience must mean participating with that experience, 'being there' – sitting on management committees, organising and joining in community events, helping at the local creche – and not just working with a group to set up a course. Real engagement works both ways and should change educators' institutions, practices and ideas.

Part of the problem for institution-based adult educators is that we operate within professional languages and practices which limit and prescribe this engagement. These may be under-pinned by particular models of human development and learning. In *Psychology and Adult Learning* (1988), Mark Tennant shows how many of the psychological studies of adult development which inform adult education are based upon ideas about how a 'healthy' personality is developed through the process of individualisation, and argues that this neglects the cultural and gendered processes of learning and identity formation. For all their good intentions, 'learner-centred' educational approaches which focus on individual learning and personal development can thus neglect the significance of these wider social forces.

More generally, our base and grounding in professional practices can get in the way of education which relates to different people's experiences. It is revealing that books by adult educators about provision for marginalised groups readily focus on forms of provision but less readily highlight or explore the voices of those adult learners themselves. Jeannie Sutcliffe's valuable writings about adult education for people with learning difficulties discuss the details of good practice and what professionals do, but say less about what people experience (Sutcliffe, 1990). By contrast, Fiona Williams and Dorothy Atkinson, sociologists rather than adult educators, use the voices of people with learning difficulties in their book, *Know Me As I Am* (1990). Many of the examples used in that book come from adult education, and they show how some of the work done in adult education is positive and challenging. But as professional educators we sometimes find it difficult to see outside of our structures, and need to include the different perspectives of adult learners.

Even when we try to work outside our institutional perspectives, the financial, procedural and political features of the institution limit what we can do. The best outreach work may develop subversive spaces, but in the end it will not transgress institutional expectations if initiative, funding and control is rooted in the centre. Working in a variety of different adult education environments it is possible to find examples of work which demonstrate the tensions between adult education practice attempting to engage with the needs and interests of adult learners, and the structures, practices and constraints of adult education institutions. The following stories are taken from attempts to work in different ways with communities in south London in the 1980s.

There was a performance poet who was engaged by the local adult education institute to work with young adults in the Brixton/Stockwell area, developing skills in Afro-Caribbean poetry. The poet chose not to work in an adult education building. The 'students' he wished to attract were disillusioned with school, and besides, so was he. So he took his work to the streets. He would work in local parks, get chatting and talk about poetry. The outcome of this work was a performance of poetry which had been worked on during these 'chats'. This was radical education, a real engagement with adult learners and their needs and interests in a form which was inviting and accessible. But while individual adult education workers enabled the project, the funding was not renewed because the tutor could not prove his student numbers. On some days he would only speak to one or two people, and it was difficult to go around park benches with a register.

Turning Pink, on the other hand, was a small theatre company set up in 1982. After attending a women's studies peace course two of the women decided to develop a consciousness-raising theatre group which would work with women through theatre to explore the range of sexualities. The group was funded by the local adult education institution to run workshops. These were very successful, and involved writing pieces with local women's groups, and performing with women at health centres, playgroups and shopping centres. The group was not funded again. Despite the fact that they kept a register (difficult enough in this sort of environment) it did not show continuity of 'students'. Most people only came once; that was the way the workshops was designed, but the system couldn't cope.

These examples illustrate very different and effective forms of education which engaged with the interests and needs of adult learners, and yet which were unacceptable within the institutional constraints of formal adult education.

Looking to the Future

Preparing this book has engendered a certain nostalgia for the radical adult education efforts of preceding decades, while reminding us that nostalgia is blinkered and that those efforts were fraught with ideological and institutional tensions. What is clear is that the context of adult education has changed dramatically in the last decade, and that we are we are working with new pressures which are both opening and closing opportunities, and squeezing adult education and learning in new directions.

On the one hand, the efforts to expand and broaden further and higher education, to emphasise the importance of vocational education, to recognise and accredit a wide range of learners and learning, and to encourage workplace education, have created new opportunities and sites of learning, and challenged the debilitating divide between academic and vocational education. Credit accumulation and transfer schemes (CATS) offer a framework where adults can move more freely between further and higher education as they wish, and are less restricted by our gatekeeping (Robertson, 1994).

On the other hand, emphasis on competence-based training and measurable, accredited outcomes is narrowing educational offerings to the needs of the marketplace, and excluding certain groups of adult learners (especially older adults). Greater centralisation and institutional competition is hampering innovative collaborations and making provision less accessible for other groups of adults, such as members of rural communities. Even in urban areas centralisation is a problem. In one south London borough all adult education is now conducted on three sites. Two of the three sites are not on local bus routes. Financial cuts have sapped morale and reduced resources for work on and for the margins. Borough and county adult education co-ordinators are disappearing and it is becoming more difficult to share information beyond college walls. Many adult educators worry that prospective changes to local authorities will further threaten statutory provision. It is becoming more difficult for radical adult educators, and adult learners, to find and exploit the spaces for adult learning which don't fit the narrow government priorities for a skilled workforce and economic competitiveness.

The picture is not entirely bleak. Adult educators are increasingly aware of the importance of developing networks with people who work outside of education. Opportunities for more creative work continue to develop in areas beyond the bounds of statutory education, especially through museums and arts organisations. Imposed changes are also challenging us to rethink what learning can be. For example, the continuing move towards accreditation may be useful for many adults and may give them the recognition which they need. Adult education has contracted in some fields, but in others there is expansion. In East Sussex, for example, provision for people with learning difficulties has grown enormously since incorporation. Staff development across colleges is being expanded because of the need to assure quality, and tutors are getting better support and recognition for their work. In this book we explore some of the contradictions of working in adult education in the 1990s, and how they can be exploited in the interests of 'different' adult learners. The next section explains the particular context of the NOW programme and the background to the projects explored in the following chapters.

Sussex and New Opportunity Work

The New Opportunities Work programme operates across the two counties of East and West Sussex. Readers who appreciate the economic and cultural geography of Britain may wonder about this focus on countering educational disadvantage in Sussex, which has been described as the one of the country's 'psychic locations', the ideal neighbourhood for wealthy commuters who wish to live in pleasant surroundings (Hall, 1988). In fact, the statistics which average out regional income and wealth conceal great inequalities and hardship, and extensive educational needs.

The larger urban communities along the south coast have been particularly badly affected by the 1990s recession. In Worthing, for example, unemployment trebled in 1992, and the heritage prettiness of the county town of Lewes conceals the highest number of unemployed people for a town of its size in the region. Cosmopolitan Brighton is home to a growing refugee population with extensive social and educational needs and has the second largest homeless, street population in the country. Within rural communities there are pockets of poverty alongside affluence, and large numbers of isolated individuals with limited access to educational opportunities (Lowerson, 1994). Sussex also has one of the largest populations of older people in the country (Census, 1991). Older adults constitute a high percentage of adult education students, and yet many older people have had limited access to educational opportunities in the past – especially women over sixty five who grew up in an age when education for girls was regarded as relatively unimportant – and are excluded from such opportunities as do exist because of immobility, declining public transport and high fee levels, or because education still seems like an alien institution. As in other parts of the country, 'care in the community' has stretched social service resources and generated a growing demand for new forms of educational provision for people with learning difficulties, in particular, for whom educational experiences have often been limited in the past.

With these new and growing demands on the services of the colleges and other traditional adult education providers, and with financial and institutional pressures limiting the range of educational provision for educationally disadvantaged groups, New Opportunities Work was clearly not misplaced in Sussex. Indeed it was welcomed by hard-pressed colleagues in the statutory and voluntary sector who perceived the initiative as enabling necessary and experimental provision for which they often had, by themselves, neither the funds, the time or the resources.

The Centre for Continuing Education (CCE) at the University of Sussex was not a natural base for a programme aimed at countering educational disadvantage. Though the more idealistic plans for the new university in the 1960s had enthused about an 'extra-mural university' which would serve the surrounding communities and be responsive to their higher education needs, in time Sussex developed a reputation for radical and rather glamorous full-time degrees. Its local and part time educational responsibilities were delegated to CCE, which became relatively isolated from the rest of the university, and which generated a successful programme of liberal adult education classes for predominantly middle class and older students in both urban and rural Sussex. Attempts in the 1970s to reach other communities – such as local council estates – were isolated and shortlived. However, CCE did develop a valuable tradition of offering part time classes for adults in partnership with other organisations, including the local education authority centres and the Workers' Education Association branches, but also with a wide range of voluntary organisations dedicated to the arts, local history and the environment.

In 1991, when CCE along with several other extra-mural departments successfully bid for University Funding Council money for work to counter educational disadvantage, this tradition of partnership provision suited the requirements for New Opportunities Work. Mary Stuart was appointed on a five year contract to coordinate the new programme. It was clear that an effective programme could only be created in partnership with the groups and organisations which already comprised or worked with so-called 'educationally disadvantaged' adults, and in the first three months of 1992 Mary researched local needs and provision, making links with Social Services workers, unemployment centres and a variety of voluntary and community groups.

Six months into the project and a programme was running which included work with individual women and women's groups; with people with disabilities and learning difficulties; with older adults who because of disability, illness or income were unable to attend regular adult education classes; with unemployed people and members of minority ethnic communities; and with men and women whose basic education had been limited. Participants were recuited through extensive publicity, though as with other similar projects, most joined courses because of personal contacts and word of mouth, because they trusted a recommendation and felt that the learning would be appropriate and accessible.

From the outset, a central principle of the NOW programme was that we should engage with people's needs and experiences, not try to fit them into ours. This has stretched our definition of education, and challenged taken-for-granted practices and procedures. Courses and classes are not the only approach. Contact with groups, advising and supporting projects set up by groups, and providing resources such as use of the university television studio, are as much a part of the programme as is traditional course provision. Such diverse approaches have both required and generated partnerships, and have created different roles, different structures, and plenty of problems and dilemmas! The following chapters will explore those issues, which can be briefly summarised as follows.

Firstly, CCE is part of a large and heirarchical educational institution with a set of loosely held assumptions about the nature and purpose of higher education. How has NOW provision been constrained by these structures and assumptions, and to what extent has it challenged the practices of both CCE and the wider institution?

Secondly, within NOW provision and at a more personal level, this engagement with difference has sometimes challenged power relations and attitudes which do not value 'other' experiences. Organisers, care workers and tutors in various contexts have often had to deal with difficult personal and social issues (of the students, and for ourselves). This has been 'scary stuff', causing us to question our self-perceptions and roles as much as that of the adults we are working with. For example, we have begun to see how even the language we use to describe our work – 'our students' – can pigeon-hole and patronise, and reduce participants' chances of defining themselves and their learning in their own terms.

Thirdly, our work in the NOW programme has highlighted the fact that difference is multiple and fractured, that there are many sources of educational marginalisation and exclusion – for example, inequalities related to gender and learning difficulties often cut across or reinforce each other. A major challenge in our work has been recognising these multiple differences and developing appropriate responses.

Fourthly, we have also recognised a significant tension between what we perceive to be subversive education – exploration of sources of oppression and of the construction of difference, and development of assertive personal and social attitudes – and the survival skills for economic security and social adjustment which students often expect and demand, and which are a government priority. Yet it is also clear that what participants in NOW provision want, and what they perceive to be of value in their lives, often changes through their explorations of identity and learning.

Fifthly, the changing political context presents both threats and opportunities for the NOW programme and other similar work. It is not yet clear whether new funding arrangements for university adult continuing education will maintain support for programmes aimed at countering educational disadvantage. Will funding pressures allow for small classes and alternative forms of provision which do not produce students and registers? Will pressures towards accreditation create assessment obstacles for disadvantaged learners or will they generate empowerment through recognition and progression? Will our partnership provision survive the centralisation of further education and the financial pressures which are biting both voluntary and statutory organisations? Higher education has, perhaps paradoxically, afforded support for innovative work which is becoming harder to sustain in further and local authority education. Will higher education itself continue to see such work as part of its profile?

Writing About Engagement With Difference

A further set of questions have been posed by the processes of writing this book. In producing the book we have tried to maintain our commitment to enabling the diversity of people's experiences to be visible and heard. The idea for the book came from Mary. As co-ordinator of the programme, she had to write an annual report on NOW's progress. Doing this alone did not reflect the range of different participants in the programme and, given the nature of reports, it would emphasise the contribution of the co-ordinator in the hope of securing a job in the university. By contrast, writing a book with some of the people involved in the programme reflected the nature of the work and offered us all an opportunity to consider our practice and challenge it further.

Having decided to take this approach, Mary became quite nervous. She had never produced a book before and was still new to the university culture of research and publication. At this point Al came into the writing project. As the CCE person responsible for continuing education research and development, he had worked with Mary since 1992, offering support, ideas and help with fundraising. He had also recently had his own first book published, and had developed some of the skills and confidence necessary for working with words towards publication. For Mary, perhaps the most frightening part of doing this book has been giving up some of the power to state what NOW was about: she had to take seriously her theoretical position about the production and ownership of knowledge. By deciding to ask people to reflect on projects they had been involved in, she was saying to tutors who teach, students who learn and members of the NOW partnership, 'here is your chance to say what you think we've been doing'.

In fact, the collaborative process of making this book has provided some of its most fruitful lessons. Each chapter explores a different NOW project from 1992 and 1993, and has been created by project participants including organisers, tutors and, in some cases, students. The chapter authors met as a group with Mary and Al for a working lunch once a week throughout the Spring term of 1994. We pored over chapter outlines and drafts, offering comments and suggestions, and found these sessions very exciting. Each set of contributors was then able to take away their draft and work it up for publication.

Working together on our chapters highlighted a number of issues. Firstly, the writing process itself exposed our own feelings of inadequacy, and reminded us that like many adult educators we have 'other' histories, experiences and identities. Through writing about our work with a wide range of people and groups, we are discovering that not only is difference itself fractured (there is not one different experience but many), but also that difference exists within us. The book's editors, for example, could not seen as traditional British academics. Mary is a mature woman 'returner' to education, and neither Al nor Mary is British; both come from the New World and share experiences of immigration and exile, and a sense of 'otherness' within British culture and society. Secondly, most of the contributors to the book have never written academically before, and for some this has been a frightening and challenging experience, as Kathy Smith recalls in her chapter:

> Having started to put pen to paper, after lots of stops and starts, I have begun again, because it occured to me that as I have never been asked to be involved in writing a book before, I feel very much alone in this and it made me realise how many of the people with learning difficulties must feel in coming to learning.

Academic writing and publishing is regarded by many people, including many adult education practitioners, as an exclusive and intimidating world: academic writing 'is for other people'! By working on our writing together we found support to overcome this feeling of inadequacy, and we learnt some of the requirements and rules of academic writing. At the same time, we wanted to avoid what we felt to be a problem with much academic writing, which denies or conceals the author's autobiographical experiences and what he or she brings to research and writing, and we determined to be present in our chapters. We hope the book will encourage both adult educators and adult students who often feel marginalised and 'different' to the people who seem to write books, and that they will see themselves both in the projects we describe and as writers about their own work.

Thirdly, and related to this sense of audience, we recognised a tension between reflection upon practice through theoretical debates, and maintaining an accessible dialogue with a readership of practitioners. Language became a major concern in our writing workshops, and we attempted to find a balance between clear, strong and assertive language on the one hand, and writing which allowed for nuance, complexity and contradiction. For some, the editing process became more problematic, and questions were posed about whose voices we are enabling to be heard. Mary and Al's compromise has been to make suggestions for changes which are intended to make the contributors' ideas clear to their readers. We hope that the contributors' voices are heard in this book.

A Thematic Structure

As one aid to readers and to help focus the issues, we have arranged the chapters according to five main themes:

- roles and relationships
- group dynamics and women's education
- defining learning – professional perceptions and learners'

abilities
- assessment and learners
- collaborative learning – community publishing.

Each section focuses on a different aspect of adult education practice, and has a short introduction to highlight the themes common to that section. There are also threads which run thoughout the book. A major concern of the book is the question of power: who has power; how is it used; and how is it contradictory? Another linking theme concerns different perspectives on learning: who defines learning; how do we value knowledges; and how do we enable learning when participants often find the process of education traumatic? A third linking theme is a notion that education is an identity-forming process. The different chapters in the book examine how we come to define ourselves through our learning experiences and how each engagement with learning further mediates our perceptions of who we are.

Roles and Relationships explores the nature of the roles set up between tutors and students, and challenges the traditional adult education relationship which recognises adult status but still creates clear boundaries between tutor and students. The chapters in this section examine learning environments where tutor-student relationships have deliberately been broken, and explore the success of this approach. Anne Bellis and Sahah Awar describe a project working with Sudanese refugees. In '"Come Back When You've Learnt Some English" – Refugees, Interpreters and Teaching English for Speakers of Other Languages', they argue that ESOL should be about access to society and not simply language acquisition. ESOL specialists and community interpreters worked with the group of refugees for a year to produce a learning package. By using interpreters, the ESOL specialists found their perceptions of the students challenged, and were forced to rethink their planning and teaching practice. In '"I Bet it was Written by a Mother": Working with Parents', Pam Coare describes the development and piloting of an open learning pack of materials for parents with children starting school. The pack was targeted at people who felt under-confident about their literacy skills. It was, at one level, produced by a group of 'professionals' with many years' experience of organising and teaching adult basic education. But these educational professionals were also a group of women, all of whom had children. Production meetings were constantly having to be cut short 'to get the kids', and all the 'professionals' admitted to being frightened of their child's teacher at some stage. This ambivalence is reflected in the perceptions of the parents who participated in the pilot of the project. When asked for feedback, one parent responded with the words, 'I bet it was written by a mother.' In 'Who is the Tutor? House-bound Learning Programmes', Kim Clancy and Mary Stuart discuss a twinned learning project in West Sussex managed by a voluntary scheme working with older people. Roles in this project are constantly interchanged. A tutor attends an adult education class and her students visit housebound partners to share their knowledge of the subject through a tutoring role. The housebound partners share the knowledge obtained through their own private study, and this information is fed back to the adult education class, thus giving the housebound student a tutoring role. The chapter assesses the experience and value of these role reversals and asks how this approach might be used in other situations.

The second section focuses on *Group Dynamics and Women's Education*, and challenges the stereotypical perception of women's education as being simply collaborative, supportive and cuddly. It explores the differences between women – differences of age, ability, class, race and sexuality – and shows how these differences can create difficulties in the learning environment. Both the chapters work from a feminist perspective. In 'Mothers and Sisters: Power and Empowerment in Women's Studies', Gerry Holloway and Mary Stuart explore the use of feminine power. The language of care is especially feminine, and in past and present women's education this language, particularly the hailing of 'mothers' and 'sisters', has been used by women to establish power over each other. The chapter takes a long hard look at a Women's Studies Access course and the power relations which developed among the students and between tutors and students. In 'Murder Your Darlings – Women's Writing: Many Voices', Jennie Fontana and Jill Masouri reflect on the writings produced by a group of women who came into formal learning after having children, and explore the varieties of experience and the extent of anger and frustration exhibited by the group. They challenge the traditional stereotype of the woman returner as simply insecure and under-confident.

Section three focuses on *Defining Learning: Professional Perceptions and Learners' Abilities*. These three chapters challenge the perceptions and responsibilities of professionals both in the education system and in the 'caring' professions. The issues are applicable to all groups of learners. Kathy Smith, in 'Our Right to Know – Women with Learning Difficulties and Sexuality Courses', explores some of the issues raised by a Body Awareness course for women. She discusses the historical context in which women with learning difficulties have been perceived both as oversexed and as children unable to 'understand' the adult world. She explores how the women themselves want to expand their knowledge but find 'new' perceptions of themselves frightening. The chapter concludes by discussing methods which can be used to support the women's growing adult status, and with the women's own thoughts on the changes which this knowledge can enable in their lives. In 'Information Technology and Enablement', David Longman and Mary Stuart consider the claim that information technology is a way of enabling people with learning difficulties. They focus on the strengths and weaknesses of the technology and suggest that the relationships between tutor and student and student and student, rather than the technology itself, form the basis for enablement. Gus Garside examines care and educational professionals' attitudes to people with learning difficulties and their specific abilities. In '"She's Doing Too Much Music" – Professional Perceptions of a Learner's Needs', he challenges stereotypes which refuse to acknowledge people's specialised ability. The chapter draws on the experience of a particularly gifted music student and her battle to become recognised as a music tutor. The chapter highlights the potential for professional training in this area.

In the fourth section we examine *Assessment and Learners*, and new pedagogies in adult education. As the 'great tradition' of liberal adult education is challenged and falters, new ideas for empowering students have been proposed. Within liberal adult education accreditation has often been regarded as another way of setting people up to fail. This section discusses how accreditation can be used to enable 'other' students, and the difficulties and challenges which accreditation poses. In 'All Change: Accreditation and "Other" Learners', Gerry Holloway explores the changing student population of ACE and how new students, particularly working class students, black students and younger students, are wanting recognition for their learning. She challenges the liberal, paternalistic view that accreditation is necessarily 'bad' for students. Mary Stuart wonders whether, '"If Experience Counts, Then Why am I Bothering to Come Here?" AP(E)L and Learning'. Some practitioners see accreditation of prior learning as an opportunity for radical educational change but recent studies suggest that students who participate in APL for credit schemes often do not 'cash in' their credit. This chapter explores the dichotomy between recognition of personal learning and the group learning experience, and suggests a way of reconciling the two.

The fifth section, *Collaborative Learning – Community Publishing*, examines the role of community groups in developing collaborative approaches to learning, particularly in the field of literacy work. Both chapters focus on projects undertaken by community publishing groups and suggest ways of facilitating greater collaboration with 'different' students. In 'Life After Stroke: Special Interest Book-writing Groups', Nick Osmond and the members of two writing groups comprising people affected by stroke – as sufferers and carers – reflect on the experiences of both participants and facilitator in a writing and publishing project. They identify the personal nature of the work undertaken and the need in such groups for mutual support and equal status. In 'Community Writing and Literacy Development', Freda Ansdell, Nan McCubbin, Sonia Plato and Judy Wallis discuss an innovative writing and publishing project which works specifically with people who have attended Adult Basic Education classes. The project emphasises the importance of creative self-expression as well as functional skills in the development of both self esteem and literacy, and explores some of the collaborative techniques used in the project.

The final chapter of the book, 'Education and Self Identity: A Process of Inclusion and Exclusion', draws the themes of the book together by examining education and learning as a process of self-development. The education system has constantly offered negative self images, in other words shame, to 'other' learners. By reflecting on the projects discussed in the book and drawing on new and challenging projects from Sweden (Harnsten, 1994) this chapter explores the potential for offering esteem, through collaboration, by challenging roles and stereotypes, and by altering the perceptions and structures of our educational system.

References

Alheit, P. and Francis, H. (eds) (1989) *Adult Education in Changing Industrial Regions*, Verlag Arbeiterbewegung und Gesellschaftswissenschaft.

Berger, J. (1972) *Ways of Seeing*, Penguin Books.

Brah, A. (1986) 'Unemployment and racism: Asian youth on the dole', in Allen, S. *et al.* (eds) *The Experience of Unemployment*, Macmillan.

Brice Heath, S. (1982) 'What no bedtime story means: narrative skills at home and school', in Mayor, B. M. and Pugh, A. K. (eds) *Language, Communication and Education*, Croom Helm.

Edwards, R. and Usher, R. (1994) 'Disciplining the subject: the power of competence', *Studies in the Education of Adults*, vol. 26, no. 1.

Evans-Pritchard, E. E. (1937) *Witchcraft, Oracles and Magic amongst the Azande*, Clarendon Press.

Gilroy, P. (1987) *'There Ain't No Black in the Union Jack': The cultural politics of race and nation*, Hutchinson.

Hall, P. (1988) 'The geography of the Fifth Kondratieff', in Massey, D. B. and Allen, J. (eds) *Uneven Re-Development: Cities and regions in transit*, Hodder and Stoughton.

Harnsten, G. (1994) *The Research Circle: Building knowledge on equal terms*, The Swedish Trade Union Confederation.

Howard, R. (1974) 'A note on S/Z', in Barthes, R. *Introduction to S/Z*, Hill and Wang.

Howard, U. (1994) 'Writing and Literacy in Nineteenth Century England: Some uses and meanings', Unpublished DPhil thesis, University of Sussex.

Johnson, R. (1979) 'Really useful knowledge': radical education and working class culture, 1790–1848', in Clarke, J., Critcher, C. and Johnson, R. (eds) *Working Class Culture: Studies in history and theory*, Hutchinson.

Jones, G. (1989) *The Social Hygiene Movement in Twentieth Century Britain*, Routledge.

Leicester, M. (1993) *Race for a Change in Continuing and Higher Education*, Open University Press.

Lovett, T. (1975) *Adult Education, Community Development and the Working Class*, Ward Lock Educational.

Lowerson, J. and Thomson, A. (eds) (1994) *Out of Sight, Out of Mind? Barriers to Participation in Rural Adult Education*, Centre for Continuing Education, University of Sussex.

McGivney, V. (1990) *Education's for Other People: Access to education for non-participant adults*, NIACE.

Opie, A. (1990) 'Qualitative research, appropriation of the 'Other' and empowerment', *Feminist Review*, 40, Spring.

Pinchbeck I. and Hewitt, M. (1973) *Children in English Society. Volume 2: From the Eighteenth Century to the Children's Act 1948*, Routledge.

Pugh, F. (1990) *The Art of the ILEA*, Inner London Education Authority.

Purvis, J. (1991) *A History of Women's Education in England*, Open University Press.

Robertson, D. (1994) *Choosing to Change: Extending access, choice and mobility in higher education*, Higher Education Quality Council.

Rousseau, J. J. (1762) *Emile and Sophie*, Everyman, 1921 edition.

Said, E. W. (1978) *Orientalism*, Routledge.

Scheff, T. (1990) *Microsociology: Discourse, emotion and social structure*, University of Chicago Press.

Sutcliffe, J. (1990) *Adults with Learning Difficulties: Education for choice and empowerment*, Open University Press.

Tennant, M. (1988) *Psychology and Adult Learning*, Routledge.

Thompson, J. (1983) *Learning Liberation: Women's response to men's education*, Croom Helm.

Ward, K. and Taylor, R. K. S. (eds) (1986) *Adult Education and the Working Class: Education for the missing millions*, Croom Helm.

Williams, F. and Atkinson, D. (1990) *Know Me As I Am: An anthology of prose, poetry and art by people with learning difficulties*, Hodder and Stoughton.

Willis, P. E. (1977) *Learning to Labour: How working class kids get working class jobs*, Saxon House.

Section One

Roles and Relationships

All learning is in some way an engagement between individuals and groups. Learning relationships can be established through direct or indirect contact. In this section the contributors are concerned with the contact which establishes the roles and relationships between educators as 'tutors' and adults as 'students'.

Both teachers and managers of adult education programmes have a certain ambivalence when they discuss their relationship with their adult students. On the one hand we recognise that adults bring with them a wealth of experience. Many of the students who participate in learning may be older and better qualified, in certain areas, than those who teach them. On the other hand, we are educators with a particular set of knowledges, some of which we are expected to impart to our students.

The issue of roles and relationships between adults within an education setting is further complicated when we, as educators, are working with people whose knowledge has been devalued by society. We have to challenge the perspectives and values that we have learnt in becoming educators. We have to ensure we are not reproducing social discriminations but are able to recognise 'other' knowledges and to incorporate this experience in our teaching practice and institutional structures.

The chapters in this sector reflect on some of the issues which affect our roles as educators and our relationships with our students. Each of the three chapters explores a different learning situation, using different subject material: cultural studies, English for Speakers of Other Languages (ESOL) and basic skills. In each the particular context creates an encounter between educator and student which is different to traditional classroom teaching. Two of the chapters share a concern with the relationships established using distance learning materials, and Chapters one and two focus on shifting power relationships between the tutor and the student group.

The first chapter in this section, *'Come Back When You've Learnt Some English'*, explores how the relationship between ESOL students and their tutor changes when a bilingual interpreter is introduced into the teaching situation. It is still the case that in educational institutions many multilingual adults are pigeonholed as simply needing English to give them access to the wider society. Anne Bellis and Sahar Awar show how an ESOL class drew on the resources of a bilingual speaker to enable greater student evaluation of the subject matter, and to explore issues about cultural awareness as well as language. By using two languages in the classroom, the students were able to get more of what they wanted from their learning. Working in partnership with an interpreter led to a series of changes in the course, challenging aspects of institutionalised racist teaching practice.

The chapter, *Who is the Tutor? Housebound Learning Programmes*, focuses on the shifting roles between tutor and students in a distance learning course. The course described in the chapter involved paired student work, telephone tutorials and audio-visual materials. Kim Clancy and Mary Stuart outline a creative approach to home-based learning and explore some of the stress encountered in work which requires complex relationships with students.

In *'I Bet it was Written by a Mother': Working with Parents*, Pam Coare discusses the development of a supported distance learning pack. The relationship between the producers and users of such learning materials is clearly a different form of engagement to that of a tutor in a classroom. Yet many of the concerns which the users raised were similar to those of any other group of students. In particular, it is evident that the personal experience of the compilers of the learning pack was considered important by the users. As we move to increase the use of distance learning packs with adult students, we need to reflect on the nature of the inter-personal relationships which distance learning establishes.

The questions raised in these chapters are not only pertinent to those educators who are working with socially and economically disadvantaged groups; they speak to all adult educators using open and distance learning approaches. Each chapter explores issues of power and how power relations change when educators try to meet students' expectations. In these specific learning contexts educators have had to engage with the adult students on more equal terms. A common concern of the authors is that when power relations between tutors and groups of students change, both are left in a state of flux, at times unsure about their identity in the engagement. This process can be positive and valuable if it is clearly negotiated and is based on a shared recognition that student autonomy rather than tutor power is the essential basis for learning.

Chapter 1

'Come Back When You've Learnt Some English': Refugees, Interpreters and Teaching English for Speakers of Other Languages

Anne Bellis and Sahar Awar

This chapter is about a two-year English for Speakers of Other Languages (ESOL) course for Sudanese refugees living in the Brighton and Hove area. The course, entitled 'Culture and Communication', was funded by the Centre for Continuing Education at the University of Sussex and took place at Friends Centre, an adult education centre in Brighton. The course, run by two ESOL tutors and a bilingual assistant, attempted to focus on learning a new culture as well as a new language, and this presented a challenge to our usual teaching methods. What follows is an account of how this project, though small in scope and limited in resources, has led us to question many of the assumptions on which our previous work was based. For us as tutors, it has raised important issues about refugee and antiracist education, the purpose of ESOL, and language and power in the classroom. Originally, the chapter was going to be written jointly by Sahar and myself, combining our different perspectives as bilingual assistant and ESOL tutor. Time and family constraints prevented Sahar from being able to make such a commitment. Rather than presenting only the tutor's view of the course, we tape-recorded and transcribed Sahar's contribution and this appears in the text in italic script. Her own account of coming to live in this country offers insights into the difficulty of adapting to a new culture, and the isolation which women with young children, in particular, can experience.

Sahar's Story

I was born and grew up in Lebanon in a small village in the mountains. The place I lived in was built by my great-great-great grandfather, so my roots were there in the village. I come from a big family: I have four younger brothers and lots of uncles, aunts and cousins who all lived around us.

We were affected by the war. Though we didn't have any factions fighting in our own village, there was lots of shelling coming from other villages. There was quite a large number of people killed: I guess about 500 people during the 17 years of war. A lot of the houses were damaged, but if we had one quiet day with no shelling, people rebuilt them again. They always felt it was their home – they would stay whatever the conditions were.

The terrible thing about war is how it will damage your brain first of all, making you expect the worst. You can't see anything except death or being badly injured. I remember one time, holding my baby daughter and just feeling: if I stop thinking about the jobs I must do around the house, my brain will go all to pieces. If the house has a hit, maybe I will die, and my daughter, or even worse, we will have a disability. But there is one good thing about this feeling, which is that you value life. Life is the most important thing really for me: nothing in the whole world is worth anyone fighting for, not money, not land, nothing material.

I came to England in 1984, but it took me a long time – about two years – to get away from feeling nervous when I heard a loud noise. For instance, when we first arrived at Heathrow Airport and went to the underground, the first two seconds the tube went I grabbed my husband and started screaming. The noise of the tube was just like a bomb coming!

My daughter was affected too, even though she was only eighteen months old. The first few months, when we lived in Eastbourne, she used to follow me round the flat, grabbing my leg or arm while I was moving from one place to another. And if I switched on the Hoover, she used to go mad. She's still having nightmares now sometimes, even ten years later.

The problem is, when you have lived through such conditions in Lebanon, you expect everyone to know what is happening there. After a short time I realised, no, people don't know what's happening. So you feel you are suffering alone.

Settling in a new country is very, very difficult, especially when you don't have anyone to show you around or anyone to help you. We didn't know any families and, of course, I didn't know the language. It was hard first of all with shopping. Because my husband (who is a surgeon) was working all day, I had to do the shopping. I remember the first time I went to buy tomatoes – it was difficult because the man was talking with a Cockney accent and I couldn't understand him. And I asked for them in kilos. After that, when he saw me, he just gave me the bag and said, 'You help yourself.'

After three months my husband went to work in Guy's Hospital in London. My daughter became sick and, after some tests at the hospital, we realised that she had TB. I didn't know what to do … I just had to give her this awful medicine, and with feeling homesick and all the other difficulties, it was quite terrible. I used to cry every day, I wanted so much to go back home. I said to my husband, 'Even with the war it is better than living here, really. Here, I'm living without hearing any bombs coming, but I'm not feeling comfortable at all, without my family and the people I know.'

My daughter was on the medicine for six or seven months and then began to get better. I was lucky to find a nursery for her. But she was so emotional and so insecure all the time I couldn't leave her. I used to learn from the children there: I asked them to teach me the nursery rhymes so I could sing them to Sara at home. I also used to read stories to her in English. The ones with a cassette are good, because you can hear how they say the words. Another thing that helped me was when someone gave us a television. I used to put the television on all day, especially the children's programmes.

The thing that I missed most at that time was the company. Back in my country, if you don't know where to go, you've always got friends to tell you, someone who knows. It wasn't until 1989, when we moved to Portslade in Sussex, that I made a good friend who told me about English classes with a creche at Friends Centre in Brighton. At that time, my third child, Marwan, was 10 months old. In the morning I had to get my daughter to school and run back to Portslade Station – it wasn't easy with two babies and all the baggage, but I was happy that I started. It was the only opportunity for me, really.

Later it became very important to me to improve my English, because I had a problem with my older son: they told me he was autistic and I had to find out all about his condition and how he was developing. I couldn't understand them (the specialists) and I couldn't make them understand me. I didn't know how to express my feelings at that time. So it was like: 'Well, that's it! I don't want anyone to explain for me – I have to find out for myself.' Because of that, I used to ask my teacher to give me as much homework as she could. And I used really to work hard.

The Students

The course at Friends Centre attracted a core of about 16–18 regular attenders, both women and men, covering an age range from early 20s to late 60s. Most of them were Coptic Christians, who, among other groups, became a persecuted minority in

Sudan when a fundamentalist Muslim regime came to power in 1989. Harassment by the authorities became commonplace, as in the experience of one of the students, described below:

> I worked for the Government for 22 years. Some problems arose because I criticised the Government's policy. The security officers took me and asked me many questions. They told me this position was only for a loyal Muslim because it needed a decision maker. They dismissed me from my post to a lower position . . . After that my husband also found a lot of problems in his shop from the security officers ... that's why we decided to come here.

The majority of students came from the northern Sudanese cities of Khartoum and Omdurman, and their occupational experiences included government administration, teaching, secretarial work, pharmacy, tailoring and dressmaking. Quite a few had run their own businesses. There was a diversity of educational background: some had experience of further or higher education while others had only basic literacy skills in their own language.

The students all faced similar problems living in this country as refugees: inadequate housing (either in Bed and Breakfast or rented accommodation in damp, crumbling and neglected properties near the seafront); difficulties getting access to health and welfare provision; and coping on a low income – they were all on income support and only entitled to claim 90 per cent of the benefit.

> It is not easy for me because I am now 54 years old – I have to start again from zero ... everything I have is in Sudan. When we left we had nothing. The Sudanese Government allowed us to take not more than 1000 American dollars ... we spent it in one week buying winter clothes for the family ...

Added to all this was the uncertainty of awaiting confirmation of 'refugee' status, and anxieties caused by incidents of racial harrassment and abuse. One of the first students to enrol on the course, a 21 year old man, was stabbed to death in a Brighton street in November 1993, in what was later admitted by police to be a racially motivated attack. This event sent shock waves throughout the Sudanese Community and has increased their sense of insecurity.

Finally there was the traumatic experience itself of being a refugee – whether this resulted from direct persecution, separation from homeland, family and friends, or the stress of adapting to a new culture with different rules. Louie (1987) warns teachers not to underestimate the 'culture shock' experienced by refugees and the extent to which 'the newcomer, finding that the views he or she has of life are no longer reinforced by the society around them, may feel threatened' (p 42). Teachers should be aware that students' cultural values may be different from their own and ' … we can do much to reduce the stress of resettlement by making these assumptions explicit'.

On the 'Culture and Communication' course, it emerged from discussions about issues such as health, that students found many of the customs and practices in this country strange and bewildering. For example, one student talked of how she felt intimidated by a health visitor coming into her home to carry out 'routine' developmental checks on her young children. There is apparently no equivalent figure to the Health Visitor in Sudan and this student experienced the visits as an intrusion. Attitudes towards child development are not universal but vary from one culture to another, and the use of 'standard' assessment techniques can be misleading.

Another area we explored in terms of cultural differences was that of looking for work. A survey investigating the job-search techniques of refugees reported that:

> Many refugees interviewed felt that they were faced with a bewildering and sophisticated system of getting a job, one of which they had little or no knowledge. It is therefore true to say that without intensive training they are competing on unequal terms with the rest of the population' (Marshall, 1989, p 20).

As most of the students had at that time never been to a Jobcentre, they agreed it would be useful to visit the local one to find out what was involved. When I phoned the Jobcentre, the initial response was one of polite incomprehension: the person I spoke to considered their procedures so straightforward and self-explanatory that she could not see the purpose of a visit. In the end, the staff were very helpful, but it was apparent that addressing the needs of bilingual speakers – and those of refugees in particular – was not something they had seriously considered. For instance, there were no bilingual staff who could act as interpreters and no literature available in any language other than English.

This was a salutary experience for me, providing an insight into how the taking-for-granted of culturally determined practices can work to the disadvantage of bilingual speakers in such an important aspect of their lives. Students have often reported that when seeking employment, the experience and qualifications gained in their own country are not taken into consideration. They are usually advised to 'Come back when you've learnt some more English'. Such a response, which throws the 'problem' back at the bilingual speaker, ignores the responsibility of such departments to look critically at their own practices and the extent to which they can exclude black and bilingual people.

ESOL: It's not just about language

It is important for a teacher to question critically not only her cultural assumptions but also the educational values on which her own practice is based. This is particularly true for ESOL, which has often been at the centre of intense ideological debates about 'race' and education. When it first developed in the 1960s, it was closely linked to Government immigration policies which aimed to 'assimilate' black people into the white majority culture (Troyna and Williams, 1986). The assimilationist approach to ESOL was based on a deficit model of black students, that is, on the assumption that they were unable to function adequately in British society because of their 'lack' of English (Bhanot and Alibhai, 1988). The narrow, stereotyped view of black and bilingual people's lives, as reflected in many early ESOL materials, is satirised by McLaughlin in her description of 'The ESL Family':

> The first thing that strikes the objective observer is that its members are appallingly accident-prone. They are constantly burning, scalding and cutting themselves or falling off ladders ... They appear to be very unhealthy. They are always telephoning the doctor and collecting prescriptions, but to little purpose, as once they get the medicine bottles home, they cannot get the tops off ... Their conversation is limited to describing problems, complaining, apologizing and occasionally asking the way. There are some things they never do: argue, express opinions, go to meetings, study, laugh, tell stories, protest, run a business (quoted in Bhanot and Alibhai, 1988).

In the 1980s, the assimilationist model of ESOL teaching was challenged by an antiracist approach. This redefined the problem by maintaining that the main barrier to progress for black people in British society lay not in their own shortcomings, but in the racism inherent in the white majority culture. Black practitioners were critical of the ESOL service and its failure to confront racism within its own practices: its ethnocentric curriculum, its patronising view of black people's lives, its predominance of white, middle-class tutors and its implicit assumption of the superiority of English over other community languages (Hussain, 1986; Alladina, 1986; Bhanot and Alibhai, 1988).

Teaching English involves more than simply technical competence. Such considerations as the types of material used, whether students are encouraged to use their mother tongue and the extent to which the syllabus is negotiated rather than imposed, have important political and social, as well as educational implications.

Bilingual Methods in the Classroom

When we first began to use Arabic and English on the course, it was as a kind of 'added-on' feature to an essentially monolingual approach. Gradually though, it came to have much more central significance. Most notably, the bilingual approach had the effect of redefining the relationship between tutors and students. My own training as a tutor had been in the direct method of language teaching, in which the students' mother tongue is actively discouraged, on the grounds that it will 'interfere' with the acquisition of English. The tutor remains very much in control of the situation. When we placed equal value on the learner's language, there was a change in the dynamics of classroom interaction: the learners became more active and assertive; everyone had the opportunity to participate and there were far more interruptions, questions, 'asides' and digressions. Bilingual classes are undoubtedly messier than monolingual ones and can be unnerving at first for a teacher used to being 'in charge'. This is no bad thing of course. I remember only too well my feelings of discomfort when the students were all sharing a joke from which I was excluded: I realised that this was how it must feel for bilingual learners a good deal of the time.

Hussain (1986) points out that an exclusive emphasis on using English 'overlooks the fact that teachers [are] dealing with adults who [are] perfectly competent speakers of a language other than English and that this competence [is] an asset rather than a handicap' (p 6). We appreciated the value of the students' first language, particularly when negotiating the syllabus and learning how their expectations of the course were influenced by their previous educational experiences. For example, coming from a more formal educational tradition (as Sahar describes later), they tended to feel more comfortable with classes that had a clear structure.

This process of negotiation also influenced our use of materials and moved us in a completely different direction from the kind of bland situations and dialogues found in standard ESOL textbooks. These often fail to take into account the sophisticated vocabulary needed by the adult learner and so we decided it would be more relevant to design our own materials, based on the students' real and immediate concerns. When dealing with the topic of health, for instance, a list of vocabulary the students considered useful included not just obvious words like 'receptionist' and 'prescription', but also the less predictable 'haemorrhoids' and 'appendectomy'.

To suggest that we took a consciously antiracist stance from the beginning of the 'Culture and Communication' course would be misleading – but by adopting a bilingual approach it seemed to develop a kind of antiracist momentum of its own. There were unresolved contradictions, however: most obviously, the relative status of the white, middle-class tutors on the one hand and the black bilingual students on the other. As Collingham (1988) points out:

> ... the ESL classroom merely replicates the structural racism of most other social institutions in Britain. Clearly this is a situation which needs to change if ESL is to reflect the multiracial composition of British society more accurately than it does at present (p 85).

Sahar's work as a poorly-paid bilingual assistant also raises the issue of the lack of appropriate training opportunities in the area, especially for much-needed bilingual tutors.

The Bilingual Assistant's Role

It has helped a lot that I have been through the same kind of experience as the students. I know that feeling that you need desperately to know the language. English teachers can teach the language and they can know what the students need to learn first. But you have to go through that experience of coming to live in another country to know what it's like. It's like a funfair ... just bring someone who has never seen the funfair before in his life and put him in the middle. He feels confused – he doesn't know where to look, what to do, which way to go and no sense of any direction. All he feels is panic – I felt like that for some time.

Another thing is that the system of education here is different from Arabic countries – especially adult education. In my country you have a textbook, read, have exercises, do your homework and that's it. Here, you try to make the priority the students' needs outside the classroom, but they want to learn and have homework, like they understood with their own system. When they talk with me, they expect that I will understand what they want straight away. But talking with the teacher, they've got first of all the difficulty of language; secondly the difficulty of making the teacher understand their point of view.

Also, don't forget that you are dealing with adults – and that's not as easy as teaching a child. We get a bit nervous if we get things wrong. Not only that, but with the quantity of information, there's a limit to how much we can concentrate on. Only having one class a week and coming back the next week with six or seven days in between, it's hard for some of them especially the elderly people – to remember and concentrate on the work they've done. It would be better to have shorter classes spread out over the week.

I have found out that being a translator is not easy. Students often ask: 'What does this mean?' I tell them that in English you've got this word; in Arabic you've got three or four words with the same meaning. Or, we have a word in Arabic and you've got three meanings for it in English. Some of the students can't easily accept that the right word to use depends on the situation. They think that one word in Arabic should have exactly the same meaning in English.

I would very much like to train to be a teacher. Eventually I would like to teach children with special needs, because of my experience with my son. Most of my friends in school wanted to be teachers – except me. I used to teach my brothers and my cousins, but I hated it. I never thought that I would be a teacher one day ... until I started at the Friends Centre. Then I started to feel the pleasure of teaching. Why? Because I was a student and I know what I expected from the teacher. But now it is important for me to do some teacher training, especially as the system is different from education in my own country. Every day there are things to learn from life, from culture, from people – from everything around you. Even if you are 100 years old, you still need to learn.

The ESOL Class: 'Access Point' or 'Ghetto'?

As the 'Culture and Communication' Project drew to a close, we were faced with the question: where should the students move on to? In her recent survey of participation of minority ethnic groups in adult education, Sargant (1993) found their reasons for studying English to be 'overwhelmingly instrumental and vocational, relating to ambitions to progress either in employment or in education' (p 21). The Sudanese students were no exception. They all had pragmatic aims of one kind or another: finding a job or training course, going into further education, helping their children with schoolwork or coping with visits to the doctor and the DSS. For them, an ESOL class was an essentially short-term measure, a first step towards other goals. As one of my colleagues put it: 'The first aim of a student in an ESOL class should be to leave it.'

Of course, leaving the class is made easier if there is an obvious progression route, such as a 'linked skills' course, in which
bilingual learners can develop their language skills alongside
some other specialisation. Such courses seem to be virtually
non-existent in the Brighton and Hove area, with the unfortu-
nate consequence that bilingual learners can often be confined
indefinitely to the 'ghetto' of a basic ESOL class. Because the
ESOL service has developed outside 'mainstream' provision,
the educational needs of bilingual learners have been effectively marginalised. The situation seems to be similar in many
other parts of the country:

> The typical scenario of a bilingual adult entering a main-
> stream college is that he or she is referred to the ESL sec-
> tion who then diagnose the student's needs solely in
> linguistic terms. No account is taken of the student's voca-
> tional or academic demands (Usher, 1989, p 32).

In reflecting on this problem, we were aware that it could
not be resolved within the isolated context of ESOL provision,
but that it raises fundamental issues about equal opportunities
for bilingual learners which concern all institutions offering
education to adults.

Conclusion

In response to the students' evaluation, the 'Culture and Communication' course will be organised in future at two different
levels. The first will be based on the language and literacy
needs of beginner students and will include more intensive bilingual support and a more formalised development of bilingual
materials. The second level will continue to focus on cultural
differences and 'access skills', and will be directed towards students with a higher proficiency in English.

With the current emphasis on certification of courses, following the Further and Higher Education Act, we hope to link the
course to some nationally recognised form of accreditation,
such as the Open College Network. The pressure towards accreditation is undoubtedly a controversial issue within Adult
Education, with many practitioners concerned that it will leave
little room for creativity or individuality (see Edwards, 1993).
Other adult educators see some potential advantages for non-
traditional learners in the new 'competence culture', regarding
it as 'a powerful tool for the extension of equal opportunities to
access to vocational qualifications' (McKelvey and Peters, 1991,
p 65). For black and bilingual learners, who often find that the
qualifications gained in their own country are not recognised

here, increased provision of accredited courses and competence-based learning should prove to be an asset. Whether this theory is reflected in practice will depend largely on the commitment of adult, further and higher education institutions to antiracist and equal opportunities policies, and the extent to which they are prepared to resource their implementation.

The 'Culture and Communication' course has perhaps raised more issues than it has resolved. To expect it to have achieved more would be unrealistic. For the true value of this kind of project to become apparent, it would have to be developed within a larger framework of educational provision, offering real choices to a diverse bilingual population. This is not just a question of basic rights but also of the underutilisation of valuable resources. The Sudanese refugees in Brighton and Hove have brought with them a wealth of skills, knowledge and experience which has so far largely been ignored by local employers and training agencies. As time goes by and the prospects of employment seem no nearer, many in the Sudanese Community are becoming discouraged and depressed:

> ... I think that after two or three years, if I don't find a job, I will be like a machine which has stopped work – it becomes old-fashioned and it can't work again ... Some people I know – especially the older generation – are starting to lose hope, and everyone must have hope ...

References

Alladina, S. (1986) 'Language communication in Britain', *Language Issues*, No 1.

Bhanot, R. and Alibhai, Y. (1988) 'Issues of Anti-racism and Equal Opportunities in ESL', in Nicholls, S. and Hoadley-Maidment, E. (eds) *Current Issues in Teaching English as a Second Language to Adults*, pp 29–33, Edward Arnold.

Collingham, M. (1988) 'Making Use of the Students' Linguistic Resources' in Nicholls, S. and Hoadley-Maidment, E. (eds) *op. cit.*, pp 81–96, Edward Arnold.

Edwards, R. (1993) 'A Spanner in the Works: Luddism and Competence', *Adults Learning*, Vol 4, No 5, pp 124–5.

Hussain, J. (1986) 'Do we Need a Policy of Languages Across the Curriculum in Adult Education?' in Naish, J. (ed.) *Language Support in Education: Report of a Conference for Skill Tutors, Subject Tutors and Language Tutors.*

Louie, G. (1987) 'Culture Shock in ESL', *Language Issues*, Vol 1, No 2, pp 42–3.

Marshall, T. (1989) *Cultural Aspects of Job-Hunting*, Refugee Council.

McKelvey, C. and Peters, H. (1991) 'NVQs and Language', *Adults Learning*, Vol 3, No 3, pp 65–6.

Sargant, N. (1993) *Learning for a Purpose: Participation in Education and Training by Adults from Ethnic Minorities*, National Institute of Adult Continuing Education.

Troyna, B. and Williams, J. (1986) *Racism, Education and the State*, Croom Helm.

Usher, G (1989) 'English as a Second Language, Language Support and Anti-racist Education: Language Policies in Further and Adult Education', *Language Issues*, Vol 3, No 1, pp 31–5.

Chapter 2

'I Bet it was Written by a Mother': Working with Parents

Pam Coare

When I was originally asked to contribute a chapter to this book, a colleague commented, 'Well, you'll get the oven cleaned.' We shared the joke because we have in common a desire to evade tasks and situations that we know could expose our weaknesses to others. We avoid putting pen to paper in case the end result is ridiculed for its style or lack of content. This insecurity also lies at the heart of our dealings with unfamiliar institutions, our often unacknowledged fear that we will be the only one who doesn't understand, that we'll not only get the answer wrong, but that we won't even know the right question to ask.

The Working with Parents project grew out of a concern to address the feelings that make us reluctant to participate in a major area of our children's lives, their school days. Schools, like many professional organisations, have mixed feelings about their clients. There is a genuine desire to include parents in the education of their children, and this is done to varying degrees in all schools, though most notably and with clearer success in primary schools. For many such schools, the education process would be greatly diminished if parents did not act as a support for classroom teachers and, with diminishing budgets, parents are a valuable resource of knowledge and experience. Yet there is also a desire among teachers to retain a 'professional' status, to maintain the mystique of the group, excluding those who are untrained in education. Professionals thus develop a shorthand, a language which protects and nurtures those within the institution. At its simplest this says 'Don't make it look or sound too easy or they'll all think they can do it.' Hence the jargon and the ever-increasing use of acronyms: it keeps us just ignorant enough to be kept firmly in our place.

Many schools are doing something to challenge this mystique, this desire for exclusivity, but if parents still feel excluded, clearly not enough is being achieved. The perception of parents who feel less confident with the language of education and the written word in general, or whose own experience of formal education has made them fearful of participation, needs to be addressed.

These feelings of exclusion and of being made to feel the over-anxious, or alternatively overbearing, parent were shared by those involved in the project. Surprisingly, this was also the common experience of those of us whose working life had been within schools or colleges, teachers and educationalists who, wearing another hat, were parents, and in particular mothers.

The Working with Parents project was an extension of a National two-year project called ADEPT (Adult Educators, Parents and Teachers), which targeted fifty local education authorities. This initial project in 1990, involved the Adult Basic Education facilitators in West Sussex with local primary and secondary schools, and focused on the ways in which schools successfully, or otherwise, kept parents informed of education policies, national debate, and school news. Many teachers involved in the pilot recognised that parents were under-confident about the role they could play in their children's education and felt excluded by the schools. Thus the second stage of the project, Working with Parents, was seen as an opportunity to redress an imbalance, to look at current school practice, and, based upon this, to produce a Learning Resource Pack for use by groups of parents.

A Parent Teacher Association?

> Somehow we must all open up to the possibility of being teachers, of assisting each other and not holding on selfishly to the little we know, or undervaluing that knowledge (Kohl, 1973).

The project had initially involved Adult Basic Education workers, as research carried out indicated that parents with limited literacy skills were most likely to feel excluded from the education of their children. Schools were noticing a particular group of parents who were reluctant to identify with the school, and who, in some instances, were the parents of the most disaffected students. These parents did not attend on occasions when teachers discussed a child's progress, did not become involved in the social activities of schools such as parent teacher associations, and failed to respond to written communications. This distancing from school life was often mirrored in the child's attitude to the institution.

Parents' unwillingness or inability to participate in school life can, of course, have many causes that have nothing to do with feelings of antipathy or lack of skills. The pressures of work and family are often the underlying causes of a failure to participate in the educational life of our children. However, for adults whose own experience of the education process has been unhappy and unrewarding, and who feel unable to compete in this field of competence, it is hardly surprising that they choose to opt out.

If the education system has rewarded some of us, has deemed us successful, it has in turn diminished and demoralized others who do not meet its expectations or goals. Too often the education system has alloted people 'boxes': failed or passed, academic or vocational, professional or parent, literate or illiterate. This is how we create the 'other' in our schools, how we identify and label those who are not like us.

The Adult Literacy Scheme, (since renamed Adult Basic Education) began in the 1970s to help, in a clearly paternalistic way, illiterate adults to climb out of their designated 'box'. Of course, most people are not illiterate: they have literacy skills, but through lack of confidence or competence, they feel unable to participate in the written world. This is a growing problem in a world that increasingly demands our sophisticated use of the printed word. This lack of basic literacy skills has a disproportionate effect on people's lives: they are more likely to be poorer that average, have fewer job opportunities and face long and frequent periods of unemployment, regardless of other skills and abilities. Research carried out both in this country and in the United States of America, has shown an intergenerational effect of poor basic skills:

> Children of parents who have limited competence in reading are between two and three times as likely to struggle and underachieve as other children. 72 per cent of children from families where parents had reading problems and who were in the lowest income group, were in the lowest reading score group. 54 per cent of children from families where parents had reading problems and who had no school qualifications, were in the lowest reading score group (ALBSU, 1993).

From their earliest days, Adult Literacy schemes throughout the country were working with adults who had sought help specifically at the time when their own children were taking their first steps in formal education. Research, therefore, showed what many parents knew and were seeking to redress: their inability to support their child in acquiring new skills and building on these throughout their early school years.

Parents who involve themselves in teaching their own children to read, and who regularly spend time reading to their children, usually produce confident readers whatever the school offers. In other words, the home background of the child has a stronger impact on whether or not he/she becomes a good reader than teachers' techniques in schools (HMI, 1991).

Informed by these ideas, the Working with Parents Resource Pack aimed for a number of positive outcomes. The Pack would address the literacy needs of parents, promote and encourage parents to develop the literacy skills of their children and equip parents with the skills and confidence to build a more equal partnership with their children's schools.

Packing

The Working with Parents pack was a collaborative effort involving staff working in the Centre for Continuing Education at the University of Sussex, in the West Sussex Adult Basic Education service and in Adult Education, who shared a common background as adult educators with experience of literacy teaching. We were also all mothers, and were, therefore, a group of five professionals who had encountered school bureaucracy as parents. These two common experiences, literacy teaching and motherhood, were drawn on continuously as the resource pack took shape, and we could share these experiences most readily when deciding which material was important and should be included, and which we felt was least relevant to the needs of those who would use the pack.

We agreed that the pack would serve as a basic resource to be used in a supported Open Learning framework, as we felt parents would be more comfortable in a collaborative, informal situation. We also expected the pack to be useful in a variety of settings, many of which would not be clearly identified with Adult Basic Education provision.

So we started at what is, for many parents, the first point of contact with their local school: the school prospectus. In an age where schools are competing for children, where finance is apportioned in direct relation to the number of parents who opt to send their children to a particular school, the prospectus has become a powerful marketing tool. It has become the public voice of the school and as such needs to speak to potential parents clearly and unambiguously about the school's hopes, aims and expectations. The prospectus is of little use if it speaks in a language that is not shared by those it is trying to influence, parents who wish to make an informed choice about their children's education. Government legislation has also required schools to include information ranging from academic performance to the cost of school uniform, which has empowered more parents in making their decision. However, many parents need to be supported through the educational maze of this new age of choice.

The working party began by looking at a selection of school prospectuses from the areas in which we lived, and in the areas in which we hoped to pilot the resource pack. It was clear from the sheer variety of these that some schools had made a conscious effort to offer clear information to parents. In many, however, the information was unclear, lengthy and wrapped in the protective jargon of the profession. A policy of 'plain English' was clearly a priority for the resource pack.

We were also aware that there were many related issues of language and access which parents needed to feel confident about if they were to support their child when starting school. At this point, we decided to identify the main elements we wanted to include in the pack, the strands that, when drawn together, would enable participating parents to have confidence to work cooperatively and effectively with the schools. The pack would be the basic resource and would be added to where necessary to meet the needs of the particular user groups. It would contain examples of school prospectuses, to enable parents to discuss with the group facilitator possible opportunities and provision, and examples of forms and letters that parents were likely to meet when their child started school. Also included was a glossary of educational terms and acronyms. If we, as professionals, were lost in the mire of attainment targets, KS2, differentiation, SATS and the cross-curriculum, what chance was there for most parents? (I should add at this point that we were forced to look up most of these terms before we could agree what they did mean!) We agreed finally to include one other element, a pre-school 'starter' kit, closely based on that offered in West Sussex to parents of children who are shortly to start school. We were aware that parents with limited literacy skills find it more difficult to provide the pre-school skills that lead to competence in reading and writing. Indeed, many parents with a broader range of literacy competences were keen to know how they could help their children prepare for school when the similar pack was first introduced in West Sussex schools. Our kit would contain a reading book to share with the child, along with an accompanying tape of the story, a booklet discussing 'towards independence', 'sharing books', and 'doing things together'. Also included was a pamphlet on helping your child with reading and writing. This was produced in a variety of languages and was our first inclusion of material for parents who did not speak English as their first language.

As the pack grew out of our shared concerns and experiences, perhaps not surprisingly, we learnt about ourselves in the process. We started to question our own parenting, to confront beliefs and prejudices, to recognise that choices are not always made for sound educational reasons, that expediency and convenience play their part. Included in the pack was the opportunity to use a computer 'Education Game' that had been devised by the BBC. To decide whether to include it we had, of course, to play the game. It was a simple idea: you progressed around a 'board', or failed to do so as you fell at an educational hurdle, only to retreat and start again. When I played with a colleague we were both confronted on numerous occasions with 'failure'. 'Your child catches chicken pox and can't go to playgroup. Go back to the beginning and lose your job'. Yes, we'd all been there or somewhere like it.

We knew then what we shared, and what it is that we share with innumerable parents. We all want the best possible educational experience for our children: we have a natural instinct to protect them from humiliation, pain and failure. We live with other demands too, though, demands of time and money, energy and self-fulfilment. We have to balance the attraction of the village school with the support of local friends and family against the broader curriculum and better facilities of the school in the town ten miles down the road. We are constrained by poor public transport and must use the local school which may not be the best one for our child, and many of us must somehow fit a job in too. It is easy to share the heartfelt cry of the mother who said to me 'I really don't want the responsibility of deciding. I wish it was like it used to be, and they just told you where the kids were going!'

There were things though that as a group we did not share with the potential users of the pack. We were all white women in stable relationships. We did not share the experience of fathers or local ethnic minority groups, nor of single parents or the homeless. These other experiences and perspectives need to be addressed if the pack is to be useful for the widest possible range of potential groups. With the increase in unemployment, and the concurrent rise in the employment of women (80 per cent of new job vacancies are for women), more men will be

able to take an active role in their children's education. They
will have more time at home with their children and will become a more common sight at the school gate. The transformation of men's parenting role will have wider personal and
social effects: 'Empowerment of socially and economically mar-
ginalized adults can be greatly enhanced by involving them
directly as parents in the schooling of their own children'
(McDonald, 1994).

We clearly identified ourselves with parents, but the parent
of our imagining was most often a mother. The material in the
pack does not seem to me to be compromised by this inherent
sexism: the issues of educational choice and literacy are equally
valid whether addressed to a male or female student, of whatever ethnic origin or income group. However, it did have implications for the piloting of the pack, as the organisations that
acted as a springboard for contact or publicity were those dealing primarily, and in some cases exclusively, with women. In
the future it will be important to promote the pack more imaginatively and not be limited by our perceived notion of 'parent'.

The Pilots

When the components of the pack had been assembled, it was
compiled by one member of the team, who augmented the material with additional examples of letters, forms, maps and prospectuses, and with suggestions as to how a group facilitator
might use the materials. Once complete, the pack was printed
in readiness for piloting with a variety of groups within West
Sussex.

Much discussion had taken place in the working party as to
the most appropriate venues and client groups. It was important to all of us that the material be presented by a facilitator
who had experience of working with people who had limited
literacy skills, and who would be both sympathetic to their
needs and informed as to appropriate methods of presentation
and support. We also intended that each pilot should, if possible, take place in a different setting, because even a small sample would provide comparative information about the impact
and shortcomings of the material. We agreed that the delivery
of the material should be by Adult Basic Education tutors and
organisers, in a variety of locations in West Sussex. Although
the group had reservations as to the effect this might have on
recruitment to the courses, we also recognised the strengths of
such organisation-based provision. ABE tutors were the people
best known to us; they had contacts with different community
groups and the expertise to make the material accessible to as

wide a group as possible.

The first of the pilots took place in a family centre in a large market town. This centre works with the parents and children of 'dysfunctional families', who are referred to the centre by the social services. Many parents experience difficulty communicating with their child, encouraging appropriate behaviour or supporting social and educational development. The local ABE organiser had previously met both the staff and clients to discuss their needs and had, therefore, built good links with both groups prior to the Working with Parents project. The idea of the project met with interest and an enthusiasm to participate. It was seen by the parents as a positive and practical way in which they could help their children. Six parents, with children ranging in age from two to twelve, participated, all of whom required help with their own literacy skills. Whilst this group was predominately women, as was to be the case with the other pilots, one father did participate. The facilitator expressed an initial concern about his position in this 'female' group, but it did not prove to be an issue for those involved. Indeed, as a single parent, struggling both financially and emotionally to raise his children alone, he shared a common purpose with the other parents present. What he shared with the other members of the group therefore was more important than what he didn't share, their gender.

The second pilot was offered at a First School which had excellent links with the local playgroup, and parents were recruited through advertisements at the playgroup. The course was marketed as 'Helping your Child at School' and attracted six parents, all with children at the school or in the attached nursery. The group was, therefore, self-selecting. No overt reference was made to communication or literacy skills, although four of the six identified that they had benefited from improving their own literacy skills on the course.

The third pilot was again housed in a primary school, this time in a small rural town where residents had some limited access to adult education opportunities. Here the course was marketed with a focus on improving skills in spelling, reading and maths to help communications with school, and eleven parents chose to participate, all of whom had children at the school.

Lastly, the fourth pilot took place in a large, urban town with a group of Asian women who were existing ABE students. The focus here was on helping parents to improve their communication skills, with the emphasis on increasing their understanding of spoken and written English and their own writing.

The response from the four groups was uniformly encouraging. Parents were very positive about the course and the material, and were able to offer suggestions to augment or improve the pack. Most identified the need for material specific to the local provision, and indeed the working party had always envisaged the pack as a resource which required additional local material. Most of the parents wished that the course had been longer than the six weekly sessions of the pilots.

They all shared a common motivation: they all wanted to help their children at school, to maximise the opportunities for their children, and for this reason the most commonly mentioned part of the pack when evaluated was that which offered parents practical suggestions for helping their children prior to, and in the early days, of their school life. This particular outcome holds a message for our playgroups and schools: when offered, many parents are grateful for support and suggestions as to how to prepare their children for the startling and challenging experience of school.

It is clear from the experience of these pilots that we need to explore an increased and improved dialogue between parents and schools, and that interest exists for a learning resource such as the 'Working with Parents' pack. However, for a resource of this kind to be used most effectively, to reach parents who will benefit from it, a number of issues with regard to delivery need to be addressed.

The End of the Story?

The Working with Parents project, growing as it did from an ALBSU initiative, focused on adult basic education providers and provision in West Sussex. This appeared, at the time, to be the most appropriate vehicle for the delivery of the pack, and indeed had many positive virtues that I have explored in previous sections. However, this may not always be the case. A great deal of ABE provision is delivered in Community Schools and adult education centres, places all too readily evoking uncomfortable memories of our own formal education. Parents with limited literacy skills are particularly vulnerable to such memories: one man, on his arrival at his first ABE session, gloomily said to me as we walked the interminable corridor to his room, 'I'd know that smell anywhere.' It could just as easily have been the echoing footsteps on concrete corridors or the peeling paint of scuffed and misused walls.

We are all products of our own educational experience, and that experience may be the reason we exclude ourselves from opportunities that present themselves in our adult lives. As educators, it is important that we do not make the exclusion inevitable by offering such provision as 'Working with Parents' exclusively in the sites of our remembered failures.

One focus of the material is on choosing the right school for your child, and if parents are to make use of this information when choosing primary schools, we are clearly looking to attract client group whose children are of pre-school age. Yet the experience of Adult Literacy and ABE provision has shown that parents are most likely to seek assistance with their literacy skills after their child is established in a primary school. Whilst not wishing to exclude parents of children already in the education system who wish to communicate more effectively with schools and to support their child's learning, as providers we may need to be more pro-active in making this resource available to parents with pre-school children. An obviously effective forum would be the network of pre-school playgroups where provision could be offered, as in the pilot, as 'Helping your Child at School', with no reference to literacy skills or 'problems'. On a practical note, this approach could also eliminate the problems of childcare while parents are working together. Alternatively, health and community centres could offer educationally neutral bases for the use of the materials.

The delivery of the pack also benefited from the presence of a facilitator, someone who could support discussion, stimulate ideas and focus attention on appropriate materials. However, the opportunity for participants to adopt this role, for parents to help and support each other, is a development we should encourage.

> Many of us underrate what we know or forget how we learned ourselves and therefore do not believe in our capacity to teach. We are trained to believe that professionals are the only ones who can teach, and that teaching requires a school. We are afraid to teach … because we might mess up the work of the professionals (Kohl, 1973).

Involvement in the working party made me re-locate my position in the process of education. We are not educators because we have a piece of paper that 'others' don't have. We are educators because we are social beings, because we are men and women, because we are parents. When one parent was asked to comment on the pack, she responded with the words, 'I bet it was written by a mother.' I take that as a sincere compliment.

References

ALBSU (1993). *Parents and Their Children: The intergenerational effect of Poor Basic Skills.*
HMI (1991) Report No 10/91, *The Teaching and Learning of Reading in Primary Schools.*
Kohl, H. (1973) *Reading: How to,* Penguin.
McDonald, T. (1994) 'Adult Empowerment: Teaching Parents to Teach', *Adults Learning,* January.

Chapter 3

Who is the Tutor? Housebound Learning Programmes

Kim Clancy and Mary Stuart

There has always been a tension between work with geographically and culturally diverse communities and the physical spaces which adult educators inhabit. The concept of 'outreach work', which is used to describe networking with communities outside our buildings, suggests that there is a right place to learn and that place is in our classrooms and offices. It is not that access to equipment and learning facilities is not important. These resources are vital, but focusing learning in 'a centre' excludes many groups of people who for one reason or another cannot or do not want to come into our buildings. The term 'outreach' comes from a Christian missionary discourse which suggests that those who do not come to 'worship' or, in adult education language, 'the centre' are in some sense wrong and need 'saving'. Outreach establishes a discourse which makes those adults who do not come into our buildings different from the norm.

Outreach is also an outdated notion. Distance learning, computer conferencing and flexible learning packages have revolutionised the nature of most adult learning for credit since the beginning of the 1980s. Most non-credit bearing adult learning has been slower to make use of these alternative methods of learning (Ecclestone, 1993). Many adult educators would argue that much of the 'specialness' of liberal adult learning is connected to the social context of a class of students and a tutor (Wiltshire, 1956; Thornton, 1976). While we recognise the validity of a social context to learning, ignoring whole groups of people who cannot physically get to the 'special learning experience' is discriminatory and elitist. This chapter focuses on an attempt to engage with a group of adults who have been educationally disadvantaged by their inability to move outside of their homes. The chapter discusses a partnership between a voluntary organisation, social services, the local adult education centre and the University of Sussex. It explores some of the tensions which arose in grappling with the diverse demands and the different ethos of the different partners as well as the participants in the learning experience. The project was originally based on an innovative project which Mary encountered while working in London.

Wandsworth Housebound Learners Scheme

While working in south London during the 1980s Mary encountered a project which both offered a social context for learning and made education accessible to learners who could not get to a local adult education centre. As part of the equal opportunities campaign established by the Inner London Education Authority (ILEA), Putney and Wandsworth Adult Education Institute (AEI) had set up a working party to look at the needs of older adults. One of the results was a recommendation to set up a housebound learners scheme. The rationale for the project recognised that although Wandsworth was an inner city borough many older people in the area were unable to travel to adult education centres for a variety of reasons, including disabilities, fear of being vulnerable to attack, and the lack of public transport routes.

It was an exciting project, pairing people who wanted to learn similar subjects, one who could attend a centre and one who could not. They became housebound partners. Two part-time co-ordinators were appointed and contacts were made with Radio 4 who 'advertised' the project and encouraged the scheme by giving the co-ordinators advanced warning of programme schedules which offered the project opportunities to use a number of documentary series as a springboard for courses. The project was extremely successful, attracting a diverse group of students, and courses were organised in 'learning to draw', 'reminiscence', and 'the history of football'. With the abolition of the ILEA Wandsworth Adult College (WAC) took over the project and the project workers continued to work with housebound adults with disabilities and degenerative diseases. At the request of the local community, the project also began to offer provision for Asian women in the area who were housebound for a variety of reasons, not necessarily age or disability.

This scheme is still active in Wandsworth although since its initial success it has been cut back as part of an overall pruning of adult education in the London Boroughs as local authorities find education too costly to sustain. There is now only one co-ordinator although the success of the programme has inspired a number of other projects, including one in Scotland, in Dorset and the project which we developed in Sussex.

Housebound Learning in Deepest Sussex

West Sussex has a large number of older residents. Many people chose Sussex as their retirement venue because they remember the county fondly from their childhood holidays; other older residents in Sussex have lived in the same town or village all their lives. There are many beautiful parts of Sussex, but they can be very isolated. Many people live in small villages without any amenities. No shops for two or three miles, very limited public transport and no recreational facilities, such as cinemas, or adult education centres. As with the Wandsworth project, older adults living in more urban areas of Sussex are also housebound and isolated through disability and fear. For some retired people old age in Sussex is a comfortable life, for many others it is a struggle. Many older people have limited financial resources and are reliant on the support of Social Services.

With the development of joint finance between the Health Authorities and Social Services in the 1980s, the adult education centre in Southwick, West Sussex approached the local Social Services department and put together a bid to develop a learning project to meet the needs of the more vulnerable older members of the community. The result was the Adur Learning Exchange (ALE), an adult education scheme which covered the Adur District Council area around the Adur River. The scheme was to be directed by a paid co-ordinator and a management committee. As ALE was a voluntary sector organisation, distinct from but working in partnership with both Social Services and education, it had a great deal of flexibility and potential. In its early stages it worked with the University of the Third Age, day centres and residential homes.

Mary's brief at the Centre for Continuing Education was to develop partnerships with other learning providers working with socially disadvantaged groups, and ALE seemed an ideal partner organisation. Despite its flexibility the project had not discarded the adult education, and for that matter Social Services, notion of getting 'learners' and 'clients' to centres. The co-ordinator felt that the educational needs of many of the particular target group of the project were not being met.

At a management committee meeting in March 1992, we discussed the Wandsworth scheme and decided to pilot a project based on the Wandsworth approach. This chapter charts the establishment and running of the pilot scheme and explores some of the difficulties in working with 'different' students outside of adult education centres or other traditional venues of learning.

Before setting up the pilot we contacted the Housebound Learners Project co-ordinator at Wandsworth. We discussed her scheme and gained a lot of valuable information on the practicalities of setting up our project. Many of the initial questionnaires which we used to identify appropriate West Sussex students were based on the Wandsworth model. Our initial concern was to establish a course which would attract a large number of both housebound learners and students who attend adult education on a regular basis who would be keen to share their learning with a housebound partner. What we didn't do was discover what housebound older learners wanted to learn. This is a common mistake with adult education, where needs analysis is perhaps seen as desirable but not possible. Organisers, generally concerned with provision and programmes, are driven by the needs of the institution, what tutors can offer and what rooms are available on what evening. What adults would like to study is haphazardly analysed by which courses attract sufficent numbers to classes and which do not.

The Pilot Scheme

A ten-week course called 'That's entertainment' was jointly organised by the Centre for Continuing Education, Adur Learning Exchange and Shoreham and Southwick Adult Education Centre, with Kim as the tutor. The course term was split into two five-week blocks, the first running from November to December 1992 and the second from January to February 1993. The venues for both teaching blocks were a community centre in Southwick and people's homes. The thematic focus of the course, entertainment in the twentieth century, was extremely broad, and was intended to interest as many potential students as possible. As educators we were concerned to offer a course which was not patronising to older adults and to avoid what has been termed the 'fluffy bunny syndrome', where older adults are only given the opportunity to study craft courses because of a medical model of education which sees therapy as the only outcome of learning. The course was to be based in a critical awareness of cultural theory and would offer older adults an opportunity to reflect on current academic discourse. The course was advertised through the different partner organisations. Social Service home helps took large print leaflets with them when they visited their clients, the adult education centre in Southwick and the Centre for Continuing Education advertised the course in their brochures and ALE sent out information to its members through its newletter. A press release was prepared and Radio Sussex interviewed the ALE co-ordinator.

In all 14 participants expressed an interest in the course. Six students attended the course at the community centre and met with Kim for two hours per week. Eight housebound students were also recruited. Each was paired with a student attending the centre. Each pair of students met weekly. A great deal of effort went into the pairing. Each student had to complete an extensive questionnaire and police checks via Social Services were organised for the students who would be visiting a housebound partner. The police check was one way of ensuring that the housebound students were 'safe' with their partner. Housebound students were visited by the ALE co-ordinator before the start of the course to explain the process of the course. Contacts were established with the library service in West Sussex who offered to enable book drops for students who wished to do additional reading and Kim spent several weeks preparing appropriate materials on video, in large print and on tape. This was to ensure that all students would have access to sufficient material to engage with the learning. Despite this introductory work problems did arise which we discuss later in the chapter.

At each of the sessions in the student's home it was the role of the student who had been to the community centre to communicate to their partner the nature of the study which had taken place in the previous session at the centre. We hoped that further discussions would develop organically from the learning materials provided, and would be determined by the particular interests of both students.

The Pairing Process

Pairing the students was an extremely difficult process and raised questions of disclosure and vulnerability. We were concerned that students would be protected going into 'strange' homes and having 'strange' visitors in their homes. Working with Social Services all participants were 'vetted' through interviews and police checks. We found this process useful and it allayed some of our concerns about students' safety but again the need for such precautions highlights the difference between education which occurs outside of the institution, where it is possible to 'control' the environment, and students working in isolation in the privacy of their own homes. Although all the students were adults, half the students were particularly vulnerable and needed to be sure they would be safe participating in this project. Despite the information which was collected and the checks, some students were still concerned that pairs could have had more information about each other before the course started. One student felt unhappy because she did not discover, until she met her partner, that she had serious disabilities. Reflecting on the point, the authors feel unsure whether this was relevant information and wonder if the discomfort derived from a social discrimination against disabled people. The incident does raise questions about what is relevant and sufficient information for the partners to have about each other before they meet.

It is worth stressing that the most rewarding partnerships were between students who already knew each other and students who shared similar interests and academic backgrounds. The intimacy of the contact does make shared interests particularly relevant but it is also important to encourage students to value a diversity of opinion. While we agree that compatabilitiy is obviously an ideal to strive for, simply trying to get students who think the same about every issue is neither possible or desirable. The pairing process needs to be delicately handled to provide all students with the opportunity to debate issues raised by the course. This may mean that different opinions can be an advantage to the learning process as it will raise awareness of the variety of beliefs between the students.

Role of the Student Attending the Centre

Of the six students who attended the community centre, one withdrew from the course after five weeks. He had been seeking a more academically orientated course of study. His co-student also withdrew. This suggests a number of issues about housebound partnership education. In traditional adult education courses, students leave courses for a variety of reasons and simply have the freedom to do so. On our pilot course the student was in some senses taking on a 'tutoring' role and was responsible for working with another student. This changes the nature of the engagement between students. Another student who came to the sessions at the community centre spent most of the course without a partner, as his housebound partner withdrew from the course after a week due to lack of interest. In some senses this is encouraging as it suggests that the housebound student was looking for an educational experience, but simply found the course was not what they wanted.

We were unable to decide how much responsibility students should have towards each other, as an important philosophical course objective was to avoid patronising older learners by doing them a good deed. The purpose of the pilot was to see if we could offer a mutually successful learning experience for both groups of students. It was naive to assume that this would automatically be the case as adults are often looking for different things from learning but it left the pilot organisers with the dilemma of incomplete partnerships.

As the course progressed it became increasingly obvious that the actual role of the students coming to the centre was unclear. Were they tutors, carers, visitors, listeners or co-students? This ambiquity was a matter for concern for these students when they reported back from their partnership sessions. There was frustration from certain students who felt they wanted to discuss the course themes but were instead forced into the role of carer/listener. These difficulties were further compounded by the partners not knowing each other at the beginning of the course. We needed a getting-to-know-each-other period but the ten-week duration of the course was not sufficient for the social contact. The one student who did know her co-students (one was her mother, the other a friend) experienced the partnership as much less problematic than the other students. Many of these relational difficulties are faced by adult education tutors when encountering a new group of students for the first time. However in traditional adult education, the tutor's role is clear, their authority is established and they are working with a group. In the partnership roles were more open and fluid. We wanted to encourage both the housebound students and their partners to contribute to the learning, through reminiscence and by sharing material and knowledge gained from the course and from outside the course. Sharing was difficult for students whose perceptions of learning were limited to traditional experiences of teachers and classrooms.

The motivation of the students who attend the centre needs to be much more carefully explored, both by the students themselves and by the course conveners. Why are they doing this course? For their own academic satisfaction? Their own interest? Or were they wanting to participate in voluntary visiting work? Most of the student who attended the centre did not have simple motivations for taking the course. Before housebound learning was further developed in West Sussex we felt it would be important to spend some time with all the students, in the group at the centre and in their partnerships, setting their targets for the course. This would enable all the students' motivations to be clear at the outset of the course and would prevent participants having unreal expectations of each other.

Effective Tutor/Student Partnerships

For partnerships to work effectively, more time needs to be allowed for the preparation and support of students. Students who will be visiting a partner in their home need an additional initial session which focuses on communication and basic teaching skills. This would help allay the fears that many students had about being a 'tutor'.

An additional session towards the end of the course was intended to help students 'say goodbye'. Students had begun to express anxiety about saying goodbye and withdrawing from their co-student. The session encouraged the group attending the community centre to explore their own fears of saying goodbye. It helped them to identify that much of the anxiety was a fear of hurting their partner. This session was helpful and will be built into courses in the future. We had not anticipated these changing roles and the particular 'counselling role' which some students felt they were involved in.

The shifting roles between students and students and students and tutor were a major aspect of the course and balancing reporting back from co-students, offering support and engaging in subject based discussions was problematic. Students who visited their partners in their homes felt as the course progressed that their role had shifted beyond that of tutor to that of counsellor. While all students did discuss with the ALE co-ordinator the boundaries of their relationship with their partners, it was impossible to keep the relationships as clearly defined. Kim was extremely aware of the intensity of the discussion which took place. The students would report in each week, sometimes positive, sometimes negative aspects of their seminars with their partners. It was so necessary for them to do this and to receive support and guidance from the tutor and the rest of the group. By the end of the session Kim was aware that she was carrying away a fair amount of anxiety and feeling from the group. Although we met to discuss the course, it would have benefited Kim far more if she had had regular timetabled sessions to 'unload' the issues she had taken away.

Course Content and Structure: 'That's Entertainment'

To attract as many students as possible, the course addressed a broad subject area. We were concerned to offer students a non-stereotypical course. Many courses which are designed for older adults do not take account of the students' intellectual abilities, focusing on a theraputic outcome for the course (Cooper and Bornat, 1988). 'That's Entertainment' explored popular culture in cinema, television, theatre, music hall and dance. Although this breadth enabled the group to cover a wide range of issues in a short space of time, it also had the drawback of only permitting a limited depth of study.

The central questions that Kim sought to explore were issues of representation, audience, memory, and 'facts in history'. Her initial approach was to pose a range of questions to establish where and how students positioned themselves in relation to popular culture, and to work outwards from these questions to an exploration of the different cultural institutions outlined in the course document. These central questions would provide a strong thematic link across the range of different entertainment industries we were examining and would allow different levels of reminiscence work to take place, depending on the inclination of each particular student.

A large proportion of the group which Kim met at the Centre were resistant to this approach and requested a more traditional, chronological approach in which the history of entertainment would be 'explained', beginning with the early roots of theatre and moving chronologically through to cinema. Work on popular culture like television and 'stars' was viewed by some students from a high/low culture, good/bad critical dichotomy. This asserted a very different perspective to Kim's, and as with all adult education, she needed to find a meeting point between herself and the students. This was of course initially only a meeting point between herself and the students who attended the community centre. There was another set of 'meeting points' within the student pairs.

Kim adapted the course, retaining the original approach, but also providing more 'facts and figures' than she had originally intended. She drew the high/low culture critical dichotomy into her teaching, introducing questions of where and how value judgements originate, who decides what is 'good', what is 'art' and how our identities/histories are implicated in the choices we make as viewers, spectators and listeners. The final session was written and led by three students. The role of 'tutor' had altered within the group sessions to become 'learner'. For most adult educators this must be seen as a positive outcome.

We include some of the course materials here to give a flavour of the course content. The materials are taken from week 5 of the course, which was half-way through the course. As well as the notes for discussion the students also had video clips to watch and discuss.

Tutor and Student Notes

Week 5

Background issues to inform your discussion on the extracts. Use these notes to help you analyse the information on the video.

What is History?

The central issue to cover this week is the relationship between the worlds of entertainment. We will particularly be looking at the relationship between cinema and history. By history, I mean the very stories which our society, our culture, our country tells itself. This ancestry is created on an individual and on a collective level.

This process is sometimes referred to as the 'popular memory'. For example, stories, memories or recollections which do not 'fit in' with the dominant 'popular memory' are often 'lost' and people forget aspects of their own past. Our society is very good at selecting its 'history'.

You may feel that 'history' is simply there, it just exists behind us, as a series of objective facts, events or truths. But how do we learn history? Through history books at school? Through people's stories? Through television documentaries? Through 'fiction' such as novels, plays or films?

The Role of Entertainment

All these forms are very carefully constructed. They do not simply *reflect reality*. They *make reality*. The writers, directors, editors, actors and so on, present particular versions of events. Conventions of storytelling, and characters are used to present a convincing story in fiction. In news, or documentary, stories are carefully selected and edited. Voice-overs are added, pictures are chosen and cropped down to size, newsreel footage is edited.

In this sense our history is 'made up', almost an invention. It is the truth but whose truth? Most of the people working in the entertainment industry behind the scenes as directors, writers, editors, are white, middle class men. Do they have a particular version of events, or do you feel that they are able to tell your stories, your history, accurately?

These are all issues that inform research being done on the relationship between 'history' and the entertainment industry. People may go to see a film or a play for pleasure, simply to be

entertained, but depending on the nature of the play or film –
are they also learning about 'history'? Are they taking away
ideas which become 'truths'?

Focus for Discussion in Your Pair

(1)   *Cinema/Memories/WW2*
What role did cinema play during the war for you? Do you
have any recollections of cinema-going during that period?
Were there particular stars who were important? Do you feel
that other cultural forms, radio for example, were more important than the cinema?

Examples of British feature films with a war/morale theme
are:

In Which We Serve (1942)
We Die at Dawn (1943)
San Demetrio, London (1943)
Waterloo Road (1944)
A famous Hollywood version of the Brits at War is:
Mrs Miniver (1942)

You have extracts of these films on your video to help you
examine the question of history and entertainment.

(2)   *Representing Women*
Have a look at the extracts from Millions Like Us. It is the final
ten minutes or so of the film. You may have seen the whole
film at some other time.

The central character, Celia, played by Patricia Roc, has left
home to live in a women's hostel and work in an aircraft engi-
neering factory. She is one of the 'mobile women' of the war.
This is an extremely moving and powerful film. It is, I think, an
excellent example of an entertaining film which is also wartime
propaganda. The need is to boost morale. The need is also to
encourage women to 'forget' the old kinds of 'femininity', for
example marriage and the home and learn a new kind of 'masculinity' by going out to work.

Questions to Discuss

Do you think Millions Like Us is a piece of entertainment or a
piece of propaganda? Or both?

How do you feel about its female characters?

Do you recollect stories of women in wartime?

Many women talk about having greater freedom and independence during the war. Do you think this was the case?

Enjoy your session and let me know how you get on!

Student Feedback

All the students completed a detailed feedback form designed to provide guidance in the organisation of future courses. The responses were very positive from all the students. The students enjoyed the course and all were interested in being involved in future housebound learning schemes. Students were also pleased that their course materials were provided in an accessible form. The range of materials needed was extensive but essential for a housebound learning project. The materials may be costly for providers and additional materials funds for housebound learning need to be allocated if a project is going to succeed.

There was broad agreement amongst the students that they needed much more information about their partners before they met. Students felt there needed to be lengthier sessions with their partners. In most cases it was suggested that the one hour session should be extended to two hours each week. Students expressed a preference for courses to be structured more traditionally. There was a tension for the students, who would have liked more time spent in sessions on the exploration of the theme and less on reporting back about sessions with their co-students. Yet on the other hand students wanted more time for guidance on their session with their co-student, particularly when roles became blurred.

Most of the housebound students expressed gratitude at having the opportunity to engage in a course of study. This gratitude could be an expression of how little education provision housebound adults are able to access. The majority of housebound students felt that the course was pitched at too academic a level. Most would have preferred more reminiscence based work. In some senses this would have been more in line with Kim's original course outline but the negotiation of the curriculum only took place with the students who attended the community centre. In retrospect the course should have been structured so that the voices of all participants were heard. In future we will encourage the partnerships to negotiate together about the content of their sessions and will make this negotiation part of the learning at the outset. Seeing all the participants on equal terms was the intention of the project, but it was difficult to achieve. To meet the needs of housebound people, we attempted to change the classroom based nature of the learning but engaging with different students' demands requires a more radical re-structuring of learning, encouraging all participants to value difference, not only tutors.

Kim's Thoughts on Being 'The Tutor'

It was a privilege to tutor this course. I gained enormous insights into both the difficulties and the rich potential for the 'learning process' when it is removed from the cosy confines of the academy. The enthusiasm and commitment of the students who attended the community centre and the warmth and generosity of the students I spoke to on the telephone strongly affected me. There is no doubt that for a number of the housebound students, the weekly sessions played an important creative role in their lives.

At times it was extremely demanding, indeed impossible, to meet the needs of different students. Their expectations of the course differed widely. The expectations of different students posed difficulties in determining the level at which to pitch the course. Wanting to be student-guided in this respect, I relied on feedback from students who came to the sessions at the community centre. This gave these students a powerful role, having to make judgements and assess the relevance of the learning for their partner. Not all the students who attended my session had similar expectations themselves. Certain students wanted an academic course, more background reading, greater emphasis on formal study. Others were less interested in this approach, in fact, some were intimidated by the requests of others, feeling themselves not academic enough by comparison. This created different levels of engagement for the students, between themselves and between myself and the students. The emphasis on more facts and figures posed difficulties in terms of the key themes underpinning the course; the more personal exploration of issues around memory, spectatorship, audience and pleasure. This more traditional approach goes against much current education pedagogy. However this tension in our approaches opened up a space to discuss education theory and made much of the engagement between students fascinating.

There were other, more practical problems. The differing physical abilities of students meant that some students could do little reading in between sessions and needed larger print or tapes. We used a wide variety of video and audio material for the sessions, and students took video and audio tapes to their partners to share the information from the sessions. This was successful, but much of the preparation was done by trial and error. It is difficult to see how this could have been avoided. Student expectations when interviewed did not match their actual behaviour during the course. Despite discussing the course content in advance with one student, we subsequently discovered that she did not own a television, and when we offered to lend her one for the duration of the course she stated a real dislike for television.

I felt I neglected my own commitment to a student-centred approach because the students demanded a more directive learning environment. In addition, to allay my anxiety of student criticism, I began to provide much more reading material which, although well received by the students attending the sessions at the community centre, made their partners feel overwhelmed.

Reflecting and Looking Forward

'That's Entertainment' was not a comfortable course for any of the participants. When we began our project none of us had any idea of the issues that it would raise. The project challenged the roles which all of us played and the insecurities and anxieties which surfaced were often difficult to handle. Yet in these moments particular insights were possible. The housebound learners project was a particularly interesting engagement with different learners. What started out as a course to enable people to learn in their own environment became a course which challenged roles within education, and which was as much a challenge for the students involved as for the tutor. We had not considered the extent to which the students' identities would be central to the success of the course. The pairing process will need to take account of not only geographic location and general interests but an acknowledgement and recognition of different experience and need. We would need to discuss issues with all students about learning approaches and expectations. Obviously it is impossible to be certain whether or not partners will 'get on', but the demands of working with another student need to be clear from the outset. Despite the difficulties, all the students who participated in the scheme would like to be involved in another housebound learners course. However any further work will need to be much more sensitive to the particular psychological anxieties which students raised, and the issues identified from the pilot require planning and time devoted to the project. Many of the issues raised in this chapter highlight the complexity of relationships in adult education. We invest so much of ourselves in our learning and as adult educators we must be more conscious of the processes of interaction and identity in education.

Since piloting the scheme ALE has been successful in gaining a grant to develop housebound learning in the area. The management committee has been able to employ another worker who will be able to focus on the particular needs of the scheme.

References

Bornat, J. and Cooper, M. (1988) 'Equal Opportunity or Special Need: Defeating the Woolly Bunny', *Journal of Educational Gerontology*, Vol. 3, No. 1.

Ecclestone, K. (1993) 'Accreditation in Adult Learning. How far can we go?' *Adults Learning*, Vol. 4, No. 7.

Thornton, A. (1976) 'Some Reflections on the "Great Tradition"', in Rogers, A. (ed.) *The Spirit and the Form*, Nottingham: Nottingham Studies in the Theory and Practice of the Education of Adults.

Wiltshire, H. (1956) 'The Great Tradition in University Adult Education', in Rogers, A. (ed.) *op. cit.*

Section Two

Group Dynamics and Women's Education

Both contributions in this section reflect on women-only, group learning environments. Since the 1970s women's education has been a priority within adult education because women have experienced, and continue to experience, discrimination in their educational opportunities (Edwards, 1993). Historically, women have been perceived to be less intelligent than men, or at least to have different knowledges and educational needs (Gilligan, 1982). Early adult education for women consisted of 'housewifery' classes while men learnt economically productive 'trades'. The critique of malestream adult education developed by second wave feminism from the 1970s included an argument for better educational access and a broader curriculum for women.

The provision of 'safe' learning environments for women also became a central concern of equal opportunities education. Women-only learning environments were developed in response to the recognition that gender power relations within classrooms favoured men. The chapters in this section do not question the need for women-only learning environments; they support such approaches but also pose difficult questions about whether or not women-only groups are necessarily 'safe'. Social interaction between women is also structured by power relations, and these chapters chart how the power dynamics within two different women-only learning environments seriously affected the learning process.

In the chapter, *Mothers and Sisters*, which focuses on a Women's Studies Access course, Gerry Holloway and Mary Stuart examine the effects of gendered socialisation on the dynamics of the group. In this context power uses the language of feminine concern and reveals itself through the gendered language of motherhood. Its roots, however, lie in the differences *between* women, those of age, class, race and sexuality. The authors argue that it is not enough to take account of gender by providing a women-only environment. To enable learning for all participants, tutors and facilitators need to be aware of the nature and roles of a group, and how 'different' women can be silenced through the language of care.

Murder Your Darlings comprises accounts of a creative writing course from two different perspectives: Jenny Fontana's tutor's story and Jill Masouri's student's story. Both accounts acknowledge the support which women can give each other, but also consider how powerful emotions such as anger are often part of student development and learning. In this particular course the anger, and tensions within the women's lives and within the group itself, was directed at a 'stand-in' tutor. The issue showed how learning situations generate power relationships between tutor and students but also among students themselves. Adults who have previously been disempowered by educational practices and structures often lose out in such conflicts. Educators should not only attend to their own roles but should also be aware of, and if need be challenge, other students' roles within a learning environment.

References

Edwards, R. (1993) *Mature Women Students: Separating or Connecting Family and Education*, London: Falmer Press.

Gilligan, C. (1982) *In a Different Voice*, Cambridge: Cambridge University Press.

Chapter 4

Mothers and Sisters: Power and Empowerment in Women's Studies

Gerry Holloway and Mary Stuart

In a recent interview in the *Observer* Nancy Kline, discussing Susan Faludi's book, *Backlash*, refused to blame men for all women's problems. This, she said, was no solution to women's oppression, it was a dead end. She argued that 'Feminism has been an instigator, not a problem solver. It's a position from which to start thinking about solutions' (August, 1993). We agree that feminism is a position from which to start thinking about solutions to problems and see that our work in teaching Women's Studies helps women to get to that position. However, the practice of feminism itself sets problems for us, problems of organisation, democracy and power, to name but a few.

Our interest in these problems is, of course, both personal and political. It is personal because we are both 'outsiders' in the academic world. Both of us are 'mature returners' to education. Mary studied for her Open University degree while living in a hostel for homeless families; Gerry is working-class and a single parent. Now we find ourselves empowered by our education. At a conference recently a woman of about our age who came from a working-class background and who had found her way later in life into academia, spoke of being afraid she would be found out by 'them'. We, too, recognised this fear, the feeling of being 'other', even among women in the world of academia, because of perceptions that intelligence relates to your particular background. These perceptions are problems that we need to tackle if we are to enable our students.

Our interest is also political because we are feminists and, through our feminism, we are interested in how power operates in a patriarchal world. Adult education has always been an area of education that has attracted women. Many of the consciousness-raising groups of the feminist movement of the 1970s and 1980s grew from adult education classes and adult education classes have often challenged traditional teaching methods and classroom hierarchies.

Mary started her career in adult education as a part-time tutor on Women's Studies courses and now convenes Women's Studies Access courses. She has been concerned to identify the extent of difference between women, both socially and culturally and has seen that these differences can often be silenced within the adult education environment in an attempt to only focus on questions of gender and of differentiation between men and women.

Gerry also began teaching women's studies for the WEA while studying for her Master's Degree. She now convenes Women's Studies Certificate courses and teaches women's studies on Access and undergraduate courses. Gerry's interest in power within women's groups stems from her experience in women's consciousness-raising groups and political organisations in the late 1970s and early 1980s. Frustrated with being overlooked at work because of her lack of formal qualifications and angry at being silenced by the universalism of articulate, educated women in the women's movement, Gerry entered university and studied women's history and the dynamics of women-only environments. Her passion is to find ways to organise and network with women in ways that recognise difference and empower *all* women.

In this chapter we explore how difference within women-only groups is structured by power and how power can be used to silence other women by calling on a universalistic discourse of 'being a woman', and how to redress that problem by raising our awareness of power imbalance not only between tutor and students but between students.

Introducing the Problem: Some Historical Issues

Feminism as we know it in this country developed at the time when patriarchy fused with capitalism and imperialism. Although it challenged patriarchal assumptions about women, it did not necessarily offer a direct challenge to capitalism and imperialism. In other words, assumptions of class and race went largely unchallenged. In the nineteenth century, the feminist project broadly fell into two different but not discrete camps. Equal rights feminism emanated from liberal notions of the rights of the individual and was directed into demands for citizenship. This form of feminism was concerned with women's access to a male-defined public sphere and did not challenge the definition of that sphere. Essentialist feminism was rooted in evangelical notions about the difference between men and women and prescribed to each sex a series of attributes and characteristics that were different but complementary. This is a neat, even if contentious, prescription that is still used by both feminists and non-feminists today.

Class was not perceived as a special problem insofar as middle and upper class women presumed it was their right, if not their duty, to instruct working-class women. The editor of the *Englishwoman's Review* went so far as to argue that all women formed one class.

> There is a sense in which we are justified in talking of women as forming one class, whether in 'the highest, the middle, or humbler ranks of life'; a sense in which women whether seamstresses, factory hands, servants, authoresses, countesses – do form one common class. There may be every variety of education, of thought, of habit – but so long as there is 'class' legislation, so long as the law makes an insurmountable difference between men and women, women must be spoken of as a separate class (*Englishwoman's Review,* May 1876).

By regarding gender as a unifying concept, and using this concept as the driving principle behind much of their activity, the early women's movement masked other problems, such as class and race. Some feminist historians have continued this practice by arguing that class is an inappropriate category when discussing women. For example, Levine plays down the importance of class in the movement by arguing that gender has been the unifying idea and claiming that women's relationship with class is associative because it is dependent on their relationship with men (Levine, 1990).

However, we argue that class is not restricted to occupational or economic status, as Levine suggests; while factors may fluctuate, the class *values* held by an individual may remain constant. Moreover, people in the nineteenth century were very conscious of their different social as well as economic status in society and used their status in very precise and important ways to achieve their aims. In this matter feminists were as conventional as anyone else. It is perhaps more helpful to consider the idea of cultural capital when thinking about power relationships between groups of women. By cultural capital we mean the acquisition of certain social knowledge (accent, dress, kin and social connections, behaviour and so on) that allows one to know *how* to participate in certain organisations and social situations. For example, Emily Davies was the daughter of an upper middle-class parson who was not wealthy and had many expenses. Nevertheless, she was never so poor that she had to take paid work. Further, her father's financial circumstances and traditional ideas about girls' education prevented her from receiving much in the way of schooling. But through her socialisation and her familial and social connections, she was able to take a leading position in the movement for higher education of women, a position no working-class woman at that time could have reached.

Gendering and Women-Only Environments

This concept of cultural capital is still relevant to studying and working in women's groups today. Although we might all be women, organising around a common oppression, we still need to realise that theorising about class, race and sexuality and about power in relationships is not just an issue 'out there' in society where we interact with men, but also an issue within our safe, all-female environment.

In any understanding of group interactions questions of personal and social 'baggage' are important considerations. What we bring with us from our past to any group environment will affect how we interact with other members of that group, and will help to shape the dynamics as the group starts to meld. Within our society a central aspect of this 'baggage' that we carry with us is the gendering process. Feminists have argued that this gendering affects every aspect of the way we behave, our position in society and the choices we make for ourselves.

Within education pedagogy, feminists have argued for the value of women-only learning environments, in response to the intrinsic power dynamics of gender, which operate detrimentally for women in a mixed-sex learning environment. We take as our starting point the importance of such environments but we also wish to question whether women-only environments are inherently empowering.

We explore the case of a Women's Studies Access course which attracted only women students. We discuss how aspects of different women's experience were used within a 'feminine' language of power to control other group members. We explore some of the reasons for these forms of power relations, in terms of the socialisation process within the group and the wider society. We also show historically how, within women's groups, this feminine language has been used to both empower and disempower women. Before we can understand these processes of empowerment/disempowerment, we need to discuss how the gendering process affects women's life chances and perceptions of themselves.

Role Patterning and Learned Helplessness

From an early age, children are assigned roles that they learn from their immediate environment and internalise the roles so they become so much a part of their experience and perception of themselves that they see this process as 'natural'. This role socialisation has two effects; it helps the child understand who they are and it helps them understand what is expected of them by society.

> The child must learn to internalise other's expectations for herself ... In this process, attributed norms are first assigned to a generalised other and then are incorporated into the child's own normative system. What was once my mother does not approve of me eating with my fingers becomes everyone who is important disapproves my eating with my fingers (Biddle, 1979).

These expectations and conceptions become understood as the 'self'. We take the meaning of who we are from our interactions with 'others' (Mead, 1932). The 'selves' that emerge are radically different for boys and girls. Even from the first few months of life, parents and care-takers are shown to treat their male and female children differently. For example, parents perceive girls to be more fragile than boys, and they will spend more time encouraging girls to smile than boys. These early perceptions mirror gender stereotypes for men and women and lay the ground work for women and men's gender identities. 'In our society, dominance and mechanical interests are characteristic of men, succourance and social sensitivity of women' (Biddle, 1979).

Many of the women on the Women's Studies Access course spoke of differential parental attitudes between themselves and their brothers as a factor that contributed to their negative self image.

> I couldn't imagine myself being brainy. My parents always said it was my brother who was the clever one. He got to go to college, I always thought I would do better doing nursing or something (Carol, a student on the Women's Studies Access Course 1993).

Sensitivity and care are attributes that encourage self denial, a constant awareness of others' needs at one's own expense. This process of self denial will encourage a sense of insecurity and lack of ability. The process of encouraging 'gentleness' within girls has been identified as a major influence upon their academic performance in school. One study by a group of social psychologists examined learned helplessness – that state where effort is reduced because failure seems certain. Rather than attempting academically difficult problems, many girls tend to avoid them, fearing failure and the subsequent loss of teacher approval (Richardson, 1988).

In researching 'School Power Cultures', Lynn Davies identifies a series of lifescripts 'written' for people in organisations, which they then 'live out' through interaction with others. People begin to have a life story written for them; teachers develop a series of expectations about the children they encounter. These become fixed over time creating a narrative in which the child is the main character. She will internalise this narrative, creating her own identity out of the script. Davies' analysis of 'pupil power' explains how students use deviant scripts to try to re-assert power over the institution that has denied them dignity (Davies, 1992). These scripts will have gender characteristics, either male/confrontational, or female/sexual innuendo or mothering. If Davies is right, even when attempting to assert themselves, girls' scripts prescribe a form of 'power' that is essentially limited, in that if it is to succeed, it relies on the 'power' of the male.

If these scripts are not dealt with, it is likely that they will become a recurrent feature of the person's behaviour patterns in later life. We can see this in the continuing limited perceptions which young women often have of their life chances. 'In a large survey of upper-elementary-school children, practically all career choices made by girls were in one of four categories: teacher, nurse, secretary, mother' (Richardson, 1988). The majority (90 per cent) of the Access students on our course had been mothers, secretaries or nurses and on an initial survey of the women's choices for university study, the majority were looking at careers in teaching or social work. Women's access to the languages of power, like their access to education, continues to be limited and their access to cultural capital continues to be denied.

A New Old Boy Network? Middle-class Feminists in the Nineteenth Century

As there are so many barriers to women's access to power it is not surprising that when they do gain some power, women form exclusive networks. This was particularly true of feminists in the nineteenth century. So how did feminist networks operate? They were very similar to 'old boy networks' and women used them in a very similar way. These networks were beneficial for middle-class women because they gave them a power base from which to organise and campaign. However, networks exclude as well as include and in a capitalist and patriarchal society this meant that working-class women had very little influence or voice. Women modelled their organisations on patriarchal institutions such as suffrage societies and trade union organisations. This model meant that the organisations were hierarchical and based on class divisions. Influential women, usually women associated with influential men, were chairs, presidents or executive committee members who decided the policy of the various organisations they sat on. At best, working-class women were employed as organisers of other working-class women but they rarely, if ever, had a role in the decision-making process or were taught how to achieve such a role, except in the Women's Co-operative Guild, to which we will return.

Middle-class women found a window into the public world of men by emphasising both equal rights and essentialist issues. On the one hand, they campaigned against the injustice of man-made laws that affected women, for example, in the Married Women's Property campaign, the campaign against the Contagious Diseases Acts and the suffrage campaigns. On the other hand, they argued that women's distinctive caring qualities and moral superiority meant that they were better suited to certain types of social reform than men, especially when it involved working with poor women and children. These qualities were reflected in the types of social reform women became involved with, such as workhouse reform, juvenile delinquency, health visiting and school boards. This essentialism also meant that middle-class women had a vested interest in maintaining inequalities between women because this unequal relationship gave them their positions of authority.

The language in which women articulated their demands for access to public concerns and social justice was rooted in the familial – in languages of motherhood and sisterhood. These languages conveyed a sense of unity while masking the inequalities between women, because motherhood and sisterhood are not concepts of equality but imply seniority if not superiority. Mothers have daughters and older sisters have younger sisters. The authority that mothers and older sisters have and had in reality resonates in the writing of nineteenth century feminists (Yeo, 1992; Fuerer, 1988). Whereas the motherhood rhetoric was usually employed in the field of social reform, for example in rescue work, the sisterhood rhetoric was often used in issues of social justice, for example, the Contagious Diseases Acts both in Britain and India, and in the Protective Legislation debate.

So why did women use a language of the family, an institution which, it has been argued, perpetuates women's oppression, when they were arguing for their rights or the rights of other women (see Barrett and McIntosh, 1982)? One argument could be that in a patriarchal society there were no other 'scripts' for women to follow. The power that women had was vested in their roles as mother or sister to men. The wife, if you follow the logic of coverture (which in this sense means the legal status of a married woman under the authority and protection of her husband and therefore without authority of her own), had no power as she was seen as being as one with her husband. However, mothers and older sisters did exercise power over children and siblings. Consequently, though there was much rhetoric about working-class and colonial women encapsulated in the slogan 'helping women to help themselves', in reality middle-class women were empowered by infantilising working-class women and black women as our poor sisters or our enslaved sisters. These relationships (mother/daughter, big sister/little sister) allowed for variations in behaviour: the 'scolding mother', the 'loving mother', the 'empowering mother', and so on (Yeo, 1992), and women who took on these roles saw the women they helped as 'dependent daughters' either needing discipline, love or education depending on the stance the 'mother' took. Power was in the hands of the 'mother' and she knew best and did not have to ask her 'daughters' their opinions. She could decide for them. For example, in the debates at the turn of this century around married women's work, the Women's Industrial Council, an organisation of predominantly middle-class women interested in the working lives of poor women, carried out an extensive survey of married working-class women throughout the country. By this time they were experts in the field of social investigation and carried out research for many organisations, yet they did not think it necessary to ask working-class women their opinions, they only wanted to collect empirical evidence of working-class women's lives (Black, 1915).

Women's Language of Care:
Its Strengths and Drawbacks

It is hardly surprising that whether or not women choose a caring role in society, the social expectation of women's behaviour is such that 'care' (in some form) is considered a 'good' quality for women to have. It is also not surprising that most discussions of women-only groups emphasise the caring qualities of such environments. We are not trying to suggest that such caring does not take place. But 'care' can mean many things, as can 'Mother' and 'Sister' as we have shown in examining women's organizations in nineteenth-century Britain.

If we examine the operation of women's language patterns, both verbal and non-verbal, there are clear gender differences which substantiate claims which suggest women tend to produce more supportive conversation patterns than men. Women and men use and control space differently and treat intimacy between people differently. In mixed-sex society this is usually detrimental to women. 'People approach women more closely and sit closer to them than they do to men. Although touching may symbolise intimacy, it also symbolises status'. 'Women are probably touched by more people in more settings than are men' (Richardson, 1988, p. 25). Women tend to be less certain when speaking, often questioning their own statements, either through intonation or by being indefinite. This will make them less able to assert themselves in a talk environment and more likely to accept others' judgements. Women's talk can of course be very empowering, creating a kind of collaboration between women, where they support each other's conversation and therefore affirm each other's self image. Care for each other and concern in the group does give members confidence to be able to communicate. 'I like the fact that it is a women-only group. I don't feel anyone's going to put me down if I say something wrong' (Denise talking about the Access course). This support provides an essential counterbalance to the fear of failure discussed earlier and offers students the beginnings of a cycle of success, giving them freedom to experiment and challenge their own and other's knowledge. This process of transformation that happens to mature students, especially mature women returners, has been well documented (see particularly Jane Thompson, 1983). What hasn't been examined is how the very language of support and care can also be used to disempower students.

The Case Study

The students on the Women's Studies Access course were recruited from the local area, many of them coming back into formal education for the first time since they were 16. Many were from working-class backgrounds. Several were single parents. Some were from more professional backgrounds although they had not succeeded at school. Most of the women were under-confident and had a low opinion of themselves. Most were grappling with years of seeing themselves as less able than their husbands, brothers, fathers or sons. For most of them, the women-friendly environment seemed, as one student put it, 'like a dream come true'. However it soon became clear to us as tutors that despite our common experience as women, the differences between all of us were enormous. These differences were of age, class, culture, sexuality, and ethnic origin. As the two classes began to form themselves, certain women took up particular roles within the group. This is not unusual. For any group to function successfully, members have to fulfil different roles. While group functions vary according to group tasks, there are certain common roles, such as facilitators, idealists, workers and supervisors each of which assumes or implies particular attributes. What was particularly interesting in our case was the way the group used these roles in an especially feminine way. The roles which group members adopted were constructed in terms of a feminine 'family'.

Women tutors often find it difficult to take on roles of leadership. Asserting authority seems contradictory to the principles of feminism and we often call on a form of 'sisterhood' between ourselves and the students. The traditional question and answer power battles of the classroom – the teacher asks questions to which they know the answer and therefore have the power to evaluate the answer (Edwards, 1980) – is abandoned for a more collegial structure, where students work in groups discussing issues and raising questions for themselves. This collegial way of operating allows students to take on more powerful roles. In the absence of the tutor taking on the role of a 'mother' on the Women's Studies course, one woman student took on that role herself. She felt she could and should 'speak' for the rest of the group. This process was quite subtle, and as tutors we were initially unaware of the process and at times colluded with it, partly because of our feelings of sisterhood. The nature of communication is itself complex and contradictory. However within our society we have a degree of common understanding of the codes in conveying messages.

The woman in question presented herself as confident, self assured and determined. She spoke 'correctly' with a middle-class accent, calling to a shared womanhood amongst us all. It was, of course, not our shared womanhood that enabled her to speak for others but the differences between us, our different class position, our ethnic background and so on. Early on, she established her seat at the table and gathered the most vulnerable students around her. She presented herself to the group as being concerned about their progress and offered her support to group members should they find work difficult. In an attempt to recognise students' knowledge, tutors usually value group members who grasp ideas and concepts quickly as they can offer an easier access point for other students who take a little longer to understand a subject. Usually this is a supportive and empowering exercise. However in this case it became a silencing process. Many of the students fell into the role of a child, exhibiting 'learned helplessness' and allowing the 'mother' student to tackle the more demanding work.

The 'mother' student had this effect by using a status discourse of non-verbal cues. By being intimate with other students she was expressing her power over them. She often put her arm round other students, offering them comfort, touching them on the arm or leg as they chatted to her about some issue. As the communication developed, the other students responded with deference, having understood the communication, dropping their eye contact or putting their head to one side. She used this technique with the women tutors as well, telling students to 'leave Mary alone, she's had a hard day', with one hand touching me gently on the shoulder while her other arm was firmly outstretched to keep the other students at bay. This particular incident totally silenced me, and although I had not communicated any such notion of having had 'a hard day', I simply smiled and left it at that.

Despite the obvious status difference between us, Mary as tutor, she as student, this student was able to exercise power over me. 'Power denotes the ability of a person to influence another, however that influence is accomplished. Authority denotes power that stems from positional membership' (Richardson, 1988). Clearly this student found a form of controlling power through 'care', which allowed her the opportunity to 'speak'' for others. Her own background, her class position and the confidence that this gave her created a status difference between her and other students, and her and us as tutors. Her speech patterns used the words of 'care' but did not exhibit the characteristics of women's language described by Lakoff, and instead were definite, clear and determined. This case study suggests that the idea of Women's Language is not just about language of women but is more about a language of powerlessness, where position and status can affect the style of speech. This language could more correctly be described as a feminine language of power that can operate to control other women. The power that the mother student was able to use may have given her confidence but it disempowered other women students and the women tutors.

Most of this process was unconscious. The woman herself was drawing upon a 'lifescript' which she had found successful in the past from her own school background. After the whole incident opened up, the 'mother student' said, 'I was worried. It was like going back to school. I couldn't stop myself, I tried to be concerned for others, because, I guess, I was worried about myself' (Jane talking to MS, July 1993). The situation developed because the students and the tutors brought with them 'baggage', forms of learned behaviour and language that automatically encouraged deference.

These behaviour patterns are constantly perpetuated through our family experiences, at school, with our peer group and as we become adults. This process becomes so 'taken for granted' that it provides us with 'a series of convenient behaviour patterns to which we can become habituated that free us from the necessity of deciding constantly among the trivial details of living' (Biddle, 1979). It is often these 'trivial details of living' that perpetuate power relations.

Challenging the Boundaries of Gender Patterning

Both the students who exhibited learned helplessness and the protective 'mother' were responding within the feminine gendering process that pervades our patriarchal society. Women-only groups are vulnerable to these types of feminine power battles, as we have shown both historically and within the contemporary society. Empowerment will not be possible unless all women are enabled to use their voice. It is important to recognise the potential for silencing which the language of femininity can offer. In order to empower women, their different experience needs to be recognised and, no matter how difficult it may be at times, women need to be encouraged to act for themselves. It is often difficult to know how we can do this in adult education and in our everyday lives. Within our case study it was the 'sisters', the students themselves, who resolved the situation within the group by challenging the 'mother's' authority and choosing 'to speak for themselves'. This was clearly the best solution. If we, as tutors, had silenced the mother student, we would have replaced her both symbolically and practically.

This dilemma is not one that can always be simply resolved. However there are, historically, more empowering models of women's organisations. In British history perhaps the most prominent and successful of these was the Women's Co-operative Guild (WCG), a mass organisation of working-class women, mainly housewives, who campaigned for various issues pertinent to their lives, for example maternity rights, suffrage, divorce reform and minimum wages. The WCG was based on the democratic ideal and structure of organising from the base upwards, and endeavoured to educate its members both about current issues and about how to participate in the democratic process of the organisation. Education was regarded as empowering and members set themselves the task of enabling as many women as possible to have not only a part in the decision-making mechanism, but also literally a voice to speak to issues they felt were important. Consequently, Virginia Woolf, when attending a WCG Conference, found to her surprise that the Guildswomen's interests did not reflect her own and that their concerns were to do with material issues that she took for granted, for example, adequate housing and decent food (Women's Co-operative Guild, 1931).

The WCG was the most successful of the British organisations of working-class women. We believe that this is because of its conscious determination not only to be autonomous of men, but also because it refused to allow middle-class women to control the organisation. Further, its institutional structures encouraged education and ensured active and democratic participation and its policy-making was informed by the experiences and attitudes of women members. The success of the WCG suggests lessons for women in education today, especially in relation to women-only and other adult education classes. For example, we need to appreciate different cultures and encourage participation by challenging the language of academia and simplistic notions of womanhood.

This chapter was first presented at the Gender and Feminist History Seminar at the University of Sussex, as a rehearsal for the Women in the Higher Education Curriculum Conference at the University of Central Lancashire. We hoped that people would consider our paper in a wider context than education and academia, as we were certainly thinking in broad terms about the issues it raises. At Sussex we were surprised to find that we raised anxieties among graduate students newly embarked on teaching who were looking for guidance on the 'right way to do it'. Others had not thought about the relationships between women in this problematic way. Interestingly, one woman explained how supportive women's groups in the 1970s had been for women who had been involved in left politics. However, our recollection of these groups was less positive, as Gerry has already indicated.

At Preston, our paper was well received by the working-class women in the group who recognised the issues we were raising. One woman did express her gratitude to middle-class women whose scholarship she valued. But gratitude has always been the expected response from working-class and black women and we are arguing that middle-class women should examine their own position in institutional and other hierarchies, and the way in which they silence other women (see also (charles), 1992). Another woman replied to our paper using complex and alienating academic language and yet she concluded by agreeing with most of our argument!

This chapter is very much 'work-in-progress' and already we are thinking about new issues concerning feminine language and power. The unconscious imperialism of middle-class activists during the nineteenth and early twentieth century is not a dead issue. Indeed we are arguing that it is a very live issue, and as educators and feminists, the power conferred on some women over other women is a central concern for us. The rhetoric of sisterhood still has currency in contemporary feminism although the debate around difference has brought inequalities to the fore (see Hinds *et al*, 1992). Many women with power have gained it through patriarchal institutions (such as academia) and have a vested interest in playing by patriarchal rules. Tutors and facilitators need to be conscious of group dynamics and power within groups, not just between tutors and students but also between students. We need to find ways of helping women to empower themselves without getting tied up in male power hierarchies and in languages and roles which prescribe power and inequality. This is not easy when we have to operate through patriarchal institutions ourselves. However, we believe that as educators we are in a special and perhaps unique position because our job is to empower people. What we need to do is work out ways of empowering other women and using the networks we create to sustain this task.

In this chapter we have shown that engaging with difference is a complicated process that needs to take on board issues about language and roles with groups. Demystifying academic processes challenges the power base which, as tutors, we often take for granted. In this encounter we were forced to challenge our own assumptions and to recognise many different sources of inequality.

References

Barrett, M. and McIntosh, M. (1982) *The Anti-Social Family*, London: Verso.

Biddle, B. (1979) *Role Theory Expectations, Identities and Behaviours*, London: Academic Press.

Black, C. (ed.) (1915) *Married Women's Work: Being the Report of an Enquiry undertaken by the Women's Industrial Council*, London: G. Bell, reprinted London: Virago, 1983.

(charles), H. (1992) 'Whiteness – The Relevance of Politically Colouring the "Non"' in Hinds, H., Phoenix, A. and Stacey, J. (eds.) *Working Out: New Directions for Women's Studies*, pp 29–35, London: Falmer Press.

Davies, L. (1992) 'School Power Cultures under Economic Constraint', *Education Review*, 44, 22.

Edwards, A. D. (1980) 'Power in the Classroom', in Pugh, K. *et al* (eds.) *Language, Communication and Education*, London: Open University Press.

Fuerer, R. (1988) 'The Meaning of 'Sisterhood': The British Women's Movement and Protective Labor Legislation, 1870–1900' *Victorian Studies*, 31, 2, Winter.

Hinds, H., Phoenix, A. and Stacey, J. (eds.) (1992) *Working Out: New Directions for Women's Studies*, London: Falmer Press.

Holcombe, L. (1983) *Wives and Property: Reform of the Married Women's Property Law in Nineteenth-Century England*, Toronto: University of Toronto Press.

Levine, P. (1990) *Feminist Lives in Victorian England: Private Roles and Public Commitment*, Oxford: Blackwell.

Llewellyn Davies, M. (ed.) (1931) *Life As We Have Known It By Co-operative Working Women*, London: Hogarth Press Ltd, reprinted London: Virago, 1984.

Mead, G. H. (1932) *Mind, Self and Society*, Chicago: University of Chicago Press.

Richardson, L. (1988) *The Dynamics of Sex and Gender: A Sociological Perspective*, London: Harper and Row.

Thompson, J. (1983) *Learning Liberation, Women's Responses to Men's Education*, London: Croom Helm.

Yeo, E. J. (1992) 'Social Motherhood and the Sexual Communion of Labour in British Social Science, 1850–1950', *Women's History Review* 1, 1, pp 63–87.

Chapter 5

Murder Your Darlings: Women's Writings, Many Voices

Jennie Fontana and Jill Masouri

A Tutor's Perspective – Jennie Fontana

Firstly I have to say that I write this as a non-academic. I can convey observations and facts but this material has not been gathered with a view to research and most of it comes from reflection and retrospective discussion with past students and tutors involved with the course.

I was first involved with 'New Horizons – A University of Sussex Centre for Continuing Education Course' in Spring 1990 as a stand-in for a tutor who was ill. Initially this was for a half-term which was then extended to a full term. I had no real brief on the students and the course and as a newcomer to adult education I was not only apprehensive but also completely unaware of the needs of such a group. In other words I was operating 'blind'. I thought I was *just* going to be running some Creative Writing classes. I can't remember much about that group in terms of 'content' but I do remember that the students produced some wonderful writings and that there was a strong feeling of warmth and support. It was a group numbering around 10 and attendance was good. There was one male in the group.

I was later asked to be involved in the New Horizons course at the Friends' Centre. The Study Skills tutor, Ruth Keynes, and myself were invited to attend a planning meeting at Sussex University. We were both pregnant. It was immediately evident that we were going to be running this 'alone' as the course convenor was moving on and the new organiser, Mary Stuart, would not be in place till the following term. It was decided that there would be other modules in the course due to Ruth's delivery date and we decided on Assertiveness and some keyboard/computer skills sessions, having five sessions each.

However I still felt as if I was operating 'blind'.

We interviewed students for the course in early September – Ruth heavily pregnant and me with seven-week-old Max in pram! I think that our initial numbers were just under 20. I don't think we turned anyone away at this stage although once the course was underway any late enquiries were put on hold for the following term so as not to disrupt the group. Almost immediately one had a sense of its vulnerability. The first term got underway with Assertiveness and Creative Writing, each having half of the time on a Tuesday morning. There was a drop in numbers early on (approximately four). I worried about this but I was reassured by the office that this was normal with most adult education groups.

Now – I say I was worried. Yes. And I worry about it still with all of the Creative Writing work that I do but in particular with such groups of women – I know what Creative Writing can do from my own very personal experience of writing. I worried that what it had touched and tapped was too much for a person to cope with. They had lifted the curtain/the blanket/the veil but could not face what they saw. As Rebecca O'Rouke identifies it is common for people to come to creative writing when they have been through major changes in their lives, like unemployment or bereavement (O'Rourke, 1994). It has to be said that Creative Writing, no matter how structured and formal (and this is actually not my approach), is about personal therapy/growth/development. And I got them into Creative Writing straight away.

In the initial blurb that students were given the tutors each wrote a summary of the modules. I think that all the women were looking for change, to rekindle their confidence, to spend some time away from the home with other adults. I think that there were some students who came because they'd always wanted to write, and some of these 'wanted to get published'. I recall many saying that the course 'looked just the thing for them'. Personally, my hidden agenda is, I think, to help put the poetry back into peoples' lives – actually as well as metaphorically.

We discussed many issues and looked at various articles and letters in newspapers (in particular *The Guardian*). We also shared stories and poems – written by women, about women's issues (but this was not exclusively so.) With this shared reading of women's writing we certainly did 'approach issues that are intrinsically personal and central to women's lives', and within the group it was most certainly the case that 'Women readers bring their lives to bear on writing, through interpretation, criticism and enjoyment' (Milloy and O'Rourke, 1991).

In most sessions we wrote. We would write using a poem or a line as a trigger or simply a phrase. I taught a technique which I use, as do many writers, which I call 'Free-writing'. This requires silence; that the pen/pencil does not leave the paper for the period of time agreed, that is, one writes regardless even if it's 'I don't know what to write, I don't know what to write'; that one writes what comes into the head – no matter what – even if it strays from the initial trigger. Immediately before these 'Free-writing' sessions we would often, but not always, go through a simple process of relaxation which I had learnt as a pre-meditation exercise.

Afterwards we would read round and it was stated from the start that at any time, with any exercise or activity that anyone could 'pass' and we would simply move on. Confidentiality was also agreed. In most sessions there would be 'passes' but these were invariably not from the same sources. I soon came to realise that the reading out loud was one of the most important elements of the group. I had never really examined why, except from my own experience of participating in writers' groups and knowing how much I looked forward to sharing what I had written, and obtaining feedback. The work group members produced was remarkable. Here is one example:

THANK YOU FOR TOUCHING MY SHOULDER

Thank you for touching my shoulder, thank you for reassuring me, for pulling me back from the edge. It's safer over there. My face burns, my mouth trembles and my armpits sweat, my stomach cramps and my feet tingle, my scalp pulls back and my forehead numbs and blurs but with a touch on my shoulder the moment passes and I stay. The panic subsides and the walls stand up straight. It is so hard to be, so hard to think and feel. Emotions are difficult slaves and terrifying ogres – I cannot contain them correctly. My vessels and flesh are on the outside raw and ready for salt. My eyes scream for a life-line and I murderously plot my escape but the words tumble out and fall into place and I belong – I'm still a child, I'm still insecure but I have a home. I am teaching myself to wait.

E. K.

In discussion with Jill, in preparation for this chapter, as well as with other students it has become absolutely apparent that this reading out loud was indeed one of the things that students really 'looked forward to'. It is certainly a way in which each gets heard. Perhaps through the writing we are able to let go – and then have control over the sharing of our feelings.

This sharing strengthens the bond in a group and boosts confidence, allowing participants plenty of safe, uncritical, approving, space in which to share their experiences. The words are their own, they are acknowledged, it is said, they have claimed it – pushed out the boundaries and surprised themselves. I didn't know I could say that/write that/feel that/write that much/read out loud!

As a tutor I have often noticed that after the first few weeks the group members appear to 'have dressed for the occasion'. On mentioning this to past students one said 'Yes. I wanted to look nice. I dressed up for this.' Another said 'I'd think about what I'd wear for it.' I always enjoyed choosing what I wore on the days I taught. We all wanted to look good for each other in our very individual ways. I find it fascinating how women use their clothes and jewellery and make-up and hair styling and accessories as a deep expression of self and their sexuality. We were in a situation where we all looked at each other (as all women do) and we wanted to look good for each other. It is not a competitive thing at all. We're not talking 'Jean Muir' here. The women in the group were being taken notice of for the first time in a long time – it was a morning out on their own. I must apologise if the following statement sounds trite but I say it born out of long experience of working with women-only groups: as we come to love and acknowledge the self so then we become beautiful.

We used various external sources as stimuli for the writing, namely the Museum and Art Gallery and Brighton Festival exhibitions – all within easy walking distance of the Friends' Centre. These outings allowed students to be together in a different space and to have time sharing thoughts and ideas in a more intimate way. For some, although Brighton residents, it was their first ever visit to the museum. For one or two this was the first 'outing' they'd had in years (this was also true when we had an evening Christmas gathering at my home). For many it was the only time they'd been out alone for several years. It was important to have this time away from the Friends' Centre as it extended the confidence of individuals and allowed them to start setting up a stronger network between themselves. This would initially be through lift-share, or 'Where's the loo?' 'I'll show you.'/'Who's the artist?' 'Didn't she live at ... ' and so on.

Out of one of the visits to the Brighton Museum and its Puppet exhibition each student made a puppet for the following meeting. This was close to being our final session. The instructions were that nothing was to be bought to make the puppet – that it was to be made out of whatever was found lying around the house – and that only they should make it. It was to be given a name. The puppets were unveiled the following week and everyone had made one. I recall one student telling of how she had put her evolving puppet in a particular place in the living-room (on top of the TV in fact) and how the family had witnessed its development and acknowledged her creativity. 'That's good mum. That's really good!' Each performed and their histories unfolded. It was a revelation! The memory of these women and their puppets and their stunning, uninhibited performances and the ingenuity of their creations is a powerful one for me. It was the way that they pulled these magnificent puppets from old plastic bags as gently as if they were cradling a baby. It was the way that these puppets revealed so much more of themselves – their alter egos. It was the way the puppet allowed their inner thoughts to bubble through and they were able to let go. Able to let go of their inhibitions and give voice, through the puppet, to what had been trapped inside.

In the following year – September 1992 – the course was structured differently. We met with Mary, the new co-ordinator, to discuss changes which we thought were appropriate and were excited when we discovered that the numbers that we enrolled went up. This was partly due to a reluctance to turn anyone away but also because we thought we were more directly meeting their needs. We began with a group of over 20 and this was too big. We lost the usual four or so within the first weeks but then the group was still too big. It was 'ticking over' fairly well but there was not as much time for everyone to read out their writings – not so much time for each to have their say. I could not remember names.

Now one of the things that I had only brushed with in the previous group was 'mothers'. I felt that we needed to deal with mothers in a more direct way. What transpired was all due to bad planning and lack of forethought on my part – however, what emerged was fascinating with several accidental elements that one might seriously consider re-using in a future group. We started looking at 'mothers', through our writing, reading and discussion. I knew that I would have to miss three sessions in a row due to other working commitments and had asked a highly skilled counsellor/writer/teacher, Sally, to run these sessions. She was met by eruption! Mothers. (I should have known better.) All the anger was rising to the surface and 'their mother' was not there. Sally got the lot.

MOTHER

Long distance calling.
I'm far, far away.
A safe distance from you.
The further away
you are,
the better I feel.
Conversation easy and light.
At ease with the distance,
miles upon miles.
Small talk, platitudes,
passing the time,
times up.
Thank God,
Good-bye, good-bye.

J.S.

I now wonder how it would have been if I had been at those classes. I wonder if they would have been able to release the anger in the same way. By 'their mother' abandoning them and not being present they were free to say what they liked. They were free to hate her – and with a safe, sympathetic, unknown, no-risk, party – Sally. I also question my own personal subconscious motives in doing this to her. The unconscious anger that members of the group placed on Sally came out in many of their writing, pieces each placing blame on different significant people in their past.

FIRE

My choleric father.
Embers smouldering
lying low – a dopey tiger
with drooping eyes and the sharpest teeth.
Your unpredictability
keeps me on my Guard
Constantly – lest the lava boils
Engulfing me till I can breathe no more.
Flames licking round
Stifling hot
and I am extinguished -
A heap of powdery ash.
Oh powerful one.

J.M.

The telephone feedback was also very interesting. Sally gave me the full and awful picture – and was dreading the following two weeks. Ruth, taking the second half of the morning with Study Skills, had missed the eruption but had been of enormous support to Sally over the telephone. However the class secretary, who had eagerly volunteered for the post which involves keeping a register and being a telephone contact for the students and tutor, told a different tale. 'Everything was alright. Not to worry. Nothing serious.' And I was slightly taken aback by the two extremes. The following two weeks were very much better and highly constructive.

By the time I got back it had 'all blown over' but we did discuss what had happened and the anger was mostly focused around my desertion of them. This was accidentally a perfect channel for their anger against the constraints in their lives, constraints which society continues to place on women. It was this very group that went on to write the pieces in a booklet entitled 'MURDER YOUR DARLINGS' from which we take our title for this chapter. The following poem reveals some of the conflicting emotions which the course sparked for the women.

WORDS

Words can harm,
And words can heal,
Words can hide,
Or words reveal,
Think about just what you say,
Sometimes the hurt won't go away.
                              C. E. J.

These women were writing for themselves: through the creative writing and reading and sharing they were, it seems, discovering/re-discovering the self. Being in an unthreatening, uncritical, safe group of women, and through the writing learning to express and acknowledge desires, needs, histories and frustrations created a rich and supportive environment for these women to initiate the changes they wanted.

'We can sit down and weep; we can go shopping,
or play at a game of constantly being wrong
with a priceless set of vocabularies,
or we can bravely deplore, but please
please come flying.'

from 'Invitation to Miss Marianne Moore'
by Elizabeth Bishop

Crossing the Bridge: A Student Perspective – Jill Masouri

I started the 'New Horizons for Women' course in September 1992. It was held on Tuesday mornings, in Brighton at The Friends' Centre, and spanned two 10-week terms, covering Study Skills, Assertiveness Training and Communication Skills. Creative Writing and Poetry was also explored throughout the course and a booklet of our own poetry and prose entitled *Murder Your Darlings* was compiled by ourselves in April 1993.

Just over 20 women enrolled: a large cross-section of all ages coming from different backgrounds and situations bringing different voices, personal histories and experiences. Most of the women had had a long break from formal learning, some rearing children. Others, due to the recession, needed to re-evaluate their direction, and some wanted to approach full-time paid work again or wished to enter higher education.

The building we met in, The Friends' Centre Quaker Meeting House, was appreciated by many. Right in the centre of town and with a large garden to sit in and a crèche, it felt friendly, approachable and secure. The cost of the sessions and the crèche were minimal and made the course accessible to many. Our coffee breaks were spent sitting in the canteen around a coal fire sharing our lives, views and news. Often we would go off into town together afterwards and continue our discussions. Meeting in an academic establishment might have felt more formal and intimidating, inhibiting the easy camaraderie that developed.

At first the group seemed huge and unwieldy – many women felt vulnerable and exposed. Obviously our needs and expectations were very different, although we shared a common bond – that of coming back into the 'world' and re-finding our voices. For some the course was a chance to off-load:

> ... some women came with a lot of personal baggage ...
> we jostled to speak and discuss our problems, needs and
> experiences ...   *J.S.*

wrote one woman afterwards. Maybe the sessions were the first time we'd felt listened to in ages. As the weeks went by, and the numbers greatly reduced, we could get to know each other more intimately, and feelings of trust and security were established – vital elements for real changes to take place.

In this section I offer a student perspective on the Creative Writing/Poetry classes led by Jennie Fontana. The quotes I've used were collected from women attending the course who were interviewed retrospectively. There was unanimous agreement that writing had enabled them to explore, articulate and subtly change their perceptions and identities.

For many of us, at first, these sessions were anticipated with nervous feelings of not being able to write, or of being creatively inadequate, anxieties around bad spelling and ungrammatical English. By showing us the technique of 'Free writing', Jennie soon had us scribbling away (Brownjohn, 1980). We were also encouraged to share parts of our work with each other, and displaying our vulnerability had the effect of bringing us closer together, as we supported and received each other's work positively.

We relied heavily on Jennie's guidance and nurturing at the beginning, and this became evident when, after a sensitive and volatile session writing about our mothers, Jennie had to leave us with a replacement tutor while she worked elsewhere for three sessions. For many it was as if our own 'mother' had abandoned us, so soon after we'd 'come back into the world again', and we were left with dredged-up emotions that were difficult to know what to do with: anger with Jennie for leaving us and shock at feeling bereft – raw feelings exposed. This seemed a crisis/turning point. Some women left and those who remained consolidated. The group became quite intense and boundaries had to be re-established. The Creative Writing continued with the 'outside' tutor but using safer and less personal subjects as stimuli, and Jennie later returned.

In many ways the group then evolved into a kind of therapy group. Being women only, the students felt safe to chat and share experiences. Many were bursting at the seams, but situations still erupted beyond safe boundaries for some and the sessions were often quite stressful, with doubts over who was taking responsibility for whom. I have since discovered that this sort of group is quite common in adult education creative writing groups, especially in groups where women are returning to formal education for the first time (Gersie and King, 1990):

> at times it felt a bit too close for comfort, hitting lots of raw nerves … what really frightened me was what the poetry section brought out of me; personal feelings lying dormant and shut out for years, blocked out of my memories, came very clear, pounding back intensely …   K.R.

However, we all gave each other time, and listened to others' stories. Some women commented on how much they looked forward to the sessions, dressing up and wearing make up. After years of being around children and interrupted conversations, some were worried about how they would talk to grown ups, saying it was the first time in a relationship outside their families:

> every time I wrote it related back to me and my family ... my relationship with my mother, father, sister, brother, husband and daughter were questioned ... it was like getting across a bridge ... we used each other's views of ourselves to boost us ... *K.P.*

Jennie continued to encourage us to write:

> ... During that first term I gathered a volume of scribbles, memories and phrases ... I was always amazed at what treasure would be teased from that secret box in my head each week ... At the beginning of the second term my sense of complacency was shattered by the death of a close relative. It felt as if a bomb had exploded in my life, and I was walking on the rubble left behind. I began to write. My notebooks began to be filled with all I could not verbalise. My pen helped release the tears and clear the confusion. In time I felt a growing need to put all of this into some coherent whole, as a tribute to the person I had lost, but also by means of making sense of my trauma. I did this in a poem, the writing of which helped put into place my raw feelings of grief, and some of them fell behind me ...

The poem that K.B. wrote was called 'Stroke', and I reproduce it here in full to give you a sense of how she used words to help her explore her grief.

STROKE

Tears burst their banks
When I see you
Slumbering fitfully
In your hospital bed.
Anger jabs at passivity
That reduces you
To a public spectacle.

Skin drags heavily
On dull bones,
Arms like hefty anchors
Pin you to the bed,
Brain waves, your only movement.
This wrecked body
Will never surface.

Fear floods inside
I take flight
Down green corridors
Shiny and new
Legs like bamboo
March jerkily
To the wretched drum
Banging in my head.

A nurse's soft tones
Hold me and reassure
They remind me
You are alive
And guide me back
To your door.

'Stroke him, feel him, touch him
Speak to him, not at, not about him
Words are his lifeline,
He can hear you.'
Closed lids darken as you approach,
He can see you
Currents of air wash over him as you move,
'He can feel you,
Stay with him.'

I hold your hand
curved and gentle,
Words, like dry biscuits,
Stick in my throat,
They edge forward
nervous feet on
Thin ice –
Then take off –
There is nothing to lose,
And no reply,
Only a warm small tear
In the corner of your eye.
'I will miss you.'

Breath in agonising gasps
Fingers sink into soft shoulders
Heady with sharp scent.
You lift your face
And have the last word,
A deep guttural groan

Of release,
Shock waves ricochet
Sending a rush of wings
Fluttering inside me,
Calm hands steady her,
We stare at nothing,
You are free.

Your ashes scattered over water
Dancing, swirling
In sharp sea breezes,
They sink in slow motion,
Below the waves,
Twisting and golden
Like dust in sun's rays
You can swim forever –
We tread water in your wake.

K.B.

By the Spring term we had each amassed several pieces of finished writing, and it was decided that we should assemble them into a booklet *Murder Your Darlings*. We realised the immeasurable value of personal discovery and empowerment that we had gained through our own writing, and through the reading of the published work of women we had discussed. We had also experienced many tensions that had arisen along the way. Issues of anger, resentment, strengths and confidence had been faced and challenged as well as women's current position in society, the roles we played and the values society attached to them – being a mother, daughter, wife, single parent, career woman, unemployed, encountering racial and sexual prejudices – and discovering our own needs.

... I thought the course wasn't going to push me, but it did the anger, releasing it – pushed me on ...   *G.M.*

... although family comes first, I discovered I still need space, time, a value for myself in my own eyes, not praised or as seen by others ...   *K.R.*

Two members of the group volunteered to collate the contributions into the booklet. We each submitted writings that we had selected ourselves, and felt reflected our own perspective.

... every single person wrote something amazing ...

C.E.J.

Seeing the end result was very satisfying and generated a very real sense of self worth, growth and achievement.

... despite my own fears and inexperience, I have achieved something for myself, even though my husband cannot understand what I do or why. This self development was mine alone ... I stuck it out and I'm very glad I did ... I think I'm ready to move on now ...   *J.M.*

And move on we did. Some of us went on to complete Access to Higher Education courses and gained university places, others returned to part- and full-time employment. Since the course finished, a group of us still keep in contact with each other, meeting occasionally to share our news and progress.

References

Brownjohn, S. (1980) *Does it Have to Rhyme?* Hodder and Stoughton.
Gersie, A. and King, S. (1990) *Storytelling in Education and Therapy,* Jessica Kingsley.
Millroy, J. and O'Rourke, R. (1991) *The Woman Reader: Learning and Teaching Women's Writing,* Routledge.
O'Rourke, R. (1994) *Written on the Margins,* University of Leeds.

Section Three

Defining Learning: Professional Perceptions and Learners' Abilities

Over the last twenty years there has been an enormous growth in the number and range of adult education opportunities for people who have been labelled as having learning difficulties. Yet 'Special Needs work', as it is often termed, is perceived to be low status work. This is partly because of the hierarchy of knowledge within education which values research and teaching in higher education above all else, and sometimes assumes that work with people with learning difficulties is or should be taught by staff who are 'not very good at their subject' or who 'can't keep students'. Even adult educators are seen pressing themselves up against the corridor wall to avoid getting too close to 'those students'. Thankfully this is changing, not least because of the recognition education with and for people with learning difficulties and disabilities has received through the Further and Higher Education Act and from the Further Education Funding Council.

The chapters in this section speak emotionally about people with learning difficulties' right to learning and their right to be treated as equal to other students. A key theme in education is assessment. Assessment of people's ability and talent takes time and real engagement. For many people with learning difficulties this assessment is undertaken without proper interaction or thought. Perceived as simply 'different' to anyone else, their abilities and talents are seen in terms of the broad classification, 'learning disability', which does not take account of the variety of skills and knowledge which, as human beings, we are all capable of developing. All adults have particular aptitudes for specific types of knowledge and skill, but for many people who have been defined as having learning difficulties these variations are not acknowledged. The chapter *'She's Doing Too Much Music': Professional Perceptions of a Learner's Needs*, focuses on this issue of difference within the label 'learning difficulty'. Gus Garside shows how seeing beyond the label can challenge definitions of what learning is and who can learn.

Many people with learning difficulties are not given choices about their learning. Both the chapters, *Our Right to Know* and *'She's Doing Too Much Music'* examine the question of student choice and the right of carers and professionals to decide what learning is appropriate for an adult who wishes to learn. In *Information Technology and Enablement*, David Longman and Mary Stuart argue that learning difficulties operate on a continuum and that many of the difficulties faced by any group of adults learning to use computers are the same, despite the particular labels the students may have acquired. This realisation sprang from an active engagement with a group of students with learning difficulties taking an introductory computer course at the University of Sussex.

The lessons learnt from the chapters in this section are generally applicable to debates about learning and teaching. Professionals' perceptions of student abilities, especially those of 'different' students who in one form or another are labelled by the education system, can limit student potential. The chapters argue that such stereotypical approaches need to be rejected by adult educators or they will simply reproduce the difficulties which so many adults have experienced in their previous encounters with education.

Chapter 6

Our Right to Know: Women with Learning Difficulties and Sexuality Courses

Kathy Smith and Mary Stuart

Policy and practice on sex education for adults with learning difficulties varies widely across the country. Concerns about political sensitivity and parental anxiety mean that in many places, sex education is taboo:

> … In some areas, sex education has been put on ice while policy documents are drawn up at County Hall level (Sutcliffe, 1990: 82).

Kathy's Reflections on Starting Up Sexuality Classes

Having started to put pen to paper, after lots of stops and starts, I have begun again, because I have never been asked to be involved in writing a book before and I feel very much alone in this and know how some people with learning difficulties must feel. The feeling is not very nice, but like the students I am going to try. So pen to paper again, I begin to think how the sexuality project all started. In 1980 I was working for the Inner London Education Authority (ILEA) in London, teaching beauty care in what was called a mainstream adult education class, when I was asked if I was interested in tutoring a course on self care designed for a group of women with learning difficulties who were living in a long-stay institution.

After I agreed I discovered that all that the carers really expected of me was to teach the women how to do their nails. I was disappointed and felt that the issues of self care for women were being defined in a stereotypical way, focusing on fashion. Feeling very ambivalent about the course, but wanting the work, I began. With 15 women in the class, teaching nail care did take up several two-hour sessions! Most of the women thoroughly enjoyed the sessions however and wanted the course to include discussions on make up and hair care. I began to realise that women with learning difficulties were seldom given the opportunity to express their sexuality in any way. Having the opportunity to examine 'style' and image was a liberation and an opportunity for them to begin to explore their own sexuality. Realising that I, too, had had stereotypical ideas, I started to enjoy the teaching.

As the course progressed I became convinced that it was essential to discuss what the students wanted out of the course. Did they really want to carry on putting nail varnish on or did they perhaps want to know more about self care, health and body awareness? The women in the group had not had the opportunity to make many choices in their lives. Most had been placed in the institution where they lived and were seldom asked about what food they might like to eat or what education they wished to participate in. Offering them a choice of topics in a class was a new idea to many group members.

During the first few weeks of the course several women's issues emerged in the sessions. Some of the women became distressed because they had lost their 'STs', and some students became angry or tearful because, 'It was that time of the month'. When I asked the women if they always suffered from pre-menstrual tension, most of them did not understand what I was talking about. I met with the staff in the home where the women were living and raised the issue of the women's lack of knowledge about their bodies. The staff's initial reaction was surprise that I was concerned that the women should have a greater awareness of the physical and emotional changes which women experience through life. There was a view that the women 'just wouldn't understand'. Some staff thought any such discussion would be harmful, creating fear and distress. I argued that ignorance creates unnecessary difficulties for people or, as Ann Craft and Marjorie Hitching identify, 'we have to deal with the reality of clients who get into all sorts of difficulties precisely because we have left them in ignorance and without protective strategies' (Craft and Hitching, 1989: 29).

However, as time went on and the group grew in confidence, the students became more demanding and wanted to know more about their own bodies and how they worked. I had no option but to develop the course in the direction which the women wanted. The big step was for me to get the staff's approval. I spent several weeks negotiating the new elements for the course. I was given a shopping list of what I could cover in my sessions: skin, hair, feet, diet, and no more ... Well, I thought, that's a start.

In the weeks and months that followed, the questions the women asked were quite amazing. Some found the discussions difficult, others would just sit very still and say nothing, but on the whole members of the group wanted to know more. The students' experiences and abilities were very diverse and we worked very patiently as a group to develop communication skills, both verbal and non-verbal, attempting wherever possible to avoid stereotypical attitudes.

The Context for the Taboo on Sex

From the middle of the nineteenth century when the classification of 'idiot' began to be more 'scientifically' specific, women who were labelled as 'feebleminded' – later to become 'mental handicap' and then 'learning difficulties' – have had society draw connections between their intelligence and their right to sexuality (Ryan, 1986).

One of the most significant features of the 1913 Mental Deficiency Act, which made provision for incarcerating people who were labelled as feebleminded, was the way the Act was gendered. Women could be 'put away' for sexual behaviour, having illegitimate children or because they were 'in need of protection'.

Expressing one's sexuality outside of marriage was a 'sin'. Sexual expression was regarded as something only for 'normal' people. In particular, any open display of sexuality, especially from women, was thought to be disgusting and abnormal (Williams, 1989). Women were put away in single sex institutions where their movements were watched to discourage overly close 'friendships' between women. Many who were put away were not allowed out of their institution into the community. In these environments women could not discuss any issues regarding their own bodies, including menstruation, secondary sexual characteristics or menopause. Knowledge of ordinary events was limited and the women were forced to rely on information which they could 'pick up' from snatches of conversation and what the women themselves encountered. One woman who was 'put away' in 1923 and who still lives in an institution told Mary:

> Well you know I didn't know anything about it. I must have been about nine or ten and I had seen the cloths on the line and had asked S why I couldn't wash those and she said, you'll know soon enough. I was only ten at the time and then when it happened, well I didn't know anything and I called out in the night S, S, I've been stabbed,

I'm bleeding, I've been stabbed. She told me to quieten
down and gave me a cloth, but I didn't know what to do
with it ... . so I just put it on my chest, I was frightened
about my heart, so I put it on my chest. I found out later
of course, but no one told you anything' (M, 1991).

While many disabled women in the early part of the twentieth century were not informed about their bodies or their sexuality (Humphries and Gordon, 1992), women with learning
difficulties were considered totally ineducable. For many of
these women, even in the 1990s sex and sexuality are taboo
subjects. Despite a legal recognition that people with learning
difficulties have adult status from 18 years old (Gunn, 1991), in
practice parents and carers of adult women can still discourage
any form of sexual pleasure including masturbation, and many
women in their 40s and 50s are still ignorant of how their bodies work and the changes which many of them are about to
face.

In the rest of this chapter we discuss the work in a number of
sexuality courses for women with learning difficulties and the
dilemmas which the tutors and students face.

Sex and Sexuality Come Out of the Closet

After a year of running the self care course, the adult education
organisers at the institute which offered the course began to
recognise that the self care course had developed and was offering students knowledge and skills far beyond its initial intention. Social workers and carers also recognised that the
students in this group were showing more confidence in themselves, and other women were keen to join the class. The shopping list of what could be covered in the course remained, but
care workers and educationalists agreed that we needed to address many of the issues raised in the self care course in a more
systematic way in a new course. As one of the adult education
organisers in the institution, Mary worked with Kathy to develop Looking Good, Feeling Fine, and in the following years
we often worked together developing and teaching new
courses in London and then in Sussex after Mary moved to the
Centre for Continuing Education.

Looking Good, Feeling Fine was developed to take account
of the range of material which we covered. Fifteen women took
the course in the first year. They were all very keen and the sessions were lively and interesting. In the first term we worked
on parts of the body which the students could see by looking at
themselves in the mirror. We used the mirror as a resource, en-

couraging the women to discuss how they looked while standing in front of it. The women were encouraged to move their arms, pull faces, examine their hair, teeth and so on. It was amazing to learn that, for many of the women in the group, looking in the mirror and seeing themselves was a new experience. Psychological theories of the self identify that a sense of personal identity grows from a recognition of yourself (Lacan, 1979; Mead, 1934). Students examined their hair, teeth, feet and body shape. For many of the women exploring how they looked helped them develop confidence in who they were. The women began to make choices about themselves, choosing to reflect who they were through their outward appearance. Several of the women who had been dressed in bobby socks and skirts took to wearing trousers. Others chose to change their hair style.

Many feminists have identified concern about personal appearance as a potential site of oppression for women (Coward, 1984). While we accept that this may be true for some women, for the women we were working with, being able to make choices about their appearance was a sign of developing self confidence and an ability to speak for themselves. So often the notion of sexuality is understood to mean the sexual act; we would argue that being more personally self aware and taking some pleasure in how you present yourself to the world is a significant aspect of a developing sexuality.

The second term of Looking Good, Feeling Fine examined the structure of the body: bones, muscles, blood and hormones. Despite the fact that all the students were adult women who had experience of menstruation, and some had experienced menopause, none of the women in the group understood the process of monthly bleeding and why it happened. Working through many of these issues created tensions for the women in the group. Having been told, as many women have been, that discussing issues about periods is 'not nice', most of the women in the group became silent, while others giggled and became visibly embarrassed when we began the section of the course. Carers expressed a concern that we were creating difficulties for the women. One carer felt that her daughter was becoming fixated on her periods and was distressed by the experience.

We were worried that we were unpicking all the work we had achieved during the first term of the course, and decided that we needed to develop the section on menstruation and menopause slowly and with sensitivity. It was essential to use pictures, and to provide clear, understandable information, as many of the women found it embarrassing to challenge us if they did not grasp what we were talking about. We realised that we had to adapt the available materials to suit the needs of the group we were working with. We were keen to use resources which were appropriate for adults, but language and terminology needed to be explained and the women needed to feel that no one would laugh or ridicule their concerns. By the end of the course most of the women spoke in support of the subject matter which we had tackled. Key workers reported that the women who had attended the course responded to their bodies' demands in a mature and confident manner. Clearly the women had understood what we had tried to communicate to them.

By the third term we were able to investigate our senses. We began to explore sensations which made us feel good, using aromatherapy, massage and soft materials. Students in the group became aware of what was pleasant to touch, what tickled, what pricked and what smelled good. Being aware of sensation helped us all explore our personal preferences and pleasures. This heightened awareness of our bodies helped group members assert their sense of themselves. For many of the women in the group, touch had been a frightening experience often associated with medical examination or being forcibly moved from one place to another. Exploring touch as a pleasurable experience gave the women a greater awareness of all parts of their bodies. When many of the women began the course, the skin on their hands and faces had been dry and red. The women all lived in institutions where maintaining personal possessions was difficult. Caring for the body is often a sign of a personal identity and theorists studying institutions have noted that inmates seldom take an interest in their appearance (Goffman, 1961). As the women became aware of pleasant sensations and understood the difference in feeling soft skin rather than sore, chapped skin, they began to use hand creams. Feminists have identified the ability to make choices about our own bodies as an important political issue (Dickson, 1985; Brownmiller, 1986). However, the argument is often phrased in a negative sense, condemning the use of cosmetics and self care products. Denying women with learning difficulties their right to use self care products seriously impairs their own sense of sexuality and pleasure.

As a result of the success of this course, and recognising that related issues needed to be addressed, other courses were developed, including a course on relationships, a course called *Positively Women* which tackled the question of being safe and confident about yourself as a women, and a course specifically focusing on health issues called *Body Awareness*. All these courses have focused on specific issues which affect women.

The Body Awareness course took the subject matter which we had examined in Looking Good, Feeling Fine a stage further, examining issues of pre-menstrual tension (PMT), emotional well being, and coping and dealing with thrush, cystitis and gynaecological issues. Visits to the doctor were an important focus for this course. The women in the group were often ignored on visits to the doctor while the professionals – their key worker and the doctor – spoke together. We became aware that assertiveness training was as important as understanding the workings of the body. The women's movement of the 1970s and 1980s focused quite correctly on the relationship between women and their doctors; as Helen Roberts noted in 1980, women visit doctors more than men. For women with learning difficulties whose lives are framed in a medical model, examining the doctor/patient relationship was even more essential.

In these courses we were constantly aware that the initial course outlines had to be adapted to meet the needs of the women we were working with. Because we were engaging with the women's needs it was often difficult to provide a clear account of the syllabus of the course – the information which the institute required for its quality assurance procedures. This created tensions in our work as our initial course information appeared to be inaccurate when the class was visited. As new quality assurance systems develop it is important that flexibility in responding to students' demands is not lost.

Confidence

Throughout our work on sexuality, we were convinced from our own experience that confidence and trust within the group are the most important elements for enabling the students to learn. Many women lack confidence in their abilities (Thompson, 1983; Ryle and Stuart, 1994). This is doubly compounded if you are also labelled as having a learning difficulty. This lack of confidence expresses itself in a variety of ways: an inability to speak up in a group; crying out of a feeling of not coping; or aggression as a way of hiding insecurity. Many people with learning difficulties feel that they do not know what is happening to them. This is either because they are not told or because information is not offered in an accessible way. A syndrome of learned and taught helplessness develops (Swain, 1989), in which people with learning difficulties accept that they will not be given information which is relevant to them. Key workers, parents and carers take that responsibility. In some ways being ignorant can create a sense of security, but it also increases a lack of confidence in yourself.

Providing women with learning difficulties with more knowledge about their bodies breaks this cycle of learned and taught helplessness. It becomes the woman's responsibility to made choices about her body. Choices about tampons or sanitary towels, hand cream or deodorant, may seen minor concerns to many women in everyday life, but for women who have had sanitary towels handed out to them on a monthly basis with no understanding or awareness of the options available, knowing more about their bodies and how they work helps the development of confidence. This is significant and important education which challenges some of the inequalities between women. Courses need to be designed to meet the needs of the students, not as dictated by professionals or education theorists who have not engaged with the specific demands of a particular group.

Trust

Working with as sensitive an issue as sexuality, it is vital to build trust between all group members. Women with learning difficulties are often very insecure about their bodies, especially as much of their physical experience of their bodies is never explained to them. Many of them are unable to read, and have a very limited knowledge of their growth. Discussions are often centred on what you are not allowed to do or on disorders of the body, and take place in the presence of a doctor. Given these parameters, developing trust is essential. Participants need to understand that they are able to speak in the group without ridicule or without being told that what they are saying is unacceptable. Building trust takes time and a degree of honesty from the tutors. Being in a women-only group helps this trust develop, especially when tutors explain that many of the concerns that the group members have are ones which they and other women share.

Group members also need to trust that issues raised in the group will remain in the group. Because women with learning difficulties are 'cared for' and are often seen as children without rights, or are considered objects of study by the medical profession, their concerns are often discussed openly among many different people. Trusting that we as tutors would not do this was important to the women sharing their worries and fears. Ensuring that we did not take issues out of the group unless the women asked us to do so was and is difficult. As trust developed several of the women revealed information about their lives which was painful and which we felt needed attention. We discussed these issues with the women concerned and sometimes got their approval to raise issues with staff, with mixed success. We have learned that it is usually more appropriate to help the women develop the confidence to tackle issues themselves. Despite the change in our practice, however, we are still unable to resolve some of the contradictions between our role as educators and our role as support workers.

Relationships

Once we began to discuss issues relating to our emotional well being, many of the women began to question us about relationships, including relationships with other women and with men. Friendships are seen as a problem in some homes for women with learning difficulties. Professionals worry that women friends might get 'too close'. As in many other areas of society, amongst professionals and carers working with women with learning difficulties fear of lesbian sexuality is enormous. It is extremely difficult to offer support to women whose feelings are confused because they have been told they are experiencing emotions which are wrong. Professionals and carers are able to decide who should be friends with whom. One woman who discussed her eating disorder with Kathy confided that she had made a friend: 'This is the first real friend I have had. I feel I can trust her.' Several weeks later the 'carers' in the home 'Rita' lived in moved her friend away, because they felt the friendship was developing into 'other things'.

As educators we are all too painfully aware that what we can offer the women we work with is often not reproduced in the rest of their lives. We discuss the group members' rights to relationships, but the women's daily experience suggests that rights are decided by their carers. We did not want to be irresponsible. Women with learning difficulties are vulnerable members of society and we appreciate that carers and parents want to protect the women in their care. We would argue that often this care can increase vulnerability. For example, parents can find it difficult to imagine that their adult daughters with learning difficulties have sexual feelings, and the women themselves find it difficult to discuss problems with their parents. If particular sexual difficulties do arise for a woman with learning difficulties and she is unable to discuss her concerns with her carers and does not understand her sexual rights, it is possible that she will be abused in some way.

Our work has and still does create tensions between carers and the adult education service we work for. At times women have even been removed from a group. However in the courses we organised we found that the question of sexual feelings and relationships became more and more prominent. When we first set up the sexuality courses we did not work closely with carers. We now feel that this was incorrect. Any sex education or sexuality course needs to have the support of parents and professional carers. Discussing the parameters and direction of a sexuality course with people who will not even be attending the course may seem an infringement of the rights of the women who have asked for the course, but unless carers can offer support and encouragement, any learning which the women engage in will be an isolated and often frightening experience.

Fear

Fear is a major part of the lives of many women with learning difficulties. Many older women have spent most of their lives in large institutions with strict regimes. Many institutions were single-sex and no sexual activity or contact was acceptable. Even in mixed-sex institutions, men and women were often not allowed to talk to each other and relationships were difficult. More recently, various studies have indicated that people with learning difficulties are particularly susceptible to sexual abuse (Brown, 1989). They are often not believed and are thought to be telling stories. One woman who consistently talked of being abused by her friend's father finally had a nervous breakdown because she was told she was 'naughty and dirty' for saying she had been raped. Stories about parental abuse have been documented by psychologists working with men and women with learning difficulties (Sinason, 1989).

Because some people with learning difficulties are watched in a way not dissimilar to the surveillance of prisoners, sexual activity is associated with fear, fear of being caught, fear of being ridiculed. In some day service centres adults with learning difficulties are told it is not appropriate to show affection at the centre. Parents are often not keen for their children, especially their daughters, to express any sexual feelings, with the result that they may be unable to express their love for someone at home. Surveillance makes ordinary sexual expression difficult. In East Sussex, Social Services policy on sexuality and the rights of adults with learning difficulties is ill defined, and while there is much good practice, many Social Services professionals are ambivalent about educationalists offering sexuality courses. Parents have withdrawn their adult 'children' from classes or have needed support in understanding new ideas and approaches. It is important to challenge carers' and professionals' attitudes to sexuality. Developing a relationship between carers and tutors which highlights the learning needs of women with learning difficulties should enable courses to present information honestly and not to ignore important aspects of sexual understanding.

Feedback and Evaluation

At the end of our courses students are asked to feed back to the tutor their thoughts and feelings about their learning. Most women were extremely positive, saying that it is their 'right to know'. However some women said they found the discussions difficult and awkward, as they had internalised a sense that their bodies were in some way 'dirty' without understanding what this might mean. Often these women found there were contradictions for them between what they were exploring in the course and their experience at home. Much of our work in London and now in Sussex raises difficult issues for the women we work with. Uncovering sexual feelings and suggesting that these sensations are normal creates a dilemma for the women. If they express themselves they may lose the favour of their parents or carers. We had initially begun working in this area at the request of the women who attended Kathy's initial self care course and became convinced of the women's right to know about sexuality, but as we have developed the work we have become aware that raising questions about sexuality for women with learning difficulties can create as many tensions for the women as ignoring their rights.

To lessen the contradictions for the women participating in the sexuality courses we decided to work with carers and professionals and have recently begun to develop courses for parents and carers to help carers explore their own fears and sexual feelings. As tutors and organisers working with women with learning difficulties we also have to examine our own perceptions and feelings. For both of us, working on this project has opened up many issues about our own sexual choices and sexual expression. We have become more aware of our own sexuality. By engaging with the women on the sexuality courses we have had our own awareness raised as much as that of the course participants. We feel we are still learning about ourselves as women. It is an voyage of self discovery, sometimes frightening but always exciting. We hope we share this sense of adventure with all the participants on our courses.

The Future

There is now some excellent material for work in this area, unlike fifteen years ago when Kathy started her first course, but much of it does not examine the complex engagement with the institutional and medicalised experience of people with learning difficulties, or the specifics of gender oppression, which is particularly surprisingly in materials dealing with sexuality and sex education. We feel it is important to draw on a feminist analysis of issues of sexuality, although even this liberatory discourse does not necessarily take account of the particular needs of disabled women (Begum, 1992).

One of the best training packs for people with learning difficulties is *My Choice, My Own Choice* (West Lambeth Health Promotions, 1992). The pack explores a number of sexual relationships for adults with learning difficulties and suggests ways of approaching parents and professionals to support the sexual choices of the people depicted in the training video. Although many of the suggestions are clearly helpful, the easy solutions which the people in the video are able to reach with the professionals and carers are far from the reality we have experienced.

A growing number of training courses and training manuals for staff working with adults with learning difficulties are also being developed. We found the training pack *Sex and Staff Training* (McCarthy and Thompson, 1994) especially useful because it examines why training is necessary and tackles a wide range of issues including staff attitudes and feelings about sex. Often it is the attitudes and contradictory feelings of people in positions of authority which create difficulties for the women on our courses and it is very useful to find material which helps staff examine their own sexual feelings and experiences.

There is a growing awareness that adults with learning difficulties have a right to sexual expression and sexual choice. One practical outcome has been the development of sensory awareness rooms in day centres, which allow centre users to explore sensations and feelings. These rooms are excellent and could be used in adult education provision as well. Closer liaison needs to be developed with carers and parents, in order to reinforce learning programmes. Educationalists have often seen themselves working in opposition to parents and carers, but this is not a useful way forward. The history of women's sexual liberation is still relatively recent and is not yet won. Women with learning difficulties are only beginning to benefit from these liberation battles. Engaging with all who have an interest in the lives of the women we work with is vital if we are to offer knowledge which the women who participate in the courses can use. Advice and information from professionals and carers must inform educational programmes and educators, professionals and carers must get support to explore the complex and difficult area of people's sexuality if they are to in turn support the growing knowledge of the women who study their sexuality. As women grow in confidence, sexuality courses may offer women with learning difficulties a real opportunity to examine their sexual choices and to act on their learning.

For reasons of safety, and at the women's request, we have not used individuals' real names in this chapter.

References

Begum, N. 'Disabled Women and the Feminist Agenda', in *Feminist Review*, Spring 1992, No. 40.

Brown, H. and Craft, A. (1989) *Thinking the Unthinkable*, London: Family Planning Association.

Brownmiller, S. (1986) *Femininity*, London: Paladin Books.

Coward, R. (1984) *Female Desire: Women's Sexuality Today*, London: Paladin Books.

Craft, A. and Hitching, M. (1989) 'Keeping Safe: Sex Education and Assertiveness Skills', in Brown, H. and Craft, A. (eds.) *Thinking the Unthinkable*, London: Family Planning Association.

Dickson, A. (1985) *The Mirror Within: A New Look at Sexuality*, London: Quartet.

Goffman, E. (1961) *Asylum: Essays on the Social Situation of Mental Patients and Other Inmates*, New York: Doubleday.

Gunn, M. J. (1991) *Sex and the Law*, London: Family Planning Association.

Humphries, S. and Gordon, P. (1992) *Out of Sight: The Experience of Disability 1900– 1950*, London: Northcote House.

Lacan, J. (1979) *The Four Fundamental Concepts of Psycho-analysis* (translated by Alan Sheridan), London: Penguin.

McCarthy, M. and Thompson, J. (1994) *Sex and Staff Training*, London: Pavilion Publishers.

Mead, G. H. (1934) *Mind, Self and Society*, Chicago: University of Chicago Press.

Ryan, J., with Thomas, F. (1987) *The Politics of Mental Handicap*, London: Free Association Books.

Ryle, M. and Stuart, M. (1994) 'An Access Curriculum for Women? A case study from Brighton', *Journal of Access Studies*, Autumn 1994.

Sinason, V. (1989) 'Uncovering and Responding to Sexual Abuse in Psychotherapeutic Settings', in Brown, H. and Craft, A., *Thinking the Unthinkable*, London: Family Planning Association.

Sutcliffe, J. (1990) *Adults with Learning Difficulties: Education for Choice and Empowerment*, Milton Keynes: Open University Press.

Swain, J. (1989) 'Learned Helplessness Theory and People with Learning Difficulties: the psychological price of powerlessness', in Brechin, A. and Walmesley, J. (eds) *Making Connections*, Sevenoaks: Hodder and Stoughton.

Thompson, J. (1983) *Learning Liberation: Women's Response to Men's Education*, London: Croom Helm.

West Lambeth Health Promotions (1992) *My Choice, My Own Choice* (video and training manual), London: Pavilion Publishers.
Williams, F. (1989) 'Mental Handicap and Oppression', in Brechin, A. and Walmesley, J. (eds) *Making Connections,* Sevenoaks: Hodder and Stoughton.

Chapter 7

Information Technology and Enablement: Microsoft Windows and Adults with Learning Difficulties

David Longman and Mary Stuart

Learning to Use Computers

The current generation of personal computers is more advanced than its predecessors in two well-advertised ways. They are more powerful in terms of hardware specifications (more memory, faster processing speeds, etc.), and with the development of Microsoft Windows™, they offer improved software facilities for interacting with the computer, to manage files, to more easily run a wider range of applications and to swap data between them. Windows also offers the now ubiquitous mouse for controlling applications, thus minimising the use of the keyboard for these tasks.

The concept of windows goes back to the late 1960s, to American research conducted by companies such as Rank-Xerox. The mouse and the graphical window together provide a direct manipulation environment in which the user is able to control many computer functions simply by pointing and clicking at graphic elements on the screen. Such an approach is intended to be more accessible, more intuitive, for the user because it is based on a range of non-specialised, universal, and basic human skills (Grief, 1988).

However, as educators we should always be cautious about such claims which largely rest on a tacit image of an idealised user. Our experience of teaching adults basic skills in using Microsoft Windows suggests that in spite of the openness of its design intentions many learners take some time to become confident and intuitive users. These issues can be magnified in highly differentiated learning groups where idealised assumptions about the material or skills to be learned are very unhelpful (Norman, 1990). This can lead to a situation where learning problems generated by design features of computer software are all too easily located with the learner, perhaps the more so if the student is already labelled as 'having' a learning difficulty.

This chapter presents an informal discussion of some observations that relate to some of these learning issues. The issues selected are not typical. We are not concerned so much with illustrating learning gains as to describe the often minute obstacles to successful computer use which are attributable to the properties of the computer environment rather than any learning difficulty experienced by the student (Suchman, 1987). If as teachers we falsely believe that using Windows and a mouse is intuitive, then we are more likely to assume that a student's difficulty rests with them and not the computing environment. The examples given in this chapter are an attempt to show how very small design details interfere with learning in accidental, that is undesigned, ways.

Learning to control the dynamic nature of Windows requires a mixture of perceptual, muscular, and intellectual aptitudes, and novices vary as to the balance they achieve in co-ordinating these processes. Although many adults begin a course fully literate and physically co-ordinated, learning to use computer software involves applying this background of established skills and expectations in the unfamiliar and, in spite of the design claims for it, counterintuitive context of Windows. Learners must sometimes cope with unexpected frustration, disappointment and anxiety.

These are not always pleasant experiences for the beginner although they pass quickly as the systematic relationship between the functional parts of the software environment is built up through instruction and training. In general it is as if the initial contact with Windows involves many learners in a learning *regression* because, for example, existing literacy skills cannot be instantly applied in the new context and many new skills must be learned. The ease with which this change occurs can vary widely. Some adults have difficulties with Windows which are related both to the character of computer applications (the conventions, the manner of presentation) and to the fact that new skills, or re-combinations of existing skills, must be acquired.

For example, whereas day-to-day reading is a fairly loose and approximate activity in which individual words are less important than the gist of the whole, in a software environment such as Windows words are used in a strictly denotative manner. Words must be read one for one, and interpreted literally as instructions to act, or as carrying important direct information for actions. For many adults an early insight is that reading a computer screen is quite different from everyday reading, that words are used in unfamiliar ways and expressions are usually terse and highly specific. Previous knowledge does not always apply. Even the process of reading texts on-screen as part of a wordprocessing activity is different. In reading text on paper, scanning down the page involves a physical movement of the head and eyes to change the angle of view. However, in a wordprocessor it is the text that is moved, not the viewing angle. Scrolling *down* a page of text in a wordprocessor has the effect of moving the text *up* on the screen, equivalent to *moving the book* when reading down a page.

For a brief moment the literate adult is placed in the position of a child acquiring its first language where words and meanings are built up interactively and experimentally over time and where new muscular co-ordinations must develop. Similar shocks can occur during the first attempts to co-ordinate the movement of the mouse with the screen pointer, and to click the mouse button appropriately. Almost all adults exclaim at the difficulty of writing their name freehand with the mouse in Windows Paintbrush. Here too the novice has a brief encounter with an experience reminiscent of a child's first attempts to write letters and words.

Adults with Learning Difficulties: A Wordprocessing Course

In this chapter we discuss our observations drawn from a Word for Windows course for a group of nine adults designated as having learning difficulties. The course ran for ten weeks, meeting on a weekday morning for two hours in the Centre for Continuing Education at Sussex University and represents the first in a new programme of computer-based courses for this group of students.

At the outset of the course we had little information about the people who had elected to take it. This is general practice with all open entry continuing education courses and this policy was adhered to despite a continuing historical tendency amongst professionals to use descriptions of individual problems and difficulties as assessment criteria (Sutcliffe, 1992). We were keen to avoid this labelling process and yet we found we had to challenge our own preconceptions because the students often met and went beyond our expectations for the course. As the course progressed a wide variation in ability and rate of learning became apparent and some individuals needed more detailed help than others.

The course was designed to encourage students to use the computer for writing in a variety of ways and they could follow their writing urge or concentrate on developing skills as they pleased. A book of written and pictorial work was produced at the end of the course and an image scanner was available for copying photographs, which lent a strong personal quality to the enterprise.

Compared with other adult groups taking a similar course this group was not radically different in the kinds of learning problems they had to solve with the computer. Although overall the rate of learning was somewhat slower, for some students the quality of the learning was considerable, and the task focus was greater. Few students on the course were highly literate but the motivation to write and to use words, and the motivation to learn to handle the wordprocessor, was as good as in any adult group and at times more intense. Significant differences appeared with some members of the group who did not use verbal communication and response (two students communicated with Makaton), and some who were very slow to take mouse or keyboard actions without positive encouragement.

All the students attended social service day centres in the East Sussex area and had never been to a university before. There are a number of universities offering courses for adults with learning difficulties, including the University of East London, University of Warwick and the pioneer of this work, the Open University (Walmsley, 1992). Some were individuals with long standing problems affecting their social and intellectual behaviour and some were individuals who had passed many years in institutional care and were now learning to live in the community.

It was interesting to observe the social integration of the students as the weeks went by. One student who was able to organise her own transport asked her taxi driver to pick her up after lunch because she wished to stay on campus and try some of the different eating places. Students spoke of 'feeling at home' in the University and talked in a casual way with other staff and students. We believe that the atmosphere of the University enabled the student group to participate intensively in their learning, and that they gained a sense of self-importance from their roles as University students. Resources in Higher Education are extensive in comparison with many colleges and this helps the students to take their learning seriously (Alexander, Hugorin and Sigler, 1985).

Of the nine students Martha, who had been arbitrarily labelled as a mentally handicapped child in the 1930s, could have done well in any introductory wordprocessing group. An intelligent woman of sixty-two with a real talent for writing and a powerful urge to write stories about her life, she would be an intellectual match for any adult class. Having been institutionalised for social reasons rather than as the result of a specifically diagnosed disability, Martha benefited both from learning to use the wordprocessor and from learning to challenge her past through her writing and asserting a new identity.

Two or three members of the group required intensive individual support but for different reasons. One student was a talented artist and could use Paintbrush to create skilful freehand drawings with little supervision, but at times her emotional fragility required additional support. This student was remarkable in that during the first workshop using Paintbrush she wrote her name freehand with the mouse, spontaneously and without evident difficulty. From the first she exhibited none of the physical difficulties associated with using the mouse and her mouse drawings demonstrated exceptional skill. Very few people are able to sit down with Paintbrush and create structured images within the first couple of hours. A second student had very poor eyesight and needed lots of help to locate keys and to identify parts of the screen. The voluntary presence of a care worker during this course was an unexpected but essential addition to the teaching team.

Yet other factors impinged on individual students and affected their learning. Sarah appeared to have great difficulty controlling the mouse because of a slight tremor and difficulty identifying parts of the screen. She had great trouble either conceiving of words to write or staying on task when one was provided. She repeatedly said that she found it very hard to think of things to write. Finally, she confided that she had 'been ill' and was still on medication.

In the following sections we describe how the students in this group experienced typical issues in learning to use Windows and especially a mouse. It became obvious as the sessions went on that this group of students was so motivated that they would succeed through perseverance where other students might give up. The important point here is that in working with people caught up in the learning disabilities cycle it is essential to challenge the educator's perceptions of the student's own learning difficulties (Harlesden CMHT, 1988). This course proceeded in the same way as any self-selecting group of adult students, and on the basis of previous experience of similar courses with adults the expectation was that this group would encounter the same sorts of difficulties and require similar sup-

port, mostly repetition of examples, and plenty of reassurance.
We now turn to look at some of the detailed micro-tasks involved in learning to use the mouse to control Word for Windows. Some modifications were made to the Windows environment, particularly by simplifying the Toolbar, menus and writing area in Word for Windows. A special template was created which also incorporated an enlarged typeface because it was clear from an early stage that two or three students had difficulty reading the smaller sizes. Adjustments were made to the mouse buttons for one student who preferred to use her left hand, and an enlarged mouse pointer was used. From the fourth week the mouse tracking speed and the double click speed were altered.

The Mouse

The mouse is the physical device used for 'pointing and clicking' at graphical elements on the screen, held flat in one hand so that it can be moved on a flat surface on its rollerball. The physical mouse is linked to a graphical pointer, usually an arrow shape, that moves on screen in synchronisation with the physical mouse. At least one button is required to select an object on the screen or to carry out some action to be executed.

There seem to be three essential combined elements to using a standard PC mouse: light, quick movements of the fingers on the mouse buttons (usually the index finger); a light grip with the breadth of the hand across the mouse usually with the thumb and fourth/fifth fingers; and moving the mouse on a flat surface. These rely on forearm and wrist control using small, gentle sweeping movements; these physical motions of the arm and hand must be visually co-ordinated with the movement of the graphical pointer to a high degree of accuracy. In the standard Word for Windows set-up although fonts can be enlarged to facilitate typing and reading, icons and functional screen text are small and densely packed. Much of the 'active' on-screen information such scroll bars, menus, or buttons, is quite subtle.

That the mouse should be used by moving it on the table top is not immediately obvious and direct instruction is often necessary. A recent example comes from a different group of senior educational administrators, a group that might be expected to fit the assumption of an idealised user. At the beginning of the first session the mouse was held it up so it could be seen by the whole group and a verbal explanation was given, combined with illustrative gestures in the air. On the instruction to start using the mouse nearly all the group held their mice in the air and started moving them around in imitation of the demonstration. The tutor had indeed assumed the self-evident nature of the mouse and had not explicitly stated that the mouse should be moved on a flat surface. In yet other cases students have been observed to hold the mouse upside down and move the rollerball with the fingers.

The Pointer

Learning to relate physical mouse movements to the movement of the screen pointer can be problematic. A lot of instructional emphasis is needed, for example by tracing the movement of the screen pointer with the finger or holding the student's hand on the mouse and moving it so that they are able to *feel* how the two things go together.

This difficulty is at least partially attributable to the quality of the standard mouse pointer itself which can be difficult to see either at rest or in motion. Even experienced users can lose sight of the pointer. One simple way to locate it, for a non-beginner, is to move the mouse but, at first, novices don't do this, and spend much time staring at the screen looking for the stationary pointer.

However, even moving the mouse does not always work. Peter's muscular co-ordination at the beginning of the course was such that whereas small rather delicate movements are more appropriate he made large, rapid sweeping movements, and as a result the pointer moved too quickly for him to see it. In addition, because the movements were large, when he came to rest the pointer often ended up just off the edge of the screen. So for Peter a simple moving and stopping strategy didn't work and created a vicious circle. When he moved the mouse the pointer would be fleetingly visible and he would stop; but his large arm movements had already moved the pointer off the edge of the screen. At first his movements were so great that adjusting the mouse tracking speed to its slowest setting had only a slight effect but by the seventh week he had learned to move the mouse and to track the screen pointer with much more success.

Apart from tracking the position of the pointer an important refinement is to learn to recognise the various shapes the pointer has according to action and context. Once again this can be a long learning curve for most people. For example, the arrow pointer will always change to a text pointer when it is moved over a screen region where the user can type. Identifying such regions on the screen is an important element of successful use of Windows and the shape of the screen pointer is a subtle but significant cue.

Gripping a Mouse

Often society perceives people with learning disabilities as 'the same as' people with physical disabilities. This is not the case and it is important to note that many of the physical difficulties about gripping the mouse are very common and not specific to any one group. The PC mouse we used in this course has two buttons and the 'best' grip (the grip which most people seem to use after some practice) holds the mouse square in the hand so the forefinger hangs over the left button (or the right button for a left hander). No force is required. The thumb and fifth finger typically straddle the body of the mouse and the ball of the palm and base of the wrist should be free so that it can be used to brake the mouse while pressing the button.

The action of pressing a button while holding the mouse rock steady is crucial because the button press is cancelled out by the slightest mouse movement. This action has few precedents in typical experience. In fact it is clear from working with many adults in this area that there is a 'natural' tendency for the hand to grip the mouse with all the fingers much as it would grip a pole. The hand swings around the mouse, with the four fingers coming together on one side and the thumb on the other. Thus no finger is naturally left free above the mouse button. Unless corrected this can hinder the novice.

However, the standard mouse design attached to most everyday PCs makes few concessions even to the diversity of human hands. For example, arching the hand over the body of the mouse can be uncomfortable for many and imposes an unusual muscular discipline on the hand. Alternative pointing devices do exist (tracker balls, joysticks and styluses) as well as different mouse shapes and it is hoped that funding can be found to carry out an evaluation of these.

Although all adult learners experience some difficulties with the standard mouse, most are able to adapt to it. This group was little different and made very good progress. A few continued to have difficulty gripping and controlling the mouse and for some this could be related to physical characteristics of the hand. June, whose hand mobility was quite restricted, could not really make the grip. This did not however prevent her from producing a volume of self motivated work during the course. In fact by the end of the course June had more or less abandoned the mouse and found the keyboard altogether easier for controlling menu operations.

Clicking the Mouse

There are three ways to use the mouse buttons, having successfully positioned the screen pointer in the right place. The *single
click* is for selecting an item or object on screen. The *double click*
both selects an item or object and carries out the action associated with it. The button can also be *held down* which has the effect of both selecting an item or object and/or moving it if the
object can be moved. A mouse click is made of two stages,
pressing and releasing the button, and the effect of these stages
differs slightly according to context. The learning task is to
know when and how the different types of button actions
should be used.

However, the physical aspects of button clicking cannot be
taken for granted. A mouse click is a light, short press, like
touch-typing, whereas many adults at first use the mouse button more like a doorbell, pressing and holding far too long.
This is not unreasonable. The common experience of buttons is
that they take effect when pressed and when this expectation is
not fulfilled the initial tendency is to hold the button longer or
to apply more pressure. In the group we were working with
two students had especially strong hands and applied great
force to the buttons, often holding them down very hard, which
perhaps springs from ordinary learnt behaviour that 'trying
hard' is associated with force. This created some difficulty in
understanding the difference between pressing and holding the
button and pressing and releasing it quickly.

Exerting more pressure on a mouse button, however, often
compounds the problem because this makes it more likely that
the mouse will move thus cancelling the potential effect of the
button press. The *double click*, used particularly for starting applications from the Program Manager in Windows, can be especially difficult to perform as it requires two clicks performed
in a short time span and with a stationary mouse. Even with
the click speed set to its slowest, several members of this group
still could not double click without help or demonstration by
week seven.

At first some learners use very gentle pressing on the mouse
button as a strategy for avoiding mouse movement but this
cannot usually be carried out quickly enough. Everyone must
find a technique for braking the mouse while double clicking
the button. Many people try a two-handed approach, first moving the mouse pointer into position, then gripping the mouse
with one hand and pressing the button with the other. This is
almost impossible to sustain because it is so inconvenient and
slow, and involves more complex hand-eye co-ordination. The

student positions the mouse pointer but looks away to co-ordinate the double-handed grip. The likelihood of accidental movement is very much greater in these circumstances and the student is caught in a frustrating spiral because the button is pressed while the eyes are diverted and therefore no correction is made to the pointer position.

By the end of the course a mixed technique had been demon-strated which involved using the mouse to select an object with a single click and finishing the action with the Enter key (usu-ally equivalent to clicking an OK button). As with all learning the technology involved needs to be made an aid to learning and independence not a barrier and by developing these alter-native strategies students found it easier to start applications from the Program Manager, avoiding the need for the double click action.

The Complexity of Windows

Everyday computers make radical assumptions about the physical and intellectual characteristics of the individual. Yet quite a number of adults have initial difficulties with using a control device like the mouse. Fine motor movements are re-quired, with a delicate muscular balance between firmness and lightness of touch, and a good degree of visual acuity. Adapta-tion involves relating the movements an individual *can* make to the actions that a system *requires* an individual to make (Nor-man, 1990). Some never accomplish it.

Windows itself is visually complex not only because there is a high rate of information but also because it is dynamic. It changes literally at the press of a button. Novices not only have to learn to appreciate the significance of these dynamic changes but also to appreciate that they are causally related to some ac-tion that they have performed, whether deliberate or acciden-tal. The novice user does not readily notice that something significant has changed on the screen, a message box for exam-ple which requires a mouse or keyboard response before con-tinuing. In such cases the student simply comes to a stop. They don't know why it isn't working but they can't see the message box.

In other cases the Paintbrush Window has been inadver-tently dragged off-screen so that only a small part is visible. The student attempts to carry on painting in what is left with-out noticing that most of the picture has apparently vanished. Other problems occur if an application has been *minimised* (it is usually no longer visible) and Program Manager returns to view. In this case beginners will intuitively double-click on the application icon intending to return to their work but instead open a second copy of the application. Oddly, this is one of the few features of Windows that seems to be genuinely intuitive but which is disallowed by the system.

Multiple menu bars are another common source of confusion. More than one application running in several overlying windows can present several menu bars to the user. Users will frequently click on the wrong menu bar, and thus activate a dormant application window. The Windows applications Paintbrush and Write do not fill the screen when they are started (*i.e.* they are not *maximised* in the terminology of Windows) and this can result in two or more menu bars being visible at the same time. Learning to control these sorts of events (multiple menu bars occur quite frequently) requires that the learner develops some sort of model of the way in which windows relate to each other and of the idea of the desktop. This is not a straightforward task for any beginner.

The students in this group, like others, must learn to integrate a dynamic system of mechanistic sequences of actions with mental models of the software environment and to acquire self-monitoring skills that enable them to keep track of their own actions. Pointing and clicking with the mouse is not merely a physical action but relies on understanding what the pointing and clicking are leading to and when is the right time to do it. In this course we concentrated on using a Print Default button on the Toolbar as the simplest way to reinforce this idea. From weeks four and five, everyone had acquired the basic understanding that a verbal instruction such as: 'move the pointer to the PRINT button and click' required them to use the mouse in certain ways, to move the pointer to the Toolbar and click on the correct button. By week seven, six of the nine students could print their own work using the Print button either independently or on verbal command.

'Difference' in Learning or a Continuum of Learning?

This paper was motivated by the discovery that many of the problems experienced by this group learning to use Windows and a mouse are extremely common across all adult groups. It is important to note the ways in which problems arise from the structure of the materials rather than from any apparent 'learning difficulties', and we hope that by delineating the characteristics of some of these problems we can discriminate more sensibly between different kinds of learning needs presented by different students. We found as the course progressed that the students quickly settled into a routine way of working, concentrating for the most part on tasks they had more or less decided on for themselves. By the final week the group had achieved a high degree of stability in the routinisation of their activity, enabling more sustained concentration on writing and drawing activities by limiting the range of new skills to be learned.

This contrasts in significant ways with other adult education classes where the tendency is to cover new wordprocessing skills right up to the last minute. In this way adult classes can leave their students less well-equipped to cope after the course has ended because the consolidation of a smaller number of crucial basic skills has not taken place. Paradoxically, the students with designated learning difficulties can probably achieve a greater depth of learning relative to their starting point, where many adults finish a course knowing too little about too much.

We came to realise as tutors that our policy of not accepting preconceived labels was correct, but perhaps more significantly for us we had to challenge ourselves in working with this group of students. The students who joined this computer course are regarded as 'different' by society and are often subject to abuse and ridicule but our experience in this context showed us that 'difference' is socially created. An incautious categorisation of these individuals might have led us to ignore the large areas of learning difficulty common to all types of students who are learning to use Windows for the first time.

At the same time individual differences forced us to pay more detailed attention to the different kinds of obstacles that students faced in learning a range of new computer skills. This chapter describes some of these obstacles and aims to challenge the myth of 'intuitive' computing that underlies commercial products such as Microsoft Windows. This myth sets up a context of learning in which certain things are pre-defined as self-evident, as not requiring to be learned. Such a context creates the conditions under which students who do not find these things self-evident are bound to fail, or be labelled as failures. We hope this discussion has illustrated ways in which the 'intuitive' character of Windows cannot be taken for granted and how some potential learning difficulties may be located in the materials, not the learner.

In working with people with learning difficulties, it is vital to be aware of our own assumptions of people's ability. During the course, we were challenged to re-think the process of learning with computers rather than assuming the students were simply exhibiting 'learning difficulties'. This recognition was further confirmed by Martha, one of the students described in this chapter. She is now co-tutoring an introductory computer course for adults with learning difficulties. Working with people with different experience can and should be an enriching and challenging experience, but often it is a way of re-affirming our own learning difficulties and prejudices. Martha spoke to us about her perceptions of the computer course. We feel her comments sum up what we have learned from engaging with the students on the computer course.

I must admit when I first came here and saw those machines, I thought I'll never get it. It all seemed so confusing. And the mouse, I didn't understand what it did. I couldn't see what it had to do with the arrow on the screen, but slowly I got to understand. You made me feel like I could do it and I became less frightened, after all if the worst comes to the worst you can just switch it (the computer) off! I have learned from my own experience of learning that computers are not monsters but can help you and I hope that I am passing that on to those I am teaching.

I'm now learning desktop publishing and using the computer I have in my room to write my life story. I can work on IBM, Amstrad and different packages. I feel I can do so much more. I might have been a slow learner in the past but I'm catching up now (Martha, October 1994).

At the students' request all names in this chapter have been changed.

References

Alexander, K., Hugerin, L. S., and Sigler, E. (1985) 'Effects of different living settings on the performance of mentally retarded individuals', *American Journal of Mental Deficiency*, 9.

Greif, I. (1988) *Computer-Supported Cooperative Work: a book of readings*, Morgan Kaufmann, San Mateo.

Harlesden CMHT (1988) *Mental Handicap in Multi-Racial Britain: Whose Learning Difficulties?*, unpublished.

Norman, D. A. (1990) *The Design of Everyday Things*, Doubleday Inc., NY, previously published as: *The Psychology of Everyday Things*.

Potts, M. and Fido, R. (1990) *A Fit Person to be Removed*, Plymouth: Northcote House.

Suchman, L. A. (1987) *Plans and Situated Actions: The problem of human-machine communication*, Cambridge University Press.

Sutfliffe, J. (1992) *Integration for Adults with Learning Difficulties: Contexts and Debates*, NIACE.

Walmsley, J. (1992) 'Opening Doors: A role for Open Learning in developing valued social roles', *British Journal of Mental Sub-normality*, July.

Chapter 8

'She's Doing Too Much Music': Professional Perceptions of a Learner's Needs

Gus Garside

A woman in her early fifties with learning difficulties used to attend two of my creative music classes on the same day, two other music classes at another institute the next day and a choir the day after. She travelled independently but came from a local day centre. If for any reason my classes had to be cancelled, she would come to the adult education building anyway and spend the day playing the piano. At home she only had a Casio keyboard, on which she would work out tunes from records, the radio or memory. One day she stopped coming to my classes. I rang the day centre and they told me that they had stopped her coming because 'she's doing too much music'. My comment that 'I bet no-one ever said that to Yehudi Menuhin' met the response 'but she's not Yehudi Menuhin'.

Between myself, the head of special needs at the College and the manager of the community home where she lived, we managed to get the decision changed. But a year later I had to fight the same battle on her behalf (and at her explicit request) again. Again we won. This time the College agreed to give her the status of my voluntary assistant – I would rather she were paid. The woman in question, who has Down's syndrome, would like to make a career in music. To her I dedicate this chapter.

The following is a consolidation of many thoughts that my working experience over the last 12 years has given rise to. Over this time, I have worked as a musician and music educationalist. For the last 9 years, much of my educational work, and some of my performance work, has been with adults and children with learning difficulties. This work has taken place in adult and further education colleges, universities, schools, day centres, concert halls, hospitals, arts centres, community centres and community homes. What follows is a response to the excitement and possibilities that I have witnessed and a possible

answer to some of the problems and frustrations that I have
felt. It is, in keeping with the requirements of academic writing,
a tidy answer – a more complex, neat and expensive answer
than would perhaps be possible in reality. Its intention is to
cover a lot of ground ... to spark ideas and debate. It is, in the
first instance, a philosophic enquiry into music education for
the adult student with learning difficulties.

Music in Education: The State of the Art

With notable exceptions, music education in England has for
sometime now been a rather elitist affair underpinned with the
concept of virtuosity and geared to the production requirements of the music of bygone centuries. The following quotation from Christopher Small's *Music, Society, Education* (1980)
puts the case clearly:

> I do not suggest that 'classical' musicians should necessar-
> ily adopt the training methods of jazz musicians, anymore
> than they should adopt those of Balinese or African play-
> ers; nonetheless, it is important that we be aware that
> other methods of musical training, both formal and infor-
> mal, do exist that have equal validity with those of the
> classical tradition of western music, and that we should
> recognise that our own methods of training musicians
> sacrifice elements of the essential musicality of man in
> pursuit of the ideals of individual virtuosity and the
> standardisation of technique. It could be that we have
> something to learn from other cultures. Virtuosity, it must
> be understood, does exist in other musical cultures but it
> is a by-product of the pursuit of music; it is only in tradi-
> tional western culture that it is an end in itself and we
> should be aware of the price we pay for it, especially in
> terms of musical communality, in terms of the ability of
> all to take an active part, not just as a listener or even as
> one who realises the ideas of others, but in the creative
> process itself.

It is little wonder that the musical development of people
with learning difficulties has never been taken very seriously. It
usually features in a rather haphazard way as part of an overall
programme. There is little or no opportunity for a person with
learning difficulties to pursue it with the kind of commitment
that some feel and that is required if one wishes to make of it
something central to one's life and more than a passing hobby.

Over recent years, there has been an intense debate around
music education with the influential growth of the community

music movement and the consequent development of education programmes around many major professional musical projects, even including leading orchestras.

Much valuable work is being done – witness the flowering of interest in and possibilities to learn actively about the music of other countries and the development of a rock music curriculum for school. It seems timely to address the needs and aspirations of those adults with learning difficulties for whom music is a passion and who would make it a vocation.

Music Therapy

In so doing we need first to examine existing musical provision for people with learning difficulties. Parallels will exist in all areas of the 'education' of people with learning difficulties, but perhaps most notably in the area of the creative arts. This has something to do with the way we perceive the creative arts and their social function.

Most books on the subject, or which touch on the subject, of music with people with learning difficulties, fall into the category of music therapy. The best known example of this is *Music Therapy* by Juliette Alvin (1975). While primarily a text on the 'healing properties of music' in relation to people with mental or physical health problems or physical disabilities, it touches several times on music with people with learning difficulties. She says:

> In a paper on backward children, J.P.B. Dobbs speaks of some of the physical chronic disabilities many of these children suffer from, namely adenoids and catarrhal troubles which affect their breathing and hearing. He has noticed that 'the breathing of subnormal children is often shallow and badly controlled ... Their general health will improve as a result of the regular systematic training in deep breathing and breath control required in singing'.

Written in 1966 and never revised, the terminology is old fashioned and unhelpful, but what is noteworthy throughout this book is the way she sees people as patients to be helped and not potential musicians. She describes her methods, saying 'they are also successful with patients whose mind is at primitive level, or not reachable with sophisticated means, such as the mentally retarded'. It is, of course, the therapeutic approach which she applies, despite saying 'mental retardation is not curable, therefore the word "therapy" may not be applicable here'.

That she wrote this in 1966 is not surprising. What is surprising and disappointing, is that the book is still marketed as a classic on which current practice may be based. Several times I've been told, in front of a student, 'oh, he won't be able to do that' or even 'you won't get very far with her'. Since confidence is essential in adult students, it is no wonder that these students had 'learning difficulties'. Of course the comments referred to, however insulting and unhelpful, underline the traditional approach to music education in requiring students to achieve standard technique. What excites me, and what I believe is vital in music (indeed in all the arts), is giving voice to the creative urge. Not standardisation but difference, recognising it and nurturing it.

Most other books that I consulted use the words 'music and the mentally handicapped' and are about working with children solely. There seems a reluctance to acknowledge and address the musical aspirations of adults with learning difficulties. Indeed there is often a reluctance to see them as adults at all, referring to them as 'boys' and 'girls', or in one instance I can recall 'my little chicks'. I've seen adults fed a musical diet that would be appropriate for three year olds. It was in the 'my little chicks' context that I developed a set of adult action songs that served the desire of the staff in the day centre in which I was working to work on co-ordination, object recognition, language development, movement and drama – all the things that action songs are about. The point is that with a little imagination it is possible, and even desirable, to develop musical material which is simple and adult. One exceptional book that I discovered is Miriam Wood's *Music for the Mentally Handicapped* from which I quote:

> We learned a great deal as we worked with our pupils; they taught us as much as we taught them. They told us verbally or non-verbally of their likes and dislikes in music. We realised our need to treat each person as an individual with equal rights, and we learned to see the potential in someone and to work to bring it out. We shared our love of music with them and they with us, and together we developed understanding and respect, one for the other (Wood, 1983: 15).

Unfortunately, even here, the material is all directed at children – there is no discussion of age appropriateness, of the differences between working with children and adults.

The contemporary development of all this work can be found in the articles written in the *Journal of British Music Therapy* where the term 'mentally handicapped' is used to this day and the emphasis is on diagnosis and help. The current principles of 'ordinary lives' and self advocacy are not addressed. It is increasingly felt, especially in the Disability Arts movement that rather than therapy, unless so requested, what people with learning difficulties want is opportunities to develop their means of creative expression via the arts.

Community Music

And so we turn to the Community Music movement. In 1991 the first *National Directory of Community Music* was published. In its introduction, Tim Joss of the Bournemouth Sinfonietta outlined the aims of Community Music:

- to provide access to music for people who are not usually able to participate in musical activity
- to offer opportunities for active participation in making and creating music
- based on partnerships where any 'professional' input is biased towards 'enabling' rather than 'leading'
- concerned with additional social purposes rather than 'music for music's sake'.

I was, for four and a half years, the artistic director of *High Spirits*, a band made up of musicians with learning difficulties. The group toured, recorded and broadcast on BBC television. But often it was the 'additional social' aspects offstage that were most memorable. Staying in a hotel up north, several miles away from their parents or community homes, was for many in the band a unique experience, as was buying me a meal in a motorway café from the money they'd earned at a gig the night before. For me going on the road with *High Spirits* turned out, in many ways, to be no different from going on the road with any other band. What was different, and this is a complex issue, was the reaction of the audiences. Used to responding to music as an expression of ability rather than sensibility they were at times dismissive, at times patronising. This wasn't always the case; sometimes they just got off on the music and the band responded by playing their best.

Within the fields of the Disability Arts movement and the Community Music movement, there are many exciting projects. Examples abound within the pages of the *Community Music Directory* and the Arts Council of Great Britain's Arts and Disability Directory *Off the Shelf and into Action*. *High Spirits* is not the only band of people with learning difficulties. I know of two others – *Heart n' Soul* in Deptford and *Special Jam* in Covent Garden.

For some years I have been involved in running adult education classes for people with learning difficulties, formerly in London and surroundings and now in East Sussex, where I run sessions at the University of Sussex's Centre for Continuing Education as part of the NOW programme.

There are also several 'Arts and Disability Organisations' who act as agencies for artists who work with a range of 'special needs' groups (for example the elderly, prisoners, people with learning difficulties, physical disabilities or mental health problems). Integration is one of the aims that they strive for. These organisations (Shape London, Artlink East, The Arts Conection, Artability, etc. – and others, such as Carousel in Brighton) additionally have a policy of providing work opportunities for people with disabilities.

But in most of these contexts music for people with learning difficulties is seen as a peripheral activity fitting in around and subject to the whims of 'Care Plans' (I refer the reader back to my opening anecdote). The issue of the context in which educational activity takes place is something to which I will return, though I would like to stress here the frustration that I, and the students, have experienced when working on a project, let us say building up to a recording date, and on the day a student is absent because his day centre staff took him or her shopping!

So What's So Special About Music?

> Once people become aware that music is in them, and not only in those who have elected to become musicians, once they take back to themselves the musical act in a spirit of delight and self affirmation, who knows what else they might insist on reclaiming and enjoying (Stevens, 1985).

The above quotation from the seminal free jazz drummer and community music pioneer John Stevens says much about why restrictions are placed upon what and how we learn about music.

> It is as personally enriching experiences, valuable in their own right, that the arts are important to the majority of students. The arts afford us means of representing, investigating and making sense of our experience. Although it would be incorrect, in strict terms, to describe the arts as languages or systems, they do operate as conveyors of meaning (Fell, 1987).

I would argue that music affords us a uniquely resonant way of representing, investigating and making sense of our experience. Being non-verbal it circumvents many of the assumptions and limitations of language. It is possible with music to respond to events in a personal and integrated way without necessarily codifying them intellectually. Several studies exist which testify to the psychological power of music. None of these are of course conclusive in their findings because responses to any profound experience is personal and individual. Music can be played solo or in a group context, where individual contributions help to shape the whole. It is clearly a powerful tool for self advocacy.

I could list several examples of students who have suddenly demonstrated previously hidden skills, both musical and otherwise, that have been released while engaged in the creative and exciting process of music-making. Perhaps the most startling for me was working with a student who had been totally silent for the six months of my project and, according to his keyworker for the two years prior to that. After a particularly fruitful and exhilarating duo with him I told him that I wanted, if he was agreeable, to lift him out of his wheelchair and onto the floor for the next piece. As the care assistant and I started to lift him, he exclaimed in a clear and assertive voice, 'Mind my balls!'

I think it is high time that we gave serious consideration to a full-time course in music or the performing arts for adults with learning difficulties. Offering courses of this nature would highlight a belief in the fundamental rights of people with learning difficulties to access and develop their talents like any other adult. It is through my years of engaging with adults with learning difficulties that I have come to see their abilities being constantly frustrated by their being labelled as different from others. It is in this spirit that I produced the following course outline for a full-time music course.

The Course

So let's look at some possible modules for such a course.

(A) Individual Instrumental Tuition

Opportunity for high standard individual tuition is so often lacking for people with learning difficulties and yet it is so vital to developing instrumental technique. I can think of two examples where this worked well: one with a singer from *High Spirits* who studied with a retired opera singer, and the drummer of the same band working alongside a drummer previously with the heavy metal group *Iron Maiden*.

(B) Group Creative Music Sessions

This is an area in which there is most existing provision for people with learning difficulties. In this course it would have two main aims – to help develop the student's ability to work in a group and to help them set their developing musical skills in a group context.

The content of this module would be threefold:

1. Improvisation: In this part of the course we could use free improvisation with 'holding forms' – that is a limited number of preset parameters that examine specific musical elements (dynamics, long/short phrases, speed, motivation, and so on). Free improvisation is the easiest way to approach music in a mixed ability culturally non-specific way and ensure that the material comes from the group.

2. Songforms: Using a repertoire of songs and tunes chosen by the group, looking at songforms and arrangements leading to:

3. Composition and Song Writing: Devising songs and tunes via creative musical exercises, discussions and brainstorms that draw on the experiences and aspirations of the group.

The creative music sessions would be, alongside individual work, a major element of the course covering a lot of ground; feeding into and drawing from other aspects of the course. It would be the breeding ground for musical creativity.

(C) Workshop Skills

This would be the third major element of the course. In the spirit of the Community Music movement, the students on this course would learn ways of passing on the skills and pleasures of music making to others with and without learning difficulties. This would, in the later stages, involve practical sessions in running workshops.

(D) Music Awareness

The main thrust of the course will be an active participation in music making. However I am aware that people with learning difficulties have more limited opportunities than many people to experience the rich variety and depth of music in the world. There is a real need for a music awareness module in which students would have an opportunity to hear and discuss with practitioners, a wide range of musics including opera, rock, jazz, Indian classical, Gamelan and so on.

This module would fall into four categories:

1. Musicians coming in to play and discuss with students various aspects of their work.

2. Where this is not, say for economic reasons, possible, we will listen to CDs and tapes and look at videos and discuss them.

3. Going out to gigs.

4. Going out to workshops led by groups of musicians with specific skill areas like the London School of Samba or the South Bank Gamelan.

This would be one of the modules that would involve an evening activity and I would see it as a fundamental aspect of the course to develop a 'night life'. The lives of too many people with learning difficulties are over-programmed by day and empty at night.

(E)   Performance Skills

This could cover aspects of choreography, body awareness and fashion as well as use of technical equipment. This module will be geared towards performances and would help students (including wheelchair-users and all those with limited mobility) to present a dynamic stage presence and to be able to set up and break down the stage equipment.

(F)   Performances

Students should have the opportunity to perform. The performances may use elements of other art forms, for example sets designed and built by theatre studies or art students in discussion with students on this course, or costumes designed and made by fashion/clothes-making students. The students from the music course would design and be involved in the printing and distribution of publicity for these gigs.

(G)   Recording

There should be at least one major recording project with opportunities to learn about recording techniques.

(H)   Instrument Making

Similarly to the above, there could be a short course on the making of simple instruments, looking at important sonic qualities and the physical requirements of students.

Entry Requirements

Applicants would be selected on the strength of their motivation and interest in the course. We would discuss their past and intended future involvement in music, their desire and interest in performing and in passing on their skills to others. This last aspect is critical as I would anticipate that such a course would be no different from most full-time music courses in that the largest proportion of the students completing it would remain skilled amateurs (whose lives will have been greatly enriched and who would be in a position to enrich the lives of others). Some may go further.

Assessment, Accreditation and Exit Routes

Without going into the detail of the why, how and who of assessment I offer the following as a basic illustration:

Objective area and method of assessment	*Level 1*	*Level 2*	*Level 3*
1. Ability to major on instrument (continuous assessment and individual performance)	Student can demonstrate control of basic concepts (rhythm, pitch where appropriate, dynamics)	Student can play basic parts or tunes	Student can play more complex parts or tunes
2. Practising alone (continuous assessment)	Student achieves control of basic concepts	Student progresses in control of basic concepts (greater number of pitches, good tone, etc.)	Student shows marked progress in instrumental facility (scales, tunes, chords)

3. Ability to work with other people to contribute ideas (continuous assessment)	Student can share and give to others space in discussion	Student can, in guided sessions, express an opinion on their own playing and on other people's in a helpful manner	Student can, in guided sessions, communicate ideas, and discuss alternatives in a helpful manner
4. Playing with other people (continuous assessment and group performance)	Student can share and give to others space in playing, and use their own space in solos	Student is musically sensitive and responsive with guidance	Student is musically sensitive and responsive without guidance
5. Running workshops (assessed practical workshop session)	Student can lead a set of basic exercises with assistance	Student can lead a set of basic exercises without assistance	Student can lead a set of basic exercises, without assistance, and assist and motivate individual group members
6. Identifying characteristics of different musics (aural test)	Reasonable identification of instrument types. Can identify basic styles (pop, jazz, classical, reggae)	Reasonable identification of instruments. Can identify broader range of styles (say Gamelan, Indian Classical, blues, Irish folk)	Good identification of instruments. Can identify an even broader range of styles and can comment on identifying characteristics

So Where Do We Go Now?

For our purposes here it would seem to me that the issue of exit routes is more pressing.

I give below a list of possible exit routes, in no particular or-

der. It is not intended as an exhaustive list and it would be
hoped that students would add to it:

Joining or forming bands. I have said there already exist three
bands, of which I am aware, the members of which have learning difficulties – *High Spirits, Heart n' Soul* and *Special Jam.* The
members of each of the first two come respectively from a single day centre. I find this restrictive and would see it as an aim
of this course to enable students, who wish to do so, to form
broader-based bands and to identify necessary support (like
Shape, London Disability Arts Forum, host Arts Centres). There
is, of course, no reason why the more able student should not
join a band with people who don't have learning difficulties. I
know of examples where this has happened.

Running Workshops. Agencies such as Shape, Artlink East,
Artability, Arts Connection, The London Disability Arts Forum
all operate as agencies for artists who work with and run workshops for groups with special needs. It is quite likely that they
could develop strategies for supporting this exit route.

Tutoring on or participating in other music courses.

Participating in courses other than music.

Jobs. It might be hoped that confidence and transferable skills
developed through this course will increase the employment
prospects of the students.

The Context

A few years ago I was running a session at a residential hospital for adults with learning difficulties. In tandem I was running a training course for nursing staff at the same
establishment. A couple of the nurses from my training sessions were present at a music session I was running. The students had profound learning difficulites and I worked closely
with each in turn, alternating solo and ensemble work. As I
came close to one student, a wheelchair-user, one of the nurses
said 'I'm sorry but he smells a bit this morning'. She went to a
cupboard, produced a spray and sprayed him from head to
foot. To say that such disrespect might hinder the learning
process is an extreme understatement but this is merely one example that I could quote. Having run music workshops in various situations I am convinced that in order for the educational
progress of students with learning difficulties to be taken seriously this work must be placed within establishments of Education and not Social Services. I've worked with the same

students in both settings and have seen their self respect, and thus their ability to learn, grow when given the oppportunity to be where learning takes place. Added to this, if any educational institution is serious about offering educational opportunities to disadvantaged groups then it must allow itself to be changed by them, not merely to go out to them, keep them at a distance. This may seem self evident and yet the ethos of modern education and the changes embodied in the Further and Higher Education Act 1992 are not conducive to such courageous and innovative work. However I do believe the case is strong and that opportunities could be created. Perhaps this would be easier at universities than elsewhere, simply because it is here that academic freedom still prevails against the rising tide of commercial pressures – the educational ethos is still placed before the business ethos.

Back to the Beginning

Let me relate how I came into working so intensively with people with learning difficulties. Like many musicians, I reached a point, where for the sake of a home life, I decided to gig less and to supplement my income with instrumental tuition. I found this intensely boring, being both repetitive and removed from the actual process of making music. Around this time I attended one of John Stevens' 'Search and Reflect' workshops. These were designed to embrace both skilled musicians and complete beginners in the immediate process of making music, and complex, demanding music at that. It was an inspirational experience and I decided that running mixed ability workshops was what I wanted to do. I set out to develop workshop skills and in the search I found myself taking part in a workshop for people with learning difficulties. I must admit to a feeling of terror that I still can't fully explain. I had never been in the presence of so many, to me, odd-looking people. I didn't know how to behave so as to not give offence. I realised that I had never been aware of people with learning difficulties before. As the workshop progressed under the skilled guidance of the tutor I became absorbed into the sensitive and vibrant music that was taking place. This was it; I never looked back!

In dealing with and realising the roots of my fear and prejudice I had to look at every aspect of 'engaging with difference'. I came to the conclusion that everything that I taught had to be clear and part of a coherent and well-thought-out structure. I had to be able to evaluate each step that I took (often with less feedback than I had expected from students previously). I had to be able to assess students' progress, and where possible, enable them to assess it for themselves. In short I had to acquire good teaching practice.

Looking back on my first experience of a group of people with learning difficulties I realise that I should have acted little differently from how I would with any other group of people. The problem was me. Similarly, appropriate education for people with learning difficulties is little different to that for other people. The issue of engaging with such difference is, as always, cultural understanding. Understanding the lives that people with learning difficulties lead, and often are forced to lead. Becoming acquainted with their lives (housing, work, etc.) is useful. Commonly it is their perceived needs that are addressed in constructing educational opportunities for people with learning difficulties rather than, as with most other people, their choices and their aspirations.

It was with all this in mind that, after some years of working with music students with learning difficulties, I began to contemplate how the aspirations of those who were serious about music could be addressed.

I hope that this chapter goes some ways to looking at important issues in the education of adults with learning difficulties both in and beyond music. More importantly I hope that, with others, I can begin to realise some of the opportunities that a course such as I have outlined could offer.

References

Alvin, J. (1975) *Music Therapy*, Hutchinson.

The Arts Business (1991) *National Directory of Community Music.*

The Arts Council (1991) *Off the Shelf and Into Action.*

Further Education Unit (1987) *Creative and Arts Activities in Further Education.*

Small, C. (1980) *Music, Society, Education*, John Calder.

Stevens, J. (1985) *Search and Reflect*, Community Music Ltd.

Wood, M. (1983) *Music for the Mentally Handicapped*, Condor Press.

Section Four

Assessment and Learners

It would be difficult to find someone working in adult education in the 1990s who will not respond, either by looking sick or becoming very animated, when the issue of assessment is mentioned. The most dramatic changes in educational practices in recent years have been concerned with assessment: assessment for credit; assessment by students; assessment by managers; and assessment by quality councils and funding bodies.

Of course assessment has always been a feature of education. Tutors have always made judgements about students' ability and progress, whether formally or informally. What has changed, however, is the nature, form and significance of formal assessment. In turn these changes are altering the experience and meaning of learning for both learners and educators.

The chapters in this section focus on two key aspects of change in contemporary adult education: the accreditation of liberal adult education and the recognition of prior experience and learning. The themes of the chapter *All Change: Accreditation and 'Other' Learners* were developed during a research project examining adult education administrators', tutors' and students' attitudes to the accreditation of liberal adult education. Historically, many of the students of so called 'liberal' or 'leisure' classes have been older adults and especially women, and many of these students are resistant to assessment and accreditation. Gerry Holloway suggests that while offering credit for learning may not appeal to this traditional group of students, it is an attractive option for other groups of learners who want or need a record of their learning.

For adults who did not gain qualifications from school, the prospect of assessment which offers qualifications and recognition can be attractive. Yet the process and effects of assessment may, of course, be contradictory. Without adequate preparation and support, traditional forms of assessment such as essays and unseen exams are often intimidating, and can exacerbate negative self-images instilled by prior educational experiences. Approaches to assessment need to take into account the previous educational experience of diverse groups of adult learners, and to support a process of affirmation and recognition rather than humiliation.

In the second chapter in this section, '*If Experience Counts, Then Why Am I Bothering to Come Here?*' Mary Stuart explores issues raised by the accreditation of prior experience and learning. Many educators who work with groups of people who are socially and economically disadvantaged regard AP(E)L as a way of creating more equitable educational opportunities and outcomes. This chapter shows how this process is more complex than is often indicated. AP(E)L raise difficult questions: what is knowledge? how do you record certain types of knowledge? and, given the boundaries of the education system, what forms of prior experience and learning can the academy realistically assess? For educators working with people who have been described as 'other' by the social institutions of education, and whose experiences do not match traditional forms of education and progression, these are especially pertinent theoretical and practical questions.

Chapter 9

All Change: Accreditation and 'Other' Learners

Gerry Holloway

In January 1993 Patricia Ambrose and I began a research project for the Centre for Continuing Education (CCE) at the University of Sussex to examine the challenge the government-
directed move towards large-scale accreditation of Continuing
Education (CE) was making to Liberal Adult Education (LAE).
Our research not only looked at CE Departments' initial responses to the Higher Education Funding Council of England
(HEFCE) proposed changes in CE funding but also examined
their perceptions of the moves towards the accreditation of
LAE and development of accredited courses (HEFCE, 1993).
This research has wider applicability in both traditional adult
education and further education. National Vocational Qualifications (NVQs) and the Open College Network (OCN) have
equally been funding led. At the time, many people in Adult
and Further Education believed that the change would destroy
adult education. Our research project offered an opportunity to
watch the unfolding changes in higher education and CE.

At the end of the research there is still a climate of uncertainty about the future funding of LAE and CE Departments'
plans still lack firm guidelines. Change, especially change
where there is so much uncertainty, generates fear, and fear of
change and uncertainty permeates our report. Departments
fear that they will have to drastically change or reduce their
programme; tutors fear that they will have to radically change
their courses and teaching methods, or worse that their liveli-
hoods are at stake; and students fear that they will be expected
to take the sort of exams that haunt their childhood memories.
At best, accreditation is seen as a pathway for non-traditional
learners into higher education, at worst it is regarded as some
sort of spectre threatening CE as we know it. However, LAE is
not without its problems and change is not always necessarily
for the worse. Accreditation, if approached imaginatively, can
be used as a way of utilising, in a practical way, the best prac-

tices of LAE and challenging traditional perceptions of learning and assessment.

In this chapter I shall firstly explore the development and definitions of LAE, its benefits and problems and examine who are the students who take these courses. Secondly, I shall discuss accreditation, the context in which it is being introduced, its potential and problems and the student population it will attract. I shall conclude by offering our interpretation of the current situation and a prognosis for the future based on our research in which we express our hope that in the future accreditation will be used in such a way that we really shall be able to engage with difference in the world of LAE. Although I have written this chapter alone, its substance owes much to the research work I carried out with Patricia Ambrose and Graham Mayhew. Their work is reflected throughout this chapter although I only refer to them when I am discussing their individual ideas and findings.

What is Liberal Adult Education?
A Brief History and a Possible Future

Ambrose argues that liberal education has its roots in the definitions of liberal education in Ancient Greece where it meant an education which differentiated a free man from a slave (Ambrose *et al.*, 1994). In other words, it was class education and as such embodies difference in an hierarchical way. Further, Ambrose defines liberal *adult* education as a form of education which 'takes into account the particular learning needs of adults, has traditionally offered open access courses designed at developing personal and social awareness rather than education for vocation' (Ambrose *et al.*, 1994). Further, she argues that it is not only chronological age that identifies LAE but also that it has been regarded as 'a special kind of education with its own general aim or purpose, related to characteristics of adulthood or the state of being an adult' (Lawson, 1976). Here difference is acknowledged in a way which is not necessarily hierarchical and therefore offers an opportunity to contest traditional assumptions about pedagogy and what constitutes knowledge. Ambrose also points out that there is an alternative definition of LAE from that of the classical Greeks which locates it as part of a tradition which Lieven has defined as having:

> emphasised the need for an education appropriate for a democratic society in which everyone is a citizen, in which everyone is free and in which everyone has a right

to that education. Here the liberal argument about education as an open ended project in which individuals discovered themselves was linked to the political project to realise a set of institutions which would enable this to happen for everyone (Lieven, 1987).

This dual definition, she argues,

> explains many of the inconsistencies in the attitude towards widening educational opportunities for adults. Alternative, more specifically vocational provision has frequently been viewed as a 'lower' form of education and treated dismissively as 'mere training' (Ambrose *et al.*, 1994)

Adult education in this country has been a site of contestation since at least the mid-19th century. At that time educational campaigners were trying to open up the universities not only to women but to part-time students as well. This was also a period when middle-class social reformers were keen to sieze the initiative from working-class radicals by offering alternative cultural forms for public consumption (Yeo, 1988). Marriott argues that the purpose of the University Extension scheme as it was called and as it was practised by Oxford and Cambridge was

> to leaven the lump, to alleviate the philistinism of provincial towns, the teaching profession, the functionaries of local government. In more dramatic terms it was to give the Democracy a sense of higher things, an antidote to anarchy and the mob-orator (Marriott, 1984).

In other words, it was an attempt to inculcate the values of a privileged elite into the masses, a political struggle about what sort of knowledge is 'real' and what sort of social and political organisations are legitimate.

At the beginning of the twentieth century, adult education classes were the only way most people could advance beyond elementary schooling. This was also a period of renewed working-class political and social activity which saw the establishment of two new organisations: Ruskin College at Oxford which sought to educate and train working-class leaders for their place in the world of politics, and the Workers' Educational Associaton (WEA) which Ambrose contends reflected the view that '... the pioneers and promoters of university adult education have been especially vulnerable to the myth that the university itself embodies the ideal of truth-seeking' (Crombie, 1983). Further she states that this attitude 'has always played a dominant part in WEA thinking and its work in conjunction with universities has been characterised by the belief that ... 'truth was one and that differences could be resolved by impartial study and discussion' (Ambrose *et al.*, 1994). So, no longer was adult education just about transmitting a specific type of knowledge from above to the masses but involved group discussion in search of an attainable universal truth which, we shall see, was another specific type of knowledge.

Ambrose argues that the type of LAE offered by university departments was defined as the 'Great Tradition' by Harold Wiltshire in 1956. She summarises the defining characteristics of the 'Great Tradition' as:

- a commitment to humane/liberal studies
- an especial concern for social studies as a way of understanding the great issues of modern life
- a non-vocational attitude
- a non-selective provision which has democratic notions of the educability of adults
- an adoption of the Socratic method in its use of small tutorial groups and guided discussion.

Although this definition was seen as old-fashioned even by Wiltshire himself, Ambrose argues that it enabled tutors to perceive their rather vague role in a definite way.

In our research, one of the questions we asked CE Departments was 'What is the value of LAE?' Our first attempt on a general questionnaire elicited vague, unsatisfactory answers which we followed up in our personal visits to selected Departments where we were able to obtain fuller replies. This led us to ask why should a question about the value of the work we do elicit such a response? If LAE is worth fighting for then surely we should be able to evaluate it? Is it because there is a sense of unease about some of our work that makes us reluctant to express our feelings on paper? Living in a state of siege where we are aware that our work is constantly in danger of attack and may indeed be threatened with extinction, we fear voicing our doubts about some of the work we do in case all our work is so labelled. This fear of 'throwing the baby out with the bath water' prevents us from articulating what we value and want to preserve in LAE and what we are willing to discard. It also encourages an either/or mentality where LAE is unchangeable and unassailable and therefore beyond evaluation rather than seeing it as part of the changing history of CE and able to adapt to changing social and political conditions.

However, there are people willing to evaluate LAE and challenge the 'Great Tradition'. Ambrose focuses on one challenge which takes the form of an epistemological debate (Crombie, 1983). Crombie's argument, Ambrose says

> states that the epistemology which has dominated western education systems is essentially Empiricist, that is to say it is derived from the assumption that there is a Cartesian split between mind and matter, that what is external is an objective, material world which can be analysed into small, specialist units of knowledge.

This system supports the view that there is a 'timeless and universal worth of guided intellectual enquiry as the road to personal development and civic maturity' which forms the basis of the university's role and that of LAE. Crombie argues an alternative epistemology which he calls 'contextualist' and describes thus:

> it is the world, reality, which has primacy in the educational process rather than formal knowledge. More precisely, perhaps, it is the 'learner-in-the-world', the experiences, challenges, problems, mysteries, and so on that motivate curiosity and enquiry. In practice, this means moving alongside the learner, entering the learner's world, in order to be able to guide and support the further exploration of reality (Crombie, 1983).

Ambrose comments that if this contextualist epistemology were applied to CE a new tradition would develop which would replace 'objective truth-seeking with the nurturance of learning, the idea of service with the role of catalyst, an individualistic focus with communalistic motives, teaching with the creation of learning situations' (Ambrose *et al.*, 1994). This will create a very different engagement between students and tutors.

Ambrose also suggests that the establishment of CE departments has made it easy for universities to assume that their community responsibilities were being looked after by worthwhile outposts. This argument asserts that it is no longer sufficient to defend the status quo of a paternalistic LAE provision. Rather we should be aware

> of the historical inadequacy of the extra-mural form in terms of its marginalisation, its atomisation, isolation and lack of resources, its failure in breaking universities from their elitism and in delivering a sufficiently powerful adult education to its potential clientele (McIlroy and Spencer, 1988).

The HEFCE changes in the funding of LAE offer a challenge

to practitioners in which these debates have a place. The arguments outlined above have significant relevance to so-called 'other' learners. Working within the parameters outlined by Crombie, individual experience is the central learning point for the learner. If that learner's experience is radically different from traditional LAE, LAE, not the learner, must change. I will discuss the changes expected and their implications for LAE later but firstly I want to turn to the students who take LAE courses at present and their reactions to the future accreditation of the courses they attend.

Who Studies in LAE Classes?

One of our discoveries in our examination of CE Departments' responses to funding changes was how little research had been carried out into students' perceptions of LAE and accreditation. We therefore decided to carry out a limited study of both tutor and student responses to the proposed changes among CE students at the University of Sussex. Graham Mayhew, a tutor organiser within CCE at Sussex, and I constructed questionnaires for tutors and subsequently for students of the tutor respondents. Graham visited the classes, explained what was happening to funding, what accreditation meant and asked the students to complete the questionnaires.

We received 272 replies from students attending 19 LAE courses. The courses they attended were on the whole typical LAE courses: Literature, Drama, Creative Writing, Art, Landscape Studies, Local Studies, Languages, Music, Information Technology, Media Studies, Archaeology and Politics. The classes took place in urban and rural centres, during the day and in the evening. As Figure 1 shows the respondents were mainly women and overwhelmingly women over the age of 50. Even though there were fewer men attending the courses they, too, were largely over 50.

The students attending the courses at Sussex are predominantly white and a large proportion have professional qualifications of some sort although given their age, many are retired (see Figure 2). We asked students whether they would want the LAE courses they attend accredited. The response was definitely no (see Figures 3, 4, 5 and 6 for breakdowns of this answer). Even amongst those who were in favour of accreditation, respondents tended to regard it as something of use to other people rather than themselves. Only a few wanted concrete evidence of their own learning. Some people were ambivalent about accreditation, either willing to accept it provided that they were not expected to take exams or write essays or be-

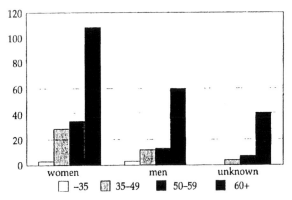

Figure 1. Breakdown of LAE students, by age and gender.

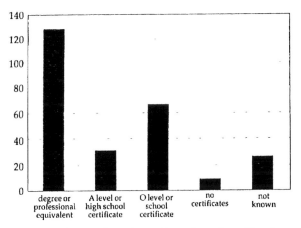

Figure 2. Breakdown of students, by educational background.

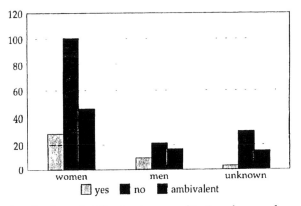

Figure 3. Students' attitudes to accreditation, by gender.

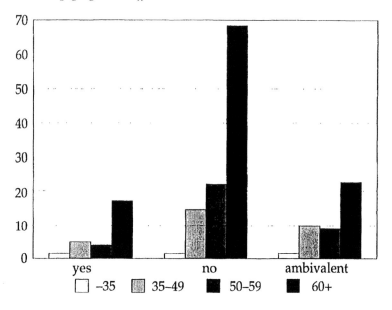

Figure 4. Women students' attitudes to accreditation, by age.

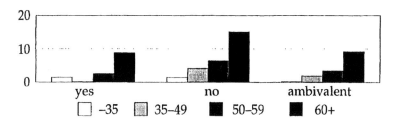

Figure 5. Men students' attitudes to accreditation, by age.

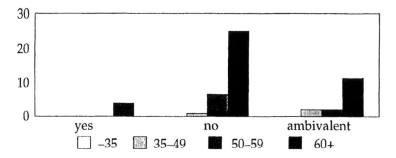

Figure 6. Attitudes towards accreditation by age, gender unknown.

cause it might keep down costs.

These responses are hardly surprising. Age can deter people from wanting accreditation. However, many retired people take Open University courses so it is possibly the added factor of the existing qualifications of most of the respondents which largely contributed to the negative response. Many commented that they attended courses in order to 'keep the brain ticking over', or regarded the class as a social occasion where they could learn with 'like-minded people'. With regard to doing work outside of the classroom, some disabled students worried about accreditation as they would not be able to do the reading and writing that they thought this would require. Younger students said that they did not have the time to study outside the classroom or would be obliged to be more selective about which classes they attended, as attendance would have to be connected with their work if they spent a lot of time on it rather than learning for pleasure. Although there is nothing wrong with the reasons that the respondents gave for attending LAE classes, it is patently obvious that many attend classes for social as well as educational reasons and that this does not sit well with the changes in funding policy. Consequently, these students may find that the changes that are bound to happen, which I will discuss in more detail later, transform LAE into something they no longer wish to attend. Furthermore, our findings from the questionnaire bore out the responses received from the CE Departments we visited who tended to feel that accreditation would appeal to new groups of students, and who had received similar responses to our questionnaire when they had tried to assess the demand for accredited courses on course evaluation forms.

The Move to Accreditation

The HEFCE Circular published in 1993 clearly states its intentions concerning the future of CE:

> The Council wishes to encourage as much non-vocational continuing education as possible to become (if not already) award-bearing, or to carry credits towards an award. It wishes at the same time to retain an amount to support a programme of non-vocational non award-bearing higher education (HEFCE 18/93).

As Ambrose observes, even though the Circular was vague about the amount of non award-bearing provision that would be retained, it was clear to CE Deparments that there was to be a fundamental shift in the balance of courses they provide and that such a shift in emphasis would have a drastic effect on the shape and quantity of much university CE provision (Ambrose *et al.*, 1994).

Our research showed that although CE Departments were developing award-bearing programmes, they were very heavily committed to providing non award-bearing courses. Most Departments provide hundreds of LAE courses while their award bearing programmes can be numbered in tens. Of course, within an award-bearing programme there are several modules but this does not alter the overall emphasis on non award-bearing provision. A few Departments had experimented with the accreditation of LAE courses but with limited success. Indeed, many respondents regarded this as a contradiction of terms because they perceived the very essence of LAE as the provision of courses designed to generate a love of learning rather than leading to formal qualifications. A member of one Department, when asked to define the value of LAE and accreditation, wrote:

> LAE offers anyone who wishes the opportunity to study what they want, when they want, and in amounts suited to their needs. Examinations and formal assessment and credit, are irrelevant to many people's needs, and may be intimidating. These factors are particularly important for older people, and for those who lack confidence and have rejected the formal system. The absence of the need for examinations enables an immense range of subjects to be offered to a very large number of people at a unit cost significantly below that which is required when credit is awarded.
>
> We see immense value in offering an increasing number of award-bearing courses for those to whom credit is important – whether *en route* to a degree, or because a Certificate or Diploma carries significance in helping participants in their jobs, voluntary work or civic role. In particular, it offers second chances to underqualified people (Ambrose *et al.*, 1994).

These views reflect those of the students we interviewed and indicate a strong resistance to changing the character of LAE through accreditation. Similar responses are also found in many adult education centres. LAE and accreditation are seen as separate and designed for different groups of students. However, change there will be. In February 1994, the HEFCE published its much awaited Circular which states:

> In 1995–6 and beyond, continuing education provision

which results in a recognised award, and also that continuing education which is accredited and can contribute to an HE award (or is credit-bearing within a credit accumulation framework), will be eligible for funding (HEFCE Circular 3/94).

The Council recognises that the

majority of non award-bearing provision currently funded by continuing education funds can be broadly categorised as liberal adult education. However the Council considers it is important also to recognise and encourage the development of provision specifically targeted at access, and at encouraging disadvantaged groups to participate in mainstream higher education. Therefore, if resources allow, supplementary funds will be made available to provide specifically for access and work targeted at disadvantaged groups to augment the existing funds in respect of liberal adult education (HEFCE Circular 3/94).

In future, the funding for non award-bearing work will not be restricted to CE Departments already providing these courses, but it will be allocated through a bidding process and therefore open to all universities. Further, the Council was not able to determine the amount available until early 1995, so there was still a great deal of uncertainty about how large the specific funding would be and how many institutions would bid for it. This means that non award-bearing provision, whether or not it is targeted at 'disadvantaged' groups, may well be restricted through lack of funds. The imposition of a division of funding between award-bearing and non award-bearing provision reinforces a hierarchy where one category of provision is privileged over another. Consequently, with this hierarchy unchallenged, whatever the HEFCE decide about the funding of non award-bearing provision, learners following non award-bearing paths will continue to be marginalised, receiving at best the 'leftovers' from the funding pot and, at worst, nothing at all. Unless there is a sea change in Government thinking towards funding the best way forward for 'disadvantaged groups' may well be to develop ways of assessing work which are not only non-threatening to learners but satisfy funding criteria for award-bearing work, thereby securing funding. Alternatively, new ways to obtain secure funding this work will need to be found.

Possible Futures for CE

In the past, CE Departments have often acted as informal agents of access into the mainstream. Most Departments have collective memories of extra-mural students going on to full-time higher education – I am one of those students. The formalisation of this process will have both benefits and problems. In recent years, CE has played a more formal role in encouraging access, often through the provision of specific Access to Higher Education courses which have brought in a younger group of students, mainly women and often from a working-class and/or ethnic minority background. These courses do require much more work from the students, tutors and clerical staff and are therefore more costly to run. Accreditation of LAE will increase workloads for those involved and careful record-keeping will be essential. Further, our research indicates that courses run in smaller rural centres may no longer be viable and the question of rural CE will need to be addressed urgently. However, CE departments will continue to have a role as 'brokers between the university and the outside community' (Spencer and Taylor, 1990) with their years of experience of developing courses jointly with voluntary organisations, FE colleges and community groups. This work may well be channelled into accredited courses in the future but accreditation, if developed sensitively, can give immense satisfaction to students who gain the confidence to continue their studies.

The findings of our small Sussex student survey reflect common perceptions in CE Departments and are borne out in other research. For example, the CE Department at Birmingham University has carried out research on a larger sample of students to find out 'more about who comes to public programme course and why'. They conclude that 61 per cent of their students were women 'and predominantly occupationally and educationally privileged'. However they also noted that of the 28 per cent of students who were in paid employment 31 per cent were interested in accreditation (unpublished findings from Birmngham, in Ambrose, *et al*, 1994).

The problem with both these surveys is that they were completed by existing students and therefore reflect the needs of a narrow group within the community. We know from our enrolment records and discussions with NOW organisers and tutors that, for example, if we had interviewed students on New Opportunities courses or Access courses we would have seen that although they are still mainly women, they are predominantly younger, more likely to be working-class and/or from ethnic minority groups and lack formal educational qualifications. It is to these groups that the accreditation of LAE might well appeal (McKelvey and Peters, 1993). Further, Birmingham found that even if younger people are well qualified they were more interested in accreditation than older students. Unfortunately, in our survey we did not have enough younger respondents to be able to reach such a conclusion but it is conceivable that young well-qualified students are less likely to be intimidated by accreditation than older people.

Students' perceptions of LAE and accreditation are often at odds with departmental and even tutors' perceptions and can be widely at variance with the Government's views. Whereas practitioners might perceive accreditation as making CE motivate the student to focus on learning rather than teaching, the students whom we surveyed tended to regard this as making greater demands on their time and having a detrimental affect on their classroom experience. Similarly, as one tutor expressed it, practitioners may well consider that it is their role 'to guide and support the further exploration of reality' and regard assessment as a means of achieving this aim but some students may feel that assessment detracts from their pleasure in learning and could put brakes on their development. So how can CE departments be able to meet a wide range of students' needs when their funding is increasingly being directed specifically towards people wanting to enter mainstream education through non-traditional pathways? And how do we address our traditional students' fears and diverse perceptions of LAE and accreditation? What will happen to our students who are emphatically opposed to accreditation of the courses they attend? Will we lose them? Should we care?

Changing Roles

One answer lies in the changing role of the university in society. As Ambrose argues,

the definition of a 'university' is undergoing radical interpretation. The abolition of the binary line has led to a broader, more diverse university system which increasingly takes account of the mature, non-traditional student population. The assumption that universities are primarily for the education of an elite of school-leavers is gradually losing ground to a recognition of the value of lifelong learning. As modularisation and credit accumulation and transfer become more widely accepted, distinctions between full-time and part-time students become meaningless (Ambrose *et al.*, 1994).

So what does this reinterpretation of the purpose and mission of universities mean for CE practitioners and, in particular, those involved with LAE? Firstly, our research shows that CE departments have a role in being the extended arm of the university; in helping those traditionally 'disadvantaged' groups who are still likely to be daunted by the prospect of entering directly into the mainstream of higher education. A programme of courses, both non award-bearing and award-bearing, will be central to the empowerment of disadvantaged groups by encouraging learning within the community and a gradual entrance into the mainstream university. Accreditation has consistently focused on the traditional body of knowledge as defined by the academy. Recognising other learners' knowledge is more likely to be possible in non award-bearing courses. Having developed their confidence and academic skills 'different' students could more readily engage with the knowledges transmitted through the academy. Within CE's broad remit, there is still a need for a distinctive university-level contribution to LAE; not all LAE need be accredited and absorbed into the mainstream.

There is also a place for accredited LAE, but as our interviews have indicated, much depends on the interpretation of accreditation. We need to be imaginative in our approach to assessment. For example, collective working methods with joint student essays and presentations, collective marking and personal logs of learning all challenge mainstream assumptions that only individually graded written work ensures standards of achievement. Furthermore, such approaches could overcome some of the fears students expressed in the questionnaires about accreditation fostering 'a more competitive atmosphere'. The issue of assessment would also be made an integral part of the course content as students would be confronted explicitly with epistemological issues as they would be required to assess not only the work of others but their own work too.

The key for the future for CE is flexibility. There is a need to move away from either/or-ism (Stephens, 1990) and to accept that students study from a mixture of motives and that the terms 'vocational' and 'non-vocational' are unnecessarily divisive. While some students may study for personal self-development, others, possibly new students to CE, may increasingly look for some form of accreditation to mark their achievement. What we must not underestimate is the fear of change currently circulating within CE departments and among our students and tutors. Many current LAE students are conventionally well qualified and do not want to study for further qualifications; they are committed to learning for pleasure. However, this does not preclude some form of assessment of their work. As discussed above, there are ways of assessing work which would make sense to people even if they are well qualified. There are, however, many people in the community who have never been reached by university LAE; further collaborative research is needed into their educational needs and into how universities can really engage with difference by attracting people from all backgrounds and age groups to study for a diverse range of purposes and in a diverse range of ways.

To see the evolution of the university into a 'learning organisation' (Duke, 1992) the contribution of CE, both award-bearing/accredited and non-award-bearing, is central. CE has long operated in a climate that is responsive to students' learning needs in the planning of curricula and could assist HE institutions adjusting to a mass system of higher education where students are likely to intersperse study with work. If the accreditation of LAE which is now well under way is flexible and imaginative it will not only be CE Departments who are fully engaging with difference but the university system as a whole.

References

Ambrose, P., Holloway, G. and Mayhew, G. (1994) *All Change: Accreditation as a Challenge to Liberal Adult Education*, Brighton: Centre for Continuing Education at the University of Sussex.
Barry, M. (1992) 'A National Strategy for Adult Education', *Adults Learning*, 3, 7, March, pp. 168–169.
Blyth, J. A. (1983) *English University Adult Education 1908–1958: The Unique Tradition*, Manchester: University of Manchester Press.
Crombie, A. E. (1983) 'Does university adult education in Britain have a future?', in Crombie, A. E. and Harries-Jenkins, G. (eds.) *The Demise of the Liberal Tradition*, Leeds: Leeds Studies in Adult and Continuing Education.
Crudden, P. and Whyte, A. (1990) 'Who is Restructuring Adult Education?, *Adults Learning*, 2, 4, December, pp. 113–115.
Department of Education and Science (1980) *Continuing Education: Post Experience Vocational Provision for those in Employment: A Paper for Discussion*, London: HMSO.
Duke, C. (1990) 'Liberal Adult Education: A Note from the Epicentre', *Adults Learning*, 1, 9, May, pp. 241–2.
Duke, C. (1992) *The Learning University: Towards a New Paradigm?*, Milton Keynes: Open University Press/SHRE.
Duke, C. and Marriott, S. (1973) *Paper Awards in Liberal Adult Education: A Study of Institutional Adaptation and its Costs*, London: Michael Joseph.
Ecclestone, K. (1993) 'Accreditation in Adult Learning? How Far Can We Go?', *Adults Learning*, 4, 7, March pp. 178–180.

Final Report of the Ministry of Reconstruction's Adult Education Committee, 1919.

Groombridge, B. (1990) 'Falling Walls: Adults and the University', *Adults Learning*, 1, 5, January, pp. 140–142.

Harries-Jenkins, G. (1983) 'University adult education into the 1980s', in Crombie, A. E. and Harries-Jenkins, G. (eds.) *op. cit.*

Higher Education Funding Council for England (1993), *Circular 18/93*, 'Continuing Education', May 1993.

Higher Education Funding Council for England (1994), *Circular 3/94*, 'Continuing Education', January 1994.

Kelly, T. (1970) (2nd edition) *A History of Adult Education in Great Britain from the Middle Ages to the Twentieth Century*, Liverpool: Liverpool University Press.

Lawson, K. (1976) 'Adult Education and Adult Learning' in Rogers, A. (ed.) *op. cit.*

Lawson, K. (1979) (revised edition) *Philosophical Concepts and Values in Adult Education*, Milton Keynes: Open University Press.

Lieven, M. (1987) 'Adult liberal education: a case study in ambivalence', *Adults Learning*, 60, 3, December, pp. 225–230.

McIlroy, J. and Spencer, B. (1988) *University Adult Education in Crisis*, Leeds: Leeds Studies in Adult and Continuing Education.

McIlroy, J. (1988) 'A turning point in university adult and continuing education', *Adult Education*, 61, 1, June, pp. 7–14.

McKelvey, C. and Peters, H. (1993) *APL: Equal Opportunities for All?* London: Routledge.

McNair, S. (1990) 'Editorial – Mass Higher Education: the Adult Agenda', *Adults Learning*, 1, 5, January, pp. 129–131.

Marriott, S. (1984) *Extramural Empires: Service and Self-Interest in English University Adult Education*, Nottingham: Department of Adult Education.

Peers, R. (1935) *The Nottingham Experiment in Adult Education 1920–1935*, Nottingham: Department of Adult Education.

Raybould, S. G. (1951) *The English Universities and Adult Education*, London: Worker's Educational Association.

Rogers, A. (1992) 'Achievements and Outcomes: Evaluation, Adult Education and Development', *Adults Learning*, 4, 3, November, pp. 69–72.

Scott, P. (1984) *The Crisis of the University*, London: Croom Helm.

Spencer, L. and Taylor, R. (1990) 'Universities and the Provision of Access Courses', *Adults Learning*, 2, 4, December.

Stanley, L. (ed.), 1990, *Feminist Praxis: Research, Theory and Epistemology in Feminist Sociology* London: Routledge.

Stanley, L. and Wise, S. (1993) (new edition) *Breaking Out Again: Feminist Ontology and Epistemology*, London: Routledge.

Steele, T. (1992) 'University Adult Education into the Mainstream: Not Waving but Drowning', *Adults Learning*, 3, 9, May, pp. 245–246.

Taylor, R. (1993) 'Accreditation and the Future of University Continuing Education', *Adults Learning*, 4, 10, June, pp. 278–279.

Thornton, A. (1976) 'Some Reflections on the "Great Tradition"', in Rogers, A. (ed.) *The Spirit and the Form*, Nottingham: Nottingham Studies in the Theory and Practice of the Education of Adults.

Tuckett, A. (1993) 'Certifiable Behaviour', *Times Higher*, March 26.

Universities Council for Adult and Continuing Education (1990), *Funding Policy for University Continuing Education in the Post-binary Context* (submission to PCFC/UFC), Warwick: UCACE.

Wagner, L. (1990) 'Adults in Higher Education: The next five years', *Adults Learning*, 2, 4, December pp. 94–96.

Westwood, S. (1989) 'Enterprise Culture and the Re-structuring of British Adult Education', *Adults Learning*, 1, 1, September, pp. 8–9.

Wiltshire, H. (1956) 'The Great Tradition in University Adult Education', in Rogers, A. (ed.) *op. cit.*

Yeo, E. (1988) 'Phases in the History of Popular Culture and Power Relations in Britain, 1789 to Present' in van Voss, L. H. and van Holthoon, F. (eds.) *Working Class and Popular Culture*, Amsterdam, Stitching Behher IISG.

Chapter 10

'If Experience Counts, Then Why am I Bothering to Come Here?': AP(E)L and Learning

Mary Stuart

Adult education has always claimed to value and recognise its students' wealth of past experiences. Most good teaching practice suggests that tutors should frame their teaching within the context of student experience (Rogers, 1986; Tennant, 1988; Knox, 1986). It does seem natural that the new 'buzz' about Accreditation of Prior Learnt Experience should be a development of this ethos of teaching adults. This was my perception of AP(E)L when I became involved in it while working in an adult education institute in the early 1990s. It made pedagogical sense to offer credit for learning that students had gained from life, but it was difficult to establish a system which would be acceptable and realistic for our institution.

Now working at the University of Sussex I have been involved, since September 1993, in developing a Recognition of Prior Learning Scheme for the University. I started the project with concerns similar to those which informed my earlier work: to develop a scheme which the university would find acceptable and which would serve the needs of a wide variety of adults who had been excluded from Higher Education in the past. As time went on, I began to see the project as more of an opportunity to investigate some of the connections between learning and knowledge, and education and experience. I feel this has enabled me to understand some of the more thorny questions posed by offering accreditation for learning which has taken place outside of educational institutions, especially those questions posed by so-called 'other' learners themselves.

The title of this chapter is one such question. A woman in her mid-forties, who had a wealth of experience working in the caring professions, wanted to study a course in Care Management. I advised her that she could perhaps claim credit for her past work experience. She replied, 'Well, if experience counts, then why am I bothering to come here?' At the time I was rather taken aback. It was not a response that I had expected and I certainly didn't give a satisfactory answer. Like many AP(E)L practitioners I was surprised that she did not simply recognise the value of AP(E)L. After all, I did! I hope that this chapter offers some more successful answers or at least addresses some of the concerns which are inherent in her question.

Why do Adults Come to Education?

I would like to emphasise the distinction between education and learning. This is an essential distinction for AP(E)L practitioners, as without it the educational institution has control over not only the definition of learning but also its practice. It is learning in practice which AP(E)L practitioners insist is not only the domain of education, but is controlled by individuals as they go through life. We learn in a wide variety of contexts in many different situations. This notion of life-long learning is also inherent in adult education pedagogy.

A more radical perception of knowledge takes the issue of control over learning even further. This perspective recognises that knowledge acquisition and understanding cannot be limited to any one educational definition of what learning is. Traditional notions of education are not fixed. They are socially created within structures of power which exclude the majority of learning experiences which are not directly visible to a professional. Educational definitions focus on learning which occurs in institutions, like school, college or university and within clearly defined subject areas and within specific curricula.

By the time adults come into a formal learning situation they have accumulated a vast amount of knowledge outside of institutions and subject boundaries, which, as adult educators, we are expected to draw on and respect. In Britain this concept of learning through life is not yet fully accepted within education establishments, particularly within Higher Education establishments. At a recent mature students' open day at the University of Sussex, a woman in her early thirties with no formal qualifications, but who had extensive experience of counselling, was told by a lecturer in psychology that she was a blank page. This highlights how much the discourse of education is still focused on learning in an institution and still does not take account of the informal learning which we all engage with throughout our lives.

Some AP(E)L practitioners are now beginning to identify that it is not only educationalists who do not readily accept the concept of learning from life, but adults themselves. This has been explained as 'low self image' (Smith and Turner, 1994). While self image is an important aspect of adults perceptions of their learning, it is only one aspect. The way adults see knowledge has more to do with our society's attitude to learning itself than with self esteem. Since the professionalisation of education in the late eighteenth century, western, industrialised society has accepted an definition of learning which is centred on the education profession's definition. This social attitude will be one which most adults will also subscribe to.

Adults come into education for a variety of reasons. These can be summarised into three categories. Firstly, they come to 'learn.' It seems to me that this reason has a lot to do with our social perception that knowledge itself is contained within education establishments. We may use different methods of explaining that 'knowledge' but it is 'owned' by education.

In *Young Children Learning* the authors argue that educationalists and parents alike see knowledge acquisition being the domain of teachers and school.

> Educational theorists, in fact, usually define education as a process entrusted by society to a specialist system involving teachers and schools ... Parents themselves often accept this view, believing that education starts at primary school and is concerned with school subjects.
> (Tizard and Hughes, 1984, p 17)

Most people, adults or children, take their definition of their intellectual capability from their interactions with education establishments. This may well give them low self esteem, but more significantly, they take for granted the definition given to them by educationalists. In other words the right of education establishments to make judgements about people's intellectual ability is not questioned. Educationalists own knowledge.

Adults also come to education to 'gain qualifications'. The so-called liberal tradition which saw qualification as limiting people's experience of learning or as being a means of 'setting people up to fail, again', does not take account of the fact that gaining qualifications is about gaining social recognition and that people want and need that recognition, for financial and status reasons. This is not some sort of false consciousness, it is building on the reality of our society, which assumes that knowledge is owned by the academy and that qualifications are a recognition that you have gained some of that knowledge. As educators we may question the validity of aspects of the assessment process, employers may even question the usefulness of the knowledge gained, but still the right of educational establishments to define and award qualifications remains. We have the luxury to question the learning, the learners do not.

The third reason why adults come into education is summed up by the statement 'I'm doing this for me'. It is a significant statement. Its speaker is fully aware that there is a difference between the social needs of learning, what you would need to present to the outside world, and a notion of personal development. It is this third notion which most adult educators I encounter really believe in. They believe in it because they are aware that the first two reasons for coming into education are based on a social construction of what learning is and that ultimately it is only if learning includes an element of the third reason, learning for ourselves, that education will have any personal meaning for people.

However learning for personal development can seem a very bland and inadequate notion to people who have little or no status or financial security in our society. It is those people who want the 'best' education, and by the 'best' they mean an education which will give them the most status and opportunities. To take the example quoted by McKelvey and Peters about British black people who still tend to be employed in low status jobs,

> Research has shown that black people recognise the importance of vocational qualifications as much as, if not more than, white people but sometimes feel that further education is not a route which can lead them to employment. This may be due to the fact that for many of them their past experience of education has been negative (McKelvey and Peters, 1993, p 36).

Crediting experience can be seen (and often is seen) as inferior learning by many in education. As Anna Paczuska identifies from her work at South Bank University:

> Because an APEL portfolio is often regarded as an alternative for those who could not get an A level, the portfolio can come to be seen as something second rate, associated with candidates who could not make it on a recognised route (Paczuska, 1993, p 79).

The student encountered by many advocates of AP(E)L who says 'I've never done anything with my life', is voicing a social perception of who owns and therefore defines knowledge. This attitude will lead to low self esteem but it is based on our social perceptions of the role of our educational institutions.

A Knowledge Revolution?
APL/AP(E)L Theory

The Accreditation of Prior Learning which is used in an increasing number of institutions across the United Kingdom has been developed and encouraged through the work of the Learning from Experience Trust (LET), under the direction of Norman Evans. The Trust grew out of work done in the United States in the 1970s. AP(E)L is now well established in America within both adult and higher education. LET has assisted projects and identified good practice in procedural developments and most of the models of AP(E)L in this country are based on work done by LET. There are various models which have been developed to suit the needs of different institutions including: distance learning APL/AP(E)L units, APL/AP(E)L policies across institutions which allow claimants to claim general higher education credits, AP(E)L co-ordinators in both Further and Higher Education, and APL/AP(E)L advisory groups within institutions. All these services offer adults potential credits for learning that has taken place outside the institution. AP(E)L can be claimed within all the acronym qualifications, NVQ, the City and Guilds, OCN, RSA certificates and HE CATS (Higher Education Credit Accumulation and Transfer Scheme) frameworks. However most of the research work that has been done around AP(E)L has concentrated on the structures for assessment of prior learning rather than questions of the relationship between the academy and knowledge.

The Knowledge Revolution (Evans, 1981) focused the discourse of AP(E)L within Britain. The debate has centred on the ownership of the practice of learning, not on who defines learning or, as Julia Waldman suggests, the current learning climate '... encompassing demonstrability seems to sit comfortably alongside the empiricism and scientific evidence so beloved of traditional education. Therefore it is likely that the values which have underpinned higher education for so long have barely shifted at all' (Waldman, 1993, p 89). In other words, AP(E)L is not challenging the traditional knowledge base as established within the academy. It is simply trying to find methods and structures to fit the alternative ways people have used to gain that knowledge into an acceptable accreditation framework for the establishments. This does not seem to be good news for people who have gained their knowledge outside of the education system, especially if that knowledge was gained within a different social framework. Cecilia McKelvey and Helen Peters in their book *APL: Equal Opportunities for All?* describe APL as a way of enabling groups of 'others' to gain recognition. In discussing APL and speakers of other languages they point out that '... the APL process can be a valuable means of gaining credit for those whose other skills exceed their skill in the use of English' (McKelvey and Peters, 1993, p 75). Unfortunately this analysis focuses on the practice of learning again, as they go on to point out that there is often not sufficient access to language support to enable speakers of other languages to make use of APL. The definition of knowledge in Britain is centred around a 'reasonable grasp of English.' In other words, knowledge that is constructed outside of 'our' framework cannot realistically be recognised and accredited as knowledge.

Experience is also a Social Construct

The learning which adults gain through life is structured in inequality. It is not only the learning which takes place within educational institutions which is sexist, racist, ablist, ageist, hetrosexist and so on, but social interaction itself. Our society has created inequalities between groups. As educators we know that the disadvantages which many of the adults we work with experience are not only educational disadvantages, but relate to how society has positioned them. Accepting this point does have quite serious implications for AP(E)L. If people's experience is defined within a social context, then certain groups of people are only going to have access to particular types of experiences and their range of options are limited by the confines of their position. In our society this will mean that women, to take one example, are much more likely to have learning experiences which focus around care and caring, for children, elderly relatives, their homes and so on. If they use their experience to claim credit the areas in which they will be able to use that credit are going to be ones which will reinforce their roles as carers. Women are only one example; the fact that experience is also socially constructed affects any group of people whose life chances have been limited through social inequalities who may wish to gain credit via an AP(E)L route. It is as if the radical pedagogy of AP(E)L is a new way of supporting structural inequalities. It is essential that we do not claim too much for AP(E)L. It is a form of assessment which has been developed within the confines of our current society. We cannot suggest that it can change the life experiences of adults who have been socially and economically disadvantaged by society. It can only offer a route to claim credit for what a person has experienced.

Student and Tutor Perceptions of 'Other' Learning

One of the most significant features of the process of knowledge being owned by the academy, both in its practice and its
definition, is the way adults who have a wealth of experience
see their own knowledge as somehow being different from and
other than 'real' knowledge which their tutors 'give' them. I
surveyed 70 students currently taking either a Certificate or a
Diploma at the University of Sussex. The courses are all 'open
entry' courses, no person registering need have qualifications
to take the course. The students varied in age, sex and ethnicity.
Some had qualifications including degrees, others had no qualifications. When responding to a questionnaire, most of the students felt that they had little or no prior learning experience
which was relevant to their present course of study. However,
when interviewed, most of the students found that there were a
wealth of skills which they were drawing on. When I asked
about the discrepancy between their responses on the questionnaire and their responses in the interview, one woman typically
replied: 'I wasn't fully aware what is meant by prior learning, I
thought it was only the sorts of things you got in education.'
This response highlights the social hegemony of institutional
definitions of knowledge .

Tutors on the same courses were also interviewed. While
most tutors felt that it was important to value the experience
which adults bring to their learning, most were extremely hesi-
tant about offering students the possibility of exemption from
aspects of the their course. A typical response was, 'I think the
most exciting courses are designed as a unity, so students need
(and I think want) to study the course as a whole.' Another tutor said that students who used AP(E)L would loose 'the critical reflection on practice which is central to the approach of the
course'.

Students cannot recognise their own learning and tutors do
not 'trust' that 'real' learning has taken place. These perceptions are built on a particular scientific modernist discourse
which focused knowledge within the domain of particular
groups in society. It is Universalist in its approach and does not
value 'other' ways of seeing. McKelvey and Peters suggest that
APL can be used to value difference but this can only be done if
perceptions about knowledge are challenged. To quote Norman Evans: 'By definition adults have not accumulated the
knowledge and skills they are offering for assessment according to the dictates of prescribed syllabuses, although they may

be asking for judgements to be made against the content of such syllabuses' (Evans, 1989, p 18). What is needed is a radical re-think about the role of the academy. Is it a place which defines knowledge per se or is it a place to explore the context of knowledge? I am happier with the notion that it is a place which explores the context of knowledge. This allows the definition of knowledge to be challenged and enables the discourse of learning to be fluid. Power relations and inequalities can be addressed in relation to the context of knowledge acquisition. This is an alternative discourse to the popularist notion of scientism. It is rooted in the enlightenment but critical in its grasp of what knowledge is. As Michel Foucault suggests, our concern should be, 'what is this Reason that we use? What are its historical effects? What are its limits, and what are its dangers?' (from an interview with Foucault by Paul Rabinow, 1983).

Practising Recognition of Prior Learning and Education as Development

With some of these concerns in mind I began to develop a scheme for the university. I felt we needed a scheme which was:

(a) soundly placed within an academic tradition which was based on a notion of different knowledges, of which academic knowledge, as it has been defined, is only one form. This would enable a discussion of the context of knowledge acquisition. The programme offering credit for adults' prior learning would therefore be based in a tradition of the sociology of knowledge which examines the socio-historical construction of knowledge

(b) person friendly. It was important that potential claimants would be able to feel comfortable about their different subjective experiences and be able to elicit their prior learning with support, as often people are not fully conscious of what they have learnt

(c) offering a variety of routes for different needs. Any scheme which claims to take account of 'other' experience must provide different options within the process. Some people may want more support than others, some may want a group experience. These different demands need to be catered for

(d) honest. If academic knowledge is only one form of knowledge, it is vital that publicity advertising the scheme should be honest and make it clear to potential claimants that credit can only be given for knowledge which fits the limited rubric of the academy. Any scheme should help claimants explore the social construction of knowledge and their relationship to this context. If this is not clear to people it is likely that claimants may well feel their life experiences are being assessed, rather than aspects of their learning being matched against academic learning

(e) cost effective, for both the individual claimant and the institution.

There are tensions in attempting to develop a scheme which both explores the context of knowledge and people's experience and which is still framed to offer credit through an academy which itself is socially and historically constructed to only recognise certain aspects of knowledge. It is that tension which needs to be made visible and clear to participants in any scheme.

Recognition of Prior Learning rather than Accreditation of Prior Learning: A Life History Approach

What we are planning for at Sussex is a scheme which uses a life history approach to the recognition of prior learning. This approach is based on recent developments in education practice, oral history and sociology in Europe, America and in Britain. It is premised on a notion that to explore your life history offers a way of contextualising learning and experience within a social framework. This approach has grown out of a feminist scholarship which has highlighted the value of researching the personal (Stanley, 1992; Middleton, 1993). Life history work allows individuals to shape and explore their own experiences within their own choice of narrative. Biographical analysis values the specific detail rather than the generalisation. It explores the construction of individual selves and how experience shapes the subjective. 'The construction of subjectivity has been central to women's history since the field emerged in the 1970s. Indeed the enduring appeal of biography lies largely in its privileged access to that process' (Dowd Hall, 1991, p 155). Pierre Dominice has been using the technique of personal biography in training Adult Educators in Geneva. He says of the approach: 'it offers a participatory approach which will help adults become more aware of and more responsible for their learning process' (Dominice, 1993).

The Recognition of Prior Learning scheme which we are developing at Sussex is working in this tradition. It will offer claimants an initial counselling interview helping them analyse their learning experiences and enable them to identify whether they wish to pursue their claim. The scheme will offer them an opportunity to further their claim by taking a module, 'Learning from Life'. This module will encourage participants to reflect on their prior learning and its relationship to the social construction of knowledge. The module's structure would use the life history approach and early on in the course participants will identify learning from a wide variety of sources. They would then produce a written account of their educational life history. This is not simply an autobiography but a structured examination of the learning experiences in their life. As with the Geneva model, 'Participants have to focus on the process of how they became themselves and how they learned what they know through the various contexts, life stages and people who were relevant to their education' (Dominice, 1993, p 197).

The second half of the course would focus more specifically on the development of appropriate evidence to claim credit for prior learning. We all tell 'our story' in different ways in different times, focusing on different aspects depending on the requirements. Participants taking the module would be asked to reflect upon a particular presentation of themselves, a presentation which would help them claim credit for their prior learning. Participants would be encouraged to situate this 'version' of themselves in the context of the very different presentations we display in different aspects of everyday life, at home, with parents, at work, with friends and so on (Goffman, 1959). This will help participants understand the process of presenting appropriate information. Discussions on the need for 'evidence' and its distinction from learning would follow. These discussions help the claimants to understand the process of assessment, which requires evidence of learning. Participants would then develop their claim for credit with a better knowledge of the process and ethos of accreditation.

It is important to separate out an individual life history, the particular learning which will be necessary for a claim for academic credit and the evidence required for the claim to succeed. Participants are not offering their lives for credit or even, for that matter, their learning. What they are offering is the evidence they have been able to accumulate which would satisfy the limited, and often mystifying, concerns of the academy.

A recent investigation of the production of the CV, a similar activity to an AP(E)L claim, by sociologists David Morgan and Nod Miller, highlighted an important issue which AP(E)L claimants and practitioners should acknowledge:

As with all auto/biographical practices, it is important finally to speculate on what is left out of the account. It is here that we come upon what Wadel has called 'the hidden work of everyday life' (Wadel, 1979). This emphasises the point that in any occupational setting, alongside the formally prescribed or routinely recognised practices, there also exist practices which are often vital to the maintenance of the organisation concerned and the cultures within it but which are not conventionally recognised (Morgan and Miller, 1993, p 142).

Any scheme should also offer claimants the opportunity to work individually on their claim, rather than work with a group, but they should be offered a support session on preparing appropriate evidence. Whether in a group environment or on their own, participants should be encouraged to see their claim as part of a mutual dialogue between themselves and the institution, both through the process of the preparation of their evidence and through the assessment of their claim. As Miller and Morgan point out about the production of the CV:

> Superficially, it might appear that the production of the CV is an individualistic act performed in a particularly individualistic context. However, not only is there scope for team work in the actual production of the CV, with the seeking or offering of advice on the part of senior colleagues or mentors, but there is also scope for team-work in the subsequent evaluation … performer and audience alike, although distant from each other, share a common culture and a common set of rules and expectations (Miller and Morgan, 1993, p 141).

The scheme should offer claimants whether successful or not the opportunity to have an evaluation of their claim and it is hoped that through the process of a course which explains the 'culture and … rules' which education demands that claimants are more able to use a RPL route.

The shift from Accreditation of Prior (experiential) Learning to Recognition of Prior (experiential) Learning is significant. Our concern was that claimants' learning would always be recognised but because of the specific context of academic knowledge it would not always be accredited. This would appear to me to be not only honest but also less invasive of people's lives.

As the Recognition of Prior Learning scheme develops, it is likely to pose extensive challenges to the process of assessment within the university, by recognising different experiences. Many AP(E)L practitioners are still grappling with the possibility of grading experiential learning. Tutors will have to engage with a greater variety of student experience and students themselves will be challenged to see their learning as being far more their responsibility.

So What About Formal Learning and Experience Then?

Some of the issues raised do answer the question posed at the beginning of the chapter about the value of experience and formal learning. A scheme which is grounded in a sociology of knowledge and an awareness of life history can focus a learner's experience within a social framework which can help them understand the context of their learning and the structures and ideology of education. Recognition of Prior Learning can be useful to learners by offering accreditation and recognition but also by enabling learners to be more responsible for their own learning.

Many of the concerns which I have raised here relate to the structure of our society and the ways in which society privileges certain types of knowledge over others. I am not trying to suggest that recognising prior learning will change the structures of our society, but exploring the questions which RPL raises, rather than simply trying to find structures which the institution will accept, does challenge the way we construct our knowledge within education. It throws into sharp focus the relationship between privilege and knowledge and forces us as educators to acknowledge our limited world view. This, for me, is a real engagement with difference and a real knowledge revolution.

References

Dominice, P. (1993) 'Composing Educational Biographies: Group Relfection Through Life Histories', ESREA Collected Papers.

Dowd Hall, J. (1992) in Alpern, S. *et al.* (eds.) *The Challenge of Feminist Biography*, Illinois: University of Illinois Press.

Evans, N. (1989) *Assessing Experiential Learning* London: FEU/Longman.

Goffman, E. (1959) *The Presentation of Self in Everyday Life* New York: Viking.

Knox, A. (1986), *Helping Adults Learn*, London: Jossey-Bass Publishers.

McKelvey, C. and Peters, H. (1993) *APL: Equal Opportunities for All?*, London: Routledge.

Middleton, S. (1993) *Educating Feminists: Life Histories and Pedagogy*, Teachers College, Columbia University.

Morgan, D. and Miller, N. (1993) 'The CV as an Autobiographical Practice', *Journal of Sociology Auto/biography Special Issue.*

Paczuska, A. (1993) 'Assessing Diversity equality issues in APEL', *Getting to the Core of APEL,* John Storan (ed.), SEEC.

Rogers, A. (1986), *Teaching Adults,* Milton Keynes: Open University Press.

Smith, P. and Turner, I. (1993) 'Experiential Learning and Undergraduate Courses', *Getting to the Core of APEL, op. cit.*

Stanley, L. (1992) *The Autobiographical 'I',* Manchester University Press.

Tennant, M. (1988) *Psychology and Adult Learning,* London: Routledge.

Waldman, J. (1993) 'Gender and APEL: Reinforcing Social and Sexual Divisions?', *Getting to the Core of APEL, op. cit.*

Section Five

Collaborative Learning – Community Publishing

This final section of the book examines the practice of two writing projects. Both projects share the aim of collaborative production of writing for publication. One project grew out of adult basic education literacy work; the other from a group of people who shared a common experience, that of being either stroke victims or stroke carers. Both projects were part of the vibrant community writing and publishing movement in East Sussex.

Adult basic education has a long history of anti-discriminatory education practice but in the chapter *Community Writing and Literacy Development*, Judy Wallis and members of Shorelink Writers challenge current developments in ABE. They show how functionalist, skills-based literacy work can limit writing development, even reinforcing the negative educational self-images of adults who have been labelled because of their struggles with reading and writing and 'standard English'. By contrast, collaborative approaches using creative and autobiographical writing, and often involving the linked processes of writing, editing and publication, facilitate the acquisition of writing skills and self-confidence precisely because they engage the writer's interest and affirm a positive relationship between writing and identity.

In the chapter *Life After Stroke: Special Interest Book-writing Groups*, Nick Osmond shows how autobiographical writing and joint publishing helped a group of people whose lives had been devastated by stroke to share their experiences and gain greater self-understanding and confidence. The chapter also explores issues of power in collaborative writing and publishing. Though members of the two book-making groups were mainly complimentary about the processes and products of their group work, as group facilitator Nick recognised that tensions in the collaborative process were generated by specific demands such as thematic coherence, word length and deadlines, and by the different roles and expectations of facilitator and group members. The recognition and negotiation of such tensions is essential to effective collaboration, both in community publishing and in adult education generally.

Chapter 11

Life After Stroke: Special Interest Book-Writing Groups

Nick Osmond

My own involvement with community publishing came about because I myself have spent much of my life in search of a community. I never felt I belonged to the middle-class Tory milieu into which I was born and which gave me direct access to the ladder of British privilege and power, in my case the pay-scale of University Lecturers (French Language and Literature). An unhappy early childhood had left me anxious and timid: unable as well as unwilling to conform to the model of masculinity and leadership for which I'd been trained in the usual series of all-male class insititutions: prep school, public school, National Service, Oxford.

As an adult I gradually came to reject the interconnected values of my family and class of origin and to align myself politically and personally with the working class. Politically this meant a recognition of the scandal of our economic system, under which the people who work to create and maintain the fabric of our human world do not own or control it; and allegiance to the socialist values of equality, respect and co-operation. But these political convictions grew from personal values of warmth, affection, imagination, communicativeness and humour, which developed in more and more conscious opposition to the ethos of my parental family. I became a trade union and community activist.

Early retirement with a pension at fifty brought me great potential freedom. I tried my hand at many things, all connected with communication and part of the quest for community. In the autumn of 1989, when I was fifty-six, I became an active volunteer with QueenSpark Books. I had always wanted, in a rather general and unfocused way, to use my literary and communication skills to facilitate the writing and expression of people who have historically been denied a voice.

History of QueenSpark Books

QueenSpark Books is a non profit-making Brighton-based organisation which, grant-aided by the Regional Arts Association and local Councils, aims to develop writing, publishing and performance in the local community. We are a Company Limited by Guarantee under the 1985 Companies Act and have a part-time paid Co-ordinator, but the rest of us are volunteers who work collectively, learning and sharing skills.

QueenSpark grew with the community politics of the seventies and was a founder member of the Federation of Worker Writers and Community Publishers. Our belief is that everyone has a history and anyone who wants to can be a writer. We publish the hidden histories of those 'ordinary' people who are usually ignored by commercial publishers and who often turn out to be quite out of the ordinary. Our list includes local autobiographies by working people, works of oral history and collections of memories with photographs. Since we began publishing in 1974 we have brought out over forty titles.

These include a number of anthologies but the concept of a collectively written book focusing on a special interest which unites the writers, was a new one. Between 1990 and 1993, working within QueenSpark, I was responsible for facilitating the writing, production and publication of two such group books, *Life after Stroke* (written by stroke survivors) and *Stroke – Who Cares?* (written by family carers).

Life After Stroke

This first project originated in 1990, when two QueenSpark authors who had suffered major strokes wrote, quite independently of each other, about their experience. Margaret Ward (aged 74), whose autobiography we had published, sent us a manuscript which included a description of her own fight for rehabilitation. At a performance event Irene Donald (54), from our Women Writers Group, read (with actions) a moving poem about recovering the use of her hand:

My wonderful hand,
that now I can lay flat on the table
and write this piece with my nimble fingers,
just three years ago my hand
was lying limply on the end of my arm.
The physios told me 'You've got to go through the pain.'
But with tears running down my cheeks I said 'I can't, I can't'.
But then I wanted to go home to be with my cats,

who had to be fed from opened tins.
So I had the incentive
and persevered with exercises and swimming,
stretching my hand out in front,
and like a frog pushed myself through the water,
and finally reaching out to the Steps to Success,
with my Wonderful Hand.

QueenSpark decided to set up a writing group of stroke people to produce a book. I led and organised the group and further members were recruited with the enthusiastic help of Sister Jan Nowak of the Brighton Stroke Rehabilitation Community Team, who was in touch with people who were making or had made a good recovery from stroke. Irene and Margaret formed a nucleus and they were joined by Marion Daniels (51), Kay Hind (68), David Morris (75), Dot Pippard (64) and George Stratton (80). We met weekly between April 1991 and July 1992, when QueenSpark formally accepted the anthology for their newly-launched 'Market Books' series, stapled card-covered booklets which sell at £1 through informal, non-commercial networks rather than in the bookshops. Without access to this kind of cheap community publishing and networking, group book projects would be much more difficult since presumably sponsors would have to be found to meet the costs of the production standards required by bookshops.

The meetings were a rich and exciting experience. People's most urgent need was to talk about what had happened and what was still happening to them. From the very first meeting we seemed to bond as a group. A warm rapport built up, and it was from these early exchanges that the writing emerged. For some members, particularly the ones with limited mobility (for whom transport was organised through the WRVS), the meetings became quite central in their lives.

Working in the group was in itself very valuable. Margaret found that sharing her feelings about her stroke with the others helped her to come to terms with it. She realised (for example) that her feelings of uselessness were quite natural but that at the same time you can get over them. She said she got strength and comfort from knowing she wasn't the only one.

Meetings usually started out with discussion of short written pieces on a common theme, and gradually a body of writings grew up around these. The writings were supplemented by transcripts of recordings of group discussions (made at four meetings). This was valuable in that a lot of fresh points came up in the heat of discussion although, as every oral historian knows, transcription is laborious and time-consuming. This extract, where we were talking about how to 're-educate' your hand, gives an idea of the lively and co-operative style of our exchanges:

Dot *I find actually talking to it helps, rather than passing silent messages, I sort of look at it and say 'Hold on to that!'* (laughs). *I find great difficulty in holding a newspaper. I think I've got it and it all goes on the floor. The mess my newspaper gets in, it's dreadful.*

Kay *So does mine.*

Marion *So you go for the tabloids only* (laughter).

Dot *I suppose it's because you can't feel you're holding it, therefore you don't feel when you're not holding it, that's the problem.*

George *Yes, and I have difficulty letting go of things.* (Demonstrates with finger crooked through handle of tea cup.) *You know, if I pick up a cup with my left hand, I have a job letting go of it.*

Margaret *Your finger doesn't slide out the same, does it? It stays bent.*

George *I often pull the cup off the table and it goes on the floor.*

Marion or Kay or Dot *So straighten out, finger.*

Given not only the decision to base the book on themes but also the sheer quantity of very disparate manuscript material that had to be processed and brought down to the 20, 000-odd words required by the Market Book format, the editing was a very considerable challenge. With the group's permission I took control of the process myself. We would have preferred group editing but this prospect I found frankly daunting, since some of the members still had considerable difficulty with short-term memory loss, sequencing and concentration. We had agreed on the themes/chapter headings, I had the skills and by this time knew the people in the group well and felt very close to them. So although it was a solitary task it didn't feel solitary because I could still hear the voices and would readily remember points connected to the passage I was working on.

There had to be a lot of fairly ruthless cutting and transposing to cut the writing to short book length and produce a sort of general story of 'strokes and how to survive them'. When the contributors met to discuss the first draft of the book they were a bit shocked at losing some of their favourite passages, but pleased with the overall result. At this point the originals of their writing were returned.

The editing plan means that the reader follows the 'stages' of the stroke experience rather than following each individual story. This has the advantage of generalising the experience. The disadvantage is that the reader can't identify with each author as an individual, though we compensated for this by placing a group photo and a biographical sketch of each contributor at the beginning of the book and tagging each segment of text with the contributor's name in bold, so although the book reads as a continuous dialogue, you can trace the story and the voice of a particular author if you want. Selections from the discussion transcripts, distinguished by italics, are woven in with the written material.

Stroke – Who Cares?

In 1992 the Centre for Continuing Education (CCE) at the University of Sussex offered to support QueenSpark by paying a tutor, under their New Opportunities Work programme, to facilitate another book-writing group and it was decided to set up a stroke carers' group to write a companion piece to *Life after Stroke*. I would again facilitate the group. Once again the book would be offered to QueenSpark as a Market Book. The title we eventually agreed on was *Stroke – Who Cares?*

The change of status from volunteer to paid convenor did not seem to make much difference to me, mainly perhaps because the money I earned was really a bonus on top of my pension, something to buy me a few extras. In fact I put in more hours on *Life after Stroke* than I did on *Stroke – Who Cares?*

Recruitment this time was through a rather different network, the Brighton Volunteer Stroke Service (VSS, now known as Dysphasic Support, a branch of the National Stroke Association), which runs clubs and trains volunteer speech therapists. By this time I knew the local organiser, Barbara Wood, through having become one of her volunteers working with a stroke person in his home and also, for a time, with people recovering from a stroke in hospital. Barbara, who had also helped with the *Life after Stroke* group, worked closely with me in planning and co-ordinating the new project. All the writers were or had been principal carers for a close relative who had had a stroke, broadly defined. They hadn't met before we came together as a group. We held weekly meetings from October 1992 to March 1993, which was the cut-off date, anything that happened after that not being included in the stories. After March we went on meeting most months to work on the editing, the introduction and the publication plan. Decisions were collective, though they were carried out by me.

There were five writers. Karen Clark (20s) was caring for her mother, Guy Pearman (early 70s) for his wife, Irene Player (50s) and Georgina Castlefranc (70s) for their husbands; Joan Roberts (early 60s) had cared for her husband until his death a few years beforehand.

As with the first group, we started writing about topics such as 'the day it happened', 'who we were'. The writings were shared by being read out by the author (or occasionally by me if someone became too emotional to continue) and, again, we soon established a warm rapport and began acting as a sort of informal support group.

The writers said that just the fact of being in a group was very helpful. One or two were dubious at first because they had very little experience of writing and did not think they would be able to write very well. But although it was hard work on occasions they found a great sense of relief in just getting everything down on paper. They felt that even if their story was never printed it would not matter; just to write all your feelings down and get them out of your system could help tremendously.

So writing the book was valuable in itself. It was like a therapy and helped the carers to see things differently. Some of them were speaking freely and openly for the first time about what had happened. Although some felt at first it was disloyal to talk about a loved one behind their back, they were able to give each other much help and encouragement simply by sharing feelings about an experience which they all knew from the inside. They knew that what they were saying was being understood.

Collaborative Editing

This time we decided that, rather than arrange the book around themes, each member would tell their own full story. For Irene's contribution we gathered extra material by taping discussion, as we found that ideas could flow more freely when people were just talking. Selections were transcribed, edited and incorporated in her story, but we didn't use transcription extensively as we had for *Life after Stroke*.

There are considerable advantages in basing the book on individual stories rather than themes. The voice, personality and particular experience of each writer comes over strongly (with strong contrasts between the stories), so the reader can identify more fully, get the feel of how it was for that person. The disadvantage of course is that there isn't the focus on each stage of the common experience which the reader finds in *Life after Stroke*. These contrasting patterns are the two broad options for editing a group book (or indeed a book of oral history) and each solution has its supporters and opponents.

During the writing of *Stroke – Who Cares?* each writer was fully in control of their own story. My role was to launch, encourage, elicit and elucidate as necessary. We kept the final shape and length of the book under continual review. At first we were aiming for about 4,000 words for each story to fit the Market Books format, but as time went on this began to seem constricting. The therapeutic benefits of the group were in conflict with publishing requirements. So after a few weeks we made the crucial decision that we would not at present worry about length, so each writer could say as much or as little as they needed to. This was particularly important for one member who was consciously dealing with feelings she hadn't fully come to terms with and just needed to keep writing without having to worry about final length or shape.

A corollary of this decision was the suggestion that we should bring out a full, uncut version and this became a possibility when we proposed, and CCE agreed to fund, twenty-five copies of a 'Library' version of the book to be distributed to public libraries and to various centres within the NHS and the VSS network, as well as to the writers. This would then be cut down to Market Book length for wider distribution.

Two of the writers had never written anything longer than a letter before and were not confident that they could write at length about their experience, but as the focus was on the process rather than the product there was no pressure to perform and they soon proved to themselves that they could write simply by ... writing! The experience of being heard with complete respect and sympathy, and the sense of affirmation and equality which that involved, soon freed these two from their initially inhibiting sense of being inadequate as writers.

The other three were already autonomous writers. One planned and wrote his piece entirely on his own, starting from a series of headings. Another contribution tended to be sprawling and voluminous; after a few weeks I suggested one or two quite drastic rearrangements and an overall plan. This was accepted and thereafter the writer was able to work more consciously and purposefully. The third writer worked quite independently; she discussed her long-term plans with the group as she went along and kept a note of our suggestions so that she could edit her work later.

My only conspicuous intervention was when I was given permission to propose cuts to bring the stories to the length required for the Market Books series. Authors had the final say. One complained about my deletion of certain pasages of philosophy which she set great store by; two others pointed out that my cuts had skewed the emphasis of their story by changing the ending. These cuts were reinstated. But once negotiations were completed the general view was that the cutting had strengthened the stories.

Group Dynamics and the Learning Process

On the whole I tried to keep a balance between equality and control.

Although my own life hadn't been touched by stroke, I had started working as a volunteer with stroke people and had recently been the principal carer of someone very close to me who was dying of cancer, so I was able to share my own feelings about these experiences with both groups and I think this brought me closer to them. I did feel I was an equal member of the groups rather than someone directing them from the outside. It is important to become part of a group by sharing your own feelings and experience. Later, when I was to facilitate a group of adult beginner writers producing a book of autobiographical short stories, I was pleased when they insisted I should write a story myself to go alongside theirs and be discussed in the same way.

On the other hand I always chaired the meetings and always had some kind of agenda so that a certain amount of ground would be covered and work produced. I kept the main end in view at all times: we were there to share and develop our thoughts and feelings, but this was in order to write a book, and this meant self-control and discipline. I tried to keep people to the point whilst at the same time allowing development of new ideas that came up in discussion. It wasn't, and didn't feel like, a group of people with equal responsibilities. After all the responsibility for the project as a whole was mine, from the initial organisation and convening, through facilitating and directing the writing, onto the editing and then the processes of typesetting and book production, right through to the organisation of the launch party and distribution (with the QueenSpark co-ordinator).

As a former University teacher and trade union activist I have had a lot of experience of running and chairing groups and meetings. I suppose this, compounded by my Public School prefect/National Service officer background (which makes brusqueness a natural cover for my shyness), meant that underpinning the friendliness there was a certain authoritarianism in my method of leading the groups. But it was a case of control by consent. When I pointed out that we wouldn't get anywhere if everyone spoke at once and that I saw my role as focusing and developing the points that came up, they agreed. 'Nick keeps us in order,' they used to say cheerfully. Because people were happy to leave overall reponsibility to me, they could concentrate on communicating with each other and on writing, which paradoxically gave them a sort of freedom.

I guess that my literacy skills (having a PhD, plus a more recently acquired Dip TEFL, and having published literary critical studies as a University teacher) were tacitly recognised. Some writers were inclined to be intimidated by this expertise but since as I've said the focus was on content and not at all on form or method, people got into 'writing it as it came'. On the whole I think they felt reassured that there was an expert at hand to sort out any problems about spelling, grammar, paragraphing, narrative structure and so on and were able to feel they could use me as a resource rather than do what I said.

I think I was successful in setting up a warm, friendly and relaxed environment for both groups. We were pleased with what we were doing and the experience of co-operation was energising. People looked forward to the meetings and from time to time we would have social gatherings to celebrate what we'd done. The comradeship of working together developed into friendship and since publication of *Life after Stroke* the group still meets from time to time, in various members' homes.

Both groups were very lively. People stimulated each other and it was natural that they wanted to get things off their chest. On one occasion in the *Stroke – Who Cares?* group a member was obviously in a crisis and needed to unburden herself and I allowed most of the meeting to be given over to that. But the principle was that everyone be treated with equal respect and have roughly the same space; that turns be taken and when it was someone's turn they be heard and given the others' full attention. This meant reflecting back what was being said and not referring it to something in the listener's experience. This discipline came very hard for one or two people who were not used to groups and there were times (especially in the *Stroke – Who Cares?* group) when I would lay down strong and explicit guidelines to this effect, which occasionally led to conflict. On the whole, though, I tried to speak as little as possible myself. Paradoxically, this was easier in the *Life after Stroke* group where people couldn't always express themselves rapidly or fluently and needed a lot of space to speak.

It is quite hard for me to say what I learned and in what ways I was challenged. I think I felt an affirmation of my ability to work co-operatively, to communicate and relate easily within a group whilst steering it to an agreed end. I didn't feel my centralising role as co-ordinator in any way disempowered people; rather the reverse. Writing a full and coherent account of your experience is empowering in itself and I was successful in facilitating this, even though my commitment to the agenda of getting a book written and edited may to some extent have closed down the options open to the group and limited its potential.

Another person might have made more use of creative writing convening skills to elicit more deeply personal contributions, and maybe in a way I pre-structured the book by suggesting topics. But members said they appreciated that this was necessary and a number of topics did come out of spontaneous discussion. In fact I'm quite pleased with the way talking and getting to know each other was the starting point for both books and seemed to lead quite naturally to writing.

'By indirections find direction out'. Writing a book wasn't the immediate aim, it wasn't at the front of our minds. People wrote because they had something they wanted to say to the other people in the group. The learning that went on, I felt, was more about people disclosing their own experience and discovering one another's than about learning writing skills. By articulating, and hearing others articulate, a particular experience, and by focusing on a common difficulty or shared pain, it was as though the experience took on a sort of validity. It was there, outside, and that somehow made it easier to deal with. The writing was a by-product and yet, precisely because we were not focusing on the skills of writing but on communication as an end product, it seemed to come out as a quite adequate expression of what people had to say.

Engaging with Difference

At the time I didn't feel I was engaging with people who were 'different'. It wasn't a class, and I wasn't conscious of the group's status as non-students. Although the word itself wasn't in my mind I definitely thought of myself as a facilitator and not a teacher. There was no question of something being passed on from my mind to theirs, in fact the idea of education didn't come into it. We met to share experience and write a book. It's clear from the transcript of discussion at the joint evaluation meeting we held after the books were published (unfortunately too long to be included) that as we went along people had in fact been learning a good deal about writing, editing, communication and co-operative work in general. But this happened as it were invisibly: learning by doing, education by stealth.

The differences between the stroke group members and students in a 'mainstream' educational setting were various. Some were practised writers in a variety of forms, from popular poems to articles in scientific journals; others were convinced they 'couldn't write'; one had severe writing problems as the result of stroke; others had recently taken up creative or autobiographical writing (obviously such groups are to an extent self-selecting). They were 'other' much more strikingly because of the way stroke had changed their lives and to some extent cut them off socially. By incorporating the stroke experience in a co-operative book they were enabled to construct and affirm a group identity as 'us'. This was both a recognition of their real and continuing disadvantage and a strong move towards rehabilitation and social integration. So their 'otherness' wasn't problematic.

Looking back I suppose the most striking aspect of both encounters was the ease and rapidity with which rapport built up. I didn't feel any sense of otherness or exclusion. Simple warmth and friendliness was perhaps the most important ingredient, but I also felt considerable empathy. I knew what it was like to be depressed, like some of the stroke people, and I'd been the principal carer for a loved one who had died. It was natural for me as a relatively open person to want to share these things, which meant that I was drawn into the group.

How did the experience affect me? I felt as though I had been entrusted with the shared expression of a profound and life-changing experience and had been worthy of the trust. It felt like co-operation and friendship, not education.

Life after the Group

As I've indicated, members of the groups have become friends and stayed in touch after the formal meetings stopped. So a very minor support network has been set up. Unfortunately though, the groups haven't continued to meet regularly, although some people, especially those who are housebound or feel a bit socially isolated, the ones for whom the weekly meetings played an important part in their life, would very much like to.

I see now that it would have been a good idea to build the aim of setting up a permanent group into the planning from an early stage. This might have meant choosing/electing people in the group to organise the meetings and activities rather than just leaving all this to the group leader, so that there was a structure for the group to continue functioning autonomously.

Of course there were those who wanted to put the stroke experience behind them and saw the writing and publishing of the book as a way of doing just that, but for others the project has been a stepping-stone to further activities. From the *Life after Stroke* group, Dot is now working as a volunteer both with adult literacy students and with a stroke person under the Dysphasic Support scheme; she has completed her autobiography and is writing regularly. Marion is also working as a volunteer in hospital reception and with one of the stroke clubs. Despite continuing health problems Margaret has gone on to write poetry and a novel; although she has written all her life this is her first venture into fiction, for which the seed was sown in our meetings. Kay has joined a U3A creative writing group; she feels that the project got her going and that she is now going from strength to strength as a writer. From the *Stroke – Who Cares?* group, Karen is the founder-member of a new writing group of single mothers which is going to produce another collective book for QueenSpark, whilst Guy has embarked on a book of his own and is using the method of putting together a long piece of writing which he learned when working on *Stroke – Who Cares?* In our evaluation meeting he said:

> I developed a certain writing style which if I ever get some spare time I will try to use to write another book ... I started with ideas more or less in chronological sequence, a thought for each chapter and worked from that and it seemed to work very well. In this book I've tried to start, I've done the same, I've got my general chapter ideas and I'm going to work from there.

The Group Book Concept

The idea of special interest book-writing projects seems to have taken root in QueenSpark. Projects currently under way are: a group of Brighton homeless people meeting at the Unemployed Centre and recruited in part through contacts with the street magazine for the homeless, *The Big Issue;* a group of single mothers (see above); and a group of women from ethnic minorities. One of our regular womens' writing groups is engaged on producing a book called *Me and My Mum.*

The customary model of book writing and publishing is of a purely imaginary exchange. A solitary author writes for a multifarious multitude of solitary readers. I once heard of a novelist on a train journey who found herself sitting opposite someone absorbed in one of her books, and couldn't help revealing herself and asking for the reader's reactions. There are public readings where the audience is allowed to put a few respectful

questions. Recently I had the rewarding and chastening experience of giving one of my short stories for comment and discussion to a literature study group which I convene. But generally
publishing is a one-way process and fruitful encounters, real
exchanges, are rare.

The group book, covering a subject in which writers and
(later) readers have a particularly strong shared interest, introduces a new model of publishing based on a community of experience. The practice of writing in groups of course is not new.
Coming together to write is often a highly rewarding and
stimulating experience. But most writing groups have a cen-
trifugal structure: each writer is still working as an individual
and what is produced belongs to her or him, so that (despite
the common writing stimulus) the writing is launched outwards. In a special interest group the forces are centripetal,
with the writers facing inwards. The work converges on a community of experience. The group book is a point of focus and
articulation for a particular community.

The stroke writers came together to draw out, share, articulate, affirm, generalise and validate a common experience, a
common suffering, which had changed their lives. They speak
with a unique authority. They write for a specific readership,
reaching out to all those whose lives have also been touched by
stroke and bringing them the feeling that they all belong to the
same community. No-one outside that community can understand in the same way, and perhaps the sense of belonging can
give strength and hope in the way no outsider can, however
caring.

The articulation and validation of the common experience
which went into the writing is, we hope, repeated in the reading in a way that will empower readers who have also been affected by stroke by helping them to understand and accept
their situation more fully and perhaps to feel more in control.
Publication and distribution are precisely targeted, not through
generalist bookshops but through the local and national stroke
networks. This leads not only to the private exchange between
writer and individual reader, but also to sharing between buyer
and borrowers (each copy is likely to be passed round several
readers) and between people discussing the book in clubs,
groups and care institutions.

We are no longer referring to a vague and much abused gen-
erality, *the* Community (frequently with a capital 'C'), which
has been ruthlessly hijacked for every conceivable type of political, social and commercial purpose, but to something much
more precise and comprehensible: *a* community of experience
or interest. The members of such communities are normally

dispersed throughout society at large. Their common interest is expressed and furthered in clubs and meetings; the special interest book is an extension and perhaps a strengthening of this integrating process. Perhaps these books by and for people whose lives have been touched by stroke will help to affirm and celebrate a community of suffering, courage and hope?

For details of QueenSpark Books ring 01273 748348 or write to 11 Jew Street, Brighton BN1 1UT.

Chapter 12

Community Writing and Literacy Development

Freda Ansdell, Nan McCubbin, Sonia Plato, Judy Wallis

It is a chilly morning in February and managers of Adult Basic Education (ABE) in East Sussex have met to discuss future funding. Needless to say there are a lot of pale and grim faces around the table. I am here as the Co-ordinator for the ABE Writing and Publishing Project to ask for contributions. My proposal is greeted by a non-committal silence. Finally a voice protests:

> What's the point of this project? In our Centre we're always getting our students to write and then having it typed up!

Why did this comment stay with me for days afterwards so that I woke up in the night with clenched teeth framing the devastating response which I should have given instead of just opening my mouth and gaping wordless like a goldfish?

Part of my anger came from an uncomfortable recognition that not so long ago my practice was not so very different. Since I first started teaching in Adult Basic Education schemes nearly twenty years ago I have been encouraging students to write about their experiences and then painstakingly typing them up on the Centre typewriter. After what seemed like an age and feeling rather like I had been through a long and exhausting labour I at last gave birth ... to a limp and fuzzy looking document scattered with poorly reproduced illustrations and worthy pieces entitled 'My summer holiday' and 'My Hobby'. It seemed like a nice idea and the students were suitably grateful but it was always something rather marginal and not part of the 'real work' of getting educated.

In 1991 I became involved in a six month project funded by South East Arts which aimed to give students in Adult Basic Education an opportunity to work intensively on their writing, often with the support of a professional writer and to encourage publication. As interest in the project grew, it became obvious that we were doing more than just giving students a nice time for a couple of months until the money ran out. The project was giving a voice to people excluded from the literary and educational establishments and the sense of confidence and self esteem which grew as a result indicated that writing and publishing work was central to adult basic education work. Moreover, we had moved a long way on from the 'getting students to write and having it typed up' school of practice. We had only touched the tip of an iceberg and six months was not sufficient to 'embed' our ideas into the ABE curriculum and to evaluate its success. We applied to have the funding extended and in the following year the project was funded by the New Opportunities Programme at Sussex University as well as South East Arts.

This chapter will explore some of the principles that came to define our writing and publishing work and will follow the progress of one particular ABE writing group which was funded by New Opportunities. These first sections are written by Judy, and the last two sections about 'Shorelink' are written by Freda, Nan and Sonia.

So What's Wrong with Getting our Students to Write and then Having it Typed Up?

When I hear the words 'we' and 'our students' I can't help shuddering. They disguise a paternalistic and protective relationship between the tutor and student. The language implies proprietorial rights and reflects a learning environment of conformity and passivity. It tacitly accepts the hierarchy of teacher and pupil. It is unthreatening, bland and mind-numbingly boring. Writing is generated by the tutor, the audience is the tutor, the editor and publisher is the tutor. It's the sort of 'nice thing which nice people do'.

Another view of ABE writing and publishing work which considers itself more enlightened, asserts that the function of such activity is chiefly therapeutic. It is undoubtedly true that for many students their writing has given them great release and has an enormous value in validating their life histories and enabling them to understand and analyse their experience. Writing does raise self esteem and confidence. However, to assume that ABE student writing only has a therapeutic value for the writer is to marginalise and patronise it. Therapy has a private and personal benefit to the individual. However, when applied to writing, the term therapeutic implies that it has no relevance in a wider social context and does not deserve to be judged by any literary criteria. Although the inspiration for writing can have its origins in a therapeutic need its outcomes may have a public and universal significance.

The 'brave new world' of ABE which demands measurable outcomes and greater cost efficiency is inevitably dismissive of personal writing and publishing work. Sue Slipman at the 1991 Adult Literacy and Basic Skills Unit Conference launched a devastating attack on student writing, describing it as

> a way of confining students to an educational ghetto. Certainly it has sometimes appeared to be the 'Valium' of basic education – an excuse for lack of planning and rigour and a poverty of expectation (*ALBSU Newsletter* Summer 1991).

My experience with the Project and with the writing groups which have been supported by New Opportunities Work proves that there is an alternative vision for writing and publishing work which the *ALBSU Newsletter* failed to recognise. Its outcomes may not be easily measurable in terms of nice neat boxes with rows of ticks in them. Neither are they particularly cheap, quick fixes to short term literacy needs. Our approach aims to tackle the very roots of educational disadvantage and seeks to re-define our relationship to the written word (see Mace, 1995).

What's Different ?

In this section I will elaborate on some of the principles which have emerged from the project over the last two years and have informed our vision of how student writing and publishing could and should be. It is a way of working which is demanding and sometimes painful, but it is also rigorous, challenging and dynamic.

So who and what are ABE students? Educationalists like nice neat little packages they can put a label on and then file away. That way everyone knows their place. A label defines difference but it does not require us to engage with that difference. In the project we have searched for a new definition emphasising what we have in common rather than what separates us. One suggestion we have used is 'people who are working on their writing.' This description encompasses the characteristics which all ABE students and many others share – a desire to continue developing their literacy skills and a lack of confidence in their writing abilities usually as a result of negative school experiences.

One student recalled:

> I had a vivid imagination and loved making up stories for my brother but when I wrote them in class the teacher made so many corrections, particularly with the spelling, that I did everything I could to avoid doing any writing.

School work was completely divorced from real issues and interests.

> I hated every minute I was at school until I got to the Tech. At the local school I had a fight with the headmistress when I was nine and threw cow dung at her. So I spent the next two years in a room on my own. The only work I did was what I found for myself. I saved my pocket money and bought myself a set of nine books on History. When I went back to class I could not focus on board or book. I was too slow to copy anything down.

In this sort of environment learning soon becomes a source of competition, of censorship and of frustration. These are the memories of education which adults bring with them when they return to learning. As tutors it is crucial that we recognise that writing is about more than the acquisition of purely neutral technical skills. A beginner writer is not a beginner thinker. It is also the means by which we give expression to our lives, our experiences, our histories and our culture. The written word has status and confers validity, it affirms your sense of identity, your place and right to power in society.

The practice of students and tutors working together on their writing as members of a community of writers has had implications for the ways in which writing groups are organised. Everyone who produces a piece of writing 'owns' that writing and decides its purpose. The group works collaboratively and decides how they want to operate together and to collectively establish guidelines for editing.

The tutor's role in the writing group is to facilitate the process, not to control it. Tutors who puts students in a passive role and impose their view of what constitutes 'good' writing, are programming their students to failure and risk creating a persistent writing block.

Ann is an example of just such an approach. She had been coming to the writing group for two terms and although she contributed perceptively to the group and recorded her own reflections on tape she would never produce more than a line of her own writing. She had been coming to other ABE classes for a number of years and when I met one of her former tutors I mentioned her enormous difficulty in putting pen to paper.

The tutor was amazed, as her experience with Ann had been of a passionate writer of prolific output with a real feel for language. The next time I had an opportunity I talked to Ann about why she had stopped writing. She became very angry and distressed and her voice trembled with emotion as she spoke: 'She wanted me to write in her language not my language.' She was talking about a previous tutor. She subsequently made a more detailed recording of the experience.

I stopped writing because of the way people tried to tell me how to write things and to change my style and to criticise the way I wrote things. They didn't like the language that I used, the way I wrote, the way I thought, even the way I felt. Writing needs to be fun, what *you* want, not what they want, the length that *you* want and how *you* want it.

For Ann there was no distinction between what she wrote and the way she wrote it. By denying her the right to express herself in the language she had chosen, she had also been denied the thoughts and feelings that had originally inspired the writing. Shortly afterwards I read out a poem that Ann had written before the writing block had descended. It was a simple but very powerful reflection on the effect of change in her local community. The rest of the group were as stunned as I had been that Ann had once been able to write with such confidence and conviction. Now she seemed bereft, effectively disenfranchised; the ownership of her language and the feelings she had struggled to express had been appropriated by someone else. The issue for tutors and students here is of gaining achievement and satisfaction through a genuine partnership and dialogue; of drawing strength from a relationship that engages with difference in a positive way and values its outcomes.

The notion of publication in our groups has become an intrinsic part of any writing activity. An opportunity to share writing, whether it is a group reading, the centre magazine or simply a piece of paper pinned to the wall, creates a sense of audience and meaningful purpose. The writing group regularly read each other's work and give feedback. It takes a lot of courage to expose yourself in this way and yet the supportive and celebratory responses from their readers are a source of motivation and encouragement to the writer that could never be supplied if the audience was solely the teacher.

'Shorelink': a Group of Beginner Writers Tell their Story

> We all felt as the weeks progressed, both our writing and
> our confidence improved so that what had at first been a
> struggle became a joy.
>   *Shorelink Writers' introduction to their first magazine.*

The following is an account of the history of one group of beginner writers and a record of how ways of working and principles of good practice have emerged. In writing this account,
members of the group discussed and put forward ideas and
contributions which were then synthesised to reflect the hopes
and views of all the Shorelink members.

Shorelink is the name we chose to represent students and tutors from Bexhill and Hastings Adult Basic Education groups
who meet together as a group of writers to share experiences
and ideas and to support each other in the struggle of writing.
It has taken us a while to see ourselves as writers with something to say which people may want to hear, but as we have
grown and developed new links with other writing and publishing groups, we have found that others have valued and
supported us and this has helped us to value ourselves.

An important and vital part of the development of Shorelink
at Bexhill and Hastings has been the availability of funding
from other sources than our own Adult Basic Education
budget, which is restricted and unable to entirely fund ongoing
writers' groups. Our continued existence is due to three factors:
external funding, the Writing and Publishing Project and, most
importantly, the very real individual commitment of students
and tutors themselves.

Shorelink began in October 1990 as two writing groups at
Bexhill and Hastings, funded for a ten week period by South
East Arts to work with a professional writer, Tony Masters. The
aim was to encourage ABE students, who might never have
written before, to use a series of location visits to stimulate
writing, develop their confidence as writers and produce an anthology of their work. We found that when the funding ran out
we had no money to produce the anthology or continue the sessions, but we did have a group of students and tutors who had
developed a real belief in the value of creative writing and a
commitment to continue to meet and write together for the rest
of the year. Running alongside the writing group was a small
publishing group whose aim was to produce the anthology for
distribution to other students and the general public. This sub-
group received support from QueenSpark in the form of three

sessions on community publishing, but was thwarted by the lack of money to print the magazine. Through this link with QueenSpark, we first came into contact with the Federation of Worker Writers and Community Publishers. By Autumn 1991 we managed to get limited funding from the ABE group budget to enable us to continue writing groups and offer places to new students for part of the year.

By 1992 we were confident enough as a group to take part in the meetings of the newly established Writing and Publishing Project and become formal members of the Federation. In the Autumn we took part in the Writing and Publishing Project's Magazine group and were finally able to publish the work of ABE writers. The offer of regular funding from the University of Sussex New Opportunities Work meant that we were able to continue to develop our own writing groups with input from professional writers and could begin to feel that we had some permanence and recognition as a group of writers. Since that time we have continued to broaden our links with other groups and have formalised ourselves as Shorelink Writers with prospective new members from Hailsham writing groups and from the local writing group at a Day Centre for people with a history of mental illness.

Most students start from a position where they are frightened to write either because of limited writing skills or extreme lack of confidence. The group reflects a very wide range of ability and interests. Some may have learning difficulties or special needs and the majority come believing that they have very little to say that will be of interest or value to others. They may join the writing groups for very different reasons: to support their work in other ABE groups or courses; to get down something they have always wanted to say; to improve their fluency, vocabulary and imagination; or to share writing with others in the group. What we have found is that everyone has a story to tell about themselves and that often this can only be expressed in a truly mutually supportive environment where each person is valued for their ability and potential. The group enables each individual to develop and extend their writing and also, through a changing view of themselves, to develop their lives through writing and activities both inside and outside the group. To those who have been denied it, self expression is a door to effective living in the world as an individual. This may sound idealistic, but we have witnessed it in action in the group. As one of our students has said, 'if Adult Basic Education is itself a bridge to further education, then for me creative writing is the easiest bridge to travel across.'

One of the reasons that Shorelink members are so keen to

encourage others to join the group is because of the value of what they have experienced and the empowerment it has given them in their daily lives and personal development.

Shorelink is organised increasingly by the students themselves, with tutors adopting a supportive and guiding role, seeking to provide continued stimulation to keep the group moving and to meet the broad range of needs and interests of the students. Something we have found helpful has been the involvement of professional poets, playwrights and writers to provoke ideas and provide encouragement. This has also been useful in raising the status of the group and plays a part along with students' own writing development in raising self esteem and valuing personal work. The group has developed its own techniques for helping the process of writing and editing which have included scribing for each other, splurging, group writing, locations, developing characterisation and autobiography. Writing is shared and editorial skills are further developed within the context of presenting work for publication.

As Shorelink has grown and developed in a wider context, opportunities for new experiences have emerged for its members. We see ourselves not only as writers but as publishers and, what is more, as writers and publishers in a national context. Over the past four years students have had to learn new skills and gain the confidence to support this role. These have ranged from organising Reading Evenings and Writing events, making videos and running Weekend Workshops, to getting to grips with using computers to publish our magazines, understanding about print-runs and marketing our publications. We have had to meet the challenge of working more formally as Shorelink in relation to well-established county and national organisations, while maintaining and strengthening our own identity through the development of closer links with people and groups within our own local community.

Shorelink is now in a situation where tutors are becoming less and less directive. Students are developing their own initiatives and directions both as individuals and as a group. We hope to extend the lessons we have learnt to other areas of Adult Basic Education and as students and tutors continue to learn and grow ourselves.

More than Just a Writing Group

These ways of working do not produce instant results. Establishing control over your own learning and independence is a slow and time-consuming process. You are having to reassess your role as the passive recipient of knowledge and received wisdom. This is a hard, frustrating and sometimes painful process because it impinges on every aspect of people's lives, altering their self image as well as their relationship to society. The writing group gives them an opportunity to reflect on and value past experience. This leads to an enormous increase in confidence and the enlargement of their interests generally. They write letters to newspapers, join local history groups, become involved in community action groups, apply for courses in Higher Education.

Bringing down the barriers between teacher and taught has had an effect on their attitudes to authority in general. Working collaboratively has given them a sense of solidarity, of shared interests and concerns as a class and a community. Achievement is not simply measured in terms of personal success but also in terms of the satisfaction gained by working in the interests of their fellows as well as themselves. Equally, such an approach makes demands on tutors as they redefine their role and give up their 'power' within the group. Their silence becomes more important than their words, their questions more significant than their answers, they listen rather than expect to be listened to. Stripped of their automatic status as leaders, tutors can feel exposed and vulnerable. The most important qualities they need are the trust and humility to acknowledge that everyone is a learner.

Group members now have a changed view of themselves as readers. They are no longer overawed by the mystique of print and now approach professional authors as travellers along the same road as themselves. By using writing techniques to persuade and enlist the sympathy and interest of the reader they have become more aware of the occasions when those same techniques are being exercised on them.

There are also risks. A new-found confidence and power may have a disruptive effect on other relationships. Those around you can feel threatened and excluded.

As one partner gains greater self esteem the delicate balance of power within a relationship shifts. One student has described how he has to do his writing when his wife has gone to bed and tensions run high on the night he comes to the writing group. Another woman's previously supportive and encouraging partner became withdrawn and aggressive as he saw his position of power in the relationship becoming eroded.

Or should we look on these as success stories? Participation in writing groups which practise the approaches we have outlined in this chapter will inevitably have wider implications for the group members. Learning and education in its broadest sense is about people's capacity for change, about re-examining your identity and about redefining terms like success and fail-ure. It is a challenge that we as tutors of the educationally dis-advantaged need to embrace with enthusiasm rather than shy away from.

References

ALBSU (1991), 'Developing a Kitemark for Basic Education and ESOL', *ALBSU Newsletter*, No. 42, p 2.

Mace, J. (ed.) (1995), *Literacy, Language and Community Publishing: Essays in Adult Education,* Clevedon: Multilingual Matters.

Conclusion

Education and Self Identity: A Process of Inclusion and Exclusion

Mary Stuart

Reflecting Further

In this book we have discussed a number of different adult learning projects, projects which in many respects mirror the range of work currently being undertaken in different adult education settings across Britain. The concerns that we have raised in the book are concerns which many adult educators share. We have brought together a number of different perspectives, not only the adult education researcher's perspective, but also those of tutors, organisers, and students involved in adult education. The book also explores some of the concerns offered by our partners in educational provision.

The complexity of the relationships involved in each project has created challenges and opportunities for engagement. Each professional, whether educator or community or social worker, has a different agenda for participating in adult education; each student has their own reasons for learning. At times there are tensions between learners, educators and partners. These difficulties and their tentative solutions are reflected in the stories in this book.

Despite the complexity of these relationships, if we are offering learning to groups who have been economically and socially disadvantaged by our society it is essential that we continue to struggle to engage with the variety of the demands which learners, tutors and partners make on educational organisations. Engaging with these demands will not always mean we can accommodate them, especially if they are conflicting. It is, therefore, particularly important to understand the nature and extent of our partnerships in learning.

Partnerships do not create equal power relations. Inequality does not only occur at the level of tutor/student contact, but also between tutors and organisers and educationalists and community workers and professionals. Planning educational provision with partners often reveals inequalities of power, about who has access to resources and the status that is attached to different groups of professionals.

This conclusion attempts to draw together these themes which run throughout the book. In particular, the conclusion will examine how power operates through the discourse of identity, how the flow of power creates and limits our social identities and how inequalities of power surface in individual identities. By identity I mean an agreed sense of who we are as individuals. Individuals develop a sense of themselves and will behave in ways which they feel reveal the 'type' of personality they have. Socially we also create an identity for our institutions. For example we have a shared knowledge in our society of what the 'medical profession' is, or what 'school' is like. In other societies these 'identities' will have different meanings. These identities are not simply fixed, they are shaped and altered by a variety of social forces, and change over time.

I will examine the extent to which education affects these identities, not only how education can affect the individual, but also how we create social identities for institutions like 'the education system', or even how we create social identities for concepts like 'education' itself. The development of our institutions, social structures and belief and philosophy systems is determined by the way we 'imagine' what concepts like education and knowledge are. I use the word 'imagine' because we are creating a social world which we can relate to, both individually and as a society. This imagining is always being redefined and contested. Yet it is in this process of 'imagining' that identity and power intersect. Through these processes of social creation funding bodies allocate resources, curricula are decided, groups and individuals are defined.

Many adult educators who want to develop an education system which offers equality of opportunity are aware that education is powerful and can change people's lives, but we often find it more difficult to be precise about the nature of that power in education. Reflection on some of our projects has enabled those of us who have participated in the writing of this book to challenge our practice and develop new ways of working which I hope are more democratic and give us a greater awareness of the nature of power in learning. The specifics of the different encounters described in the book have certainly helped me to re-think the process of developing educational provision. The work of the NOW programme has moved on since I decided to work on this book. The programme has expanded and is part of an Education Equality Unit which has two co-ordinators, focusing on community provision and learner support. We are continuing to work with new partners, which still creates challenges for us and our institution. We are exploring new ways of offering appropriate support for learning and teaching and developing educational guidance and counselling to increase the learners' options.

In the final section of this chapter I discuss some of this new thinking in our work, in particular the democratic practice of education as a process of research. I will draw on the Swedish experience of 'research circles' (Harnsten, 1994), a group learning process which enables a shared identity between all the participants, which offers esteem to individuals and which enables exploration of learning in a way that is critical and democratic.

The Process of Socialisation and Education: Offering Shame or Esteem

The way individuals identify who they are is drawn from a variety of different components, including gender, cultural heritage and family background. Intersecting with and drawing on these different aspects of our-selves is a 'sense'or perception of our 'intelligence'. Our language is permeated with words which reflect the centrality of intelligence to an individual identity. Being 'streetwise', a 'cleverclogs', 'dumb', 'stupid' and so on, are all expressions which adults and children use in establishing and maintaining relationships and a sense of identity in relation to others around them. What is particularly significant about this process is that 'intelligence' is not only defined and used in the confines of education, it is also constantly being redefined and challenged in all aspects of everyday life. This does not lessen the importance of the professional educator's definition of someone's intelligence. It makes their definition more important, because it is constructed in a social framework which we all recognise and connect to our own identity, and because the professional definition also carries with it the weight of social status. These definitions of our 'intelligence', whether defined by our peers, our carers or by professionals, are developed in power relationships. Individuals are being offered a social definition of who they are within a hierarchy. These social material structures are perpetuated through the processes of self identity, and the social definition of 'your place' is internalised to become a part of who you are.

From an early age we begin to establish an 'intelligence'

identity. Our parents and carers will often praise our achievements in crawling, walking, potty training and so on, with
statements about how 'clever' we are. Most psychologists see
these early experiences as being central to the shaping of our
identity. George Herbert Mead, a social psychologist working
in the 1930s in America, developed a theory which explains this
process of internalising others' 'ideas' about who we are and
making them our own. He saw interaction between people,
both at an individual level and at a social level, as being central
to the development of a 'self'. He suggested that we internalise
others' perceptions of who we are and symbolically 'create'
ourselves (Mead, 1934). This process is not haphazard but is
mediated through attachments to specific individuals or 'significant others' and through our interactions with a more general symbolic level of 'the society', what he termed the
'generalised other'. This theory helps explain how power in society operates within individuals because it suggests that it is
through the very process of how we see ourselves and are defined by others, that we are placed within a social hierarchy.
Our social institutions create the material parameters within
which we are able to function in society, our class position, our
gender, our ethnicity and so on, and through the process of
forming our self identity we unconsciously internalise the
power relations from the society or as Mead called it the 'generalised other'.

A number of theorists have used Mead's idea of the self generated through a process of symbolic interactions (Goffman,
1961; Plummer, 1983). Erving Goffman saw the process of socialisation developing through a desire to avoid embarrassment. The notion of embarrassment can be seen in relation to a
scale of shame on the one hand and esteem on the other. In an
attempt to avoid experiencing shame, we internalise experiences
as they occur and we 'relive' these experiences again and again,
each time the experience 'teaches' us about who we are. Working in this tradition, Thomas Scheff (1990) identifies education as
one of the major identity-forming processes that we encounter
in our modernist world. It is in the education system that the
operation of shame and esteem can often be seen most clearly.

In this book we have tried to identify a variety of groups
who have been offered shame by education. They have been
seen as less able to learn. Sometimes this shaming has not been
deliberate, as discussed in relation to housebound learners in
Chapter three, but by emphasising the importance of learning
in an education establishment, housebound people have been
excluded and internalise a sense of themselves as being difficult
and a 'nuisance' to the educationalists. The following statement

is taken from one of the participants' feedback sheets from the That's Entertainment course which is described in Chapter three. 'I am so grateful to you all for setting up this course. I understand it must have been difficult to accommodate people like me. I do so hope you can find the time to set up another course especially on music' (Mrs S, 1993). Mrs S sees herself as 'difficult', and places blame for the lack of educational opportunities for housebound people upon herself. We have created a social 'imagining' that education occurs within education buildings. Mrs S takes this social imagining for granted. By accepting this view of education Mrs S has come to see herself, and not the structures of education, as the problem.

In some cases the shaming of certain groups of learners has been a deliberate process by professionals. Take, for example, the story recounted in Gus Garside's chapter, *'She's Doing too Much Music'*. Here a woman with 'learning difficulties' is disempowered and shamed because a 'professional' does not see that she has or can have any musical ability. The dominant social definition that only 'intelligent' people should have access to learning is confirmed in this story. In the professional's eyes, education can only be useful for limited therapeutic purposes for people with learning difficulties.

The way we use our definition of intelligence is a particularly potent way of offering individuals or groups either pride or shame. Since the professionalisation of education in the nineteenth century, teachers, tutors and other educators have become 'significant others' in the shaping of our identities. They are awarded certain rights in defining aspects of who and how we see ourselves. When adults are asked about their memories of education, many focus on particular teachers or tutors who affected their learning either positively or negatively (Howard, 1994; Mass Observation Education Directive Responses, 1991). It is crucial that the effects which significant individuals in education have on the process of self identity are examined in our practice. This point is highlighted in Chapter two, *'I Bet it was Written by a Mother'* and in Chapter five, *Murder your Darlings*. In both these chapters the identity of the tutors affects the learning of the adults involved.

However the tutor's role and identity is only one aspect of the process through which education forms identities. In the next section I will examine the 'purpose' of adult education and how the debate on purpose has shaped a social identity for adult education in Britain. I will explain how this social identity has determined access and curricula for adults and how the provision which has been offered has affected individuals and groups of learners.

Adult Education and Excluded Groups

In the introduction Al Thomson and I examined the history of education provision in Britain and how, from the development of a professional education service, battles were fought over who had rights to education. Adult education developed in the context of seemingly contradictory discourses. These were, on the one hand, a work ethic discourse, which focused on a structural need to develop the skills of the workforce, and, on the other hand, a discourse of useful leisure, which argued that adults should spend their free-time on improving their minds (Cross, 1990). This contradiction remains with us today. The recent Further and Higher Education Act (1992) argued for a skills development, and many adult educators and organisations like ALBSU and NIACE have valued aspects of the move towards a more 'professional' and instrumental adult education across all sectors. Others have argued that the ideas of a so-called 'liberal adult education' which were hegemonic during the earlier part of this century are being lost by focusing on market-related skills in adult, further and higher education.

Despite the supposed contradictions between the two discourses, historically and in the present, there are some similar principles which run through both an adult education based on skills and an adult education based on personal development. During the early part of this century when educationalists were debating the purpose of 'adult education', there was much discussion about who should participate in this education. In *Civilisation and its Discontents*, Freud wrote about the dangers of leisure and saw free-time as a opportunity for the individual to 'regress' to childhood. He was particularly concerned about the libido of the 'masses' who, he believed, needed the example of elites to get them to 'perform work and undergo the renunciation on which the existence of civilisation depends' (Freud, 1930: 141). For Freud and other social scientists, leisure was not a desirable option for the working class and therefore education should have a very limited vocational role for the majority of the population. Learning should be confined to the 'reality principle', specific skills training was what was required for the 'masses'. Laurence P. Jacks, on the other hand, argued in favour of learning for leisure for the 'masses'. Yet his argument was, like Freud's, about control. It was through a liberal adult education that people would learn a 'discipline of the body and mind' which would help them develop a creative life (Cross, 1990).

In many ways these two discourses about the purpose of adult learning are similar. They both define certain groups in society and suggest ways in which their behaviour should be controlled and organised. Proponents of both skills-based and liberal adult education emphasise that they are offering opportunities to adults. However it seems to me that the debate over skills versus liberal adult education is a limited one. While offering opportunities to some, both discourses exclude certain individuals and groups from learning what they wish to study. Both discourses 'imagine' a social identity for particular groups in society and 'imagine' a particular identity for 'education'. In discussing the purpose of adult education, it is significant that the education debate continues to define groups of learners in stereotypical ways. For example people with learning difficulties have only recently won the right to education and the curriculum which is offered is still prescribed by professionals, as identified in the chapter *Our Right to Know: Women with Learning Difficulties and Sexuality Courses*. The perception that bilingual speakers are unable to learn job-related skills until they have 'learnt some more English', as discussed by Anne Bellis and Sahar Awar in Chapter one, is a similar gatekeeping exercise.

Through challenging who has access to the range of educational opportunities, the distinctions between learning for leisure and learning for work diminish. Groups of learners which have been excluded from education through a social acceptance of one discourse of education in the past are looking for an education discourse in the 1990s that will meet their needs and which may include instrumental skills for work as well as personal development study. We need to create a different education discourse which caters for diverse learners' needs and which does not use definitions of learning and education to exclude particular individuals and groups from the opportunity to learn.

Working on the Margins, Moving to the Centre: Reflecting on NOW

It would fanciful to imagine that the projects outlined in this book are anything but peripheral to the university in which we work. This is the case for most adult educators working with groups which have been socially and economically disadvantaged. However the nature of education is changing. In Britain we are working towards a mass higher education system (McNair, 1994). The reduction in statutory grants is forcing students studying in HE to look for places in universities which are close to their home in order to keep costs down. Universities are having to look more to their local communities and to adults who wish to study part-time to maintain or increase their student numbers. For people who work with under-represented groups in higher education, this is an opportunity to enhance access to further study and to have the programmes of learning which we have developed with marginalised groups recognised by our institutions. The potential for better progression routes between adult education, further education and higher education is enormous. Offering work-based learning gives many working class adults an opportunity to learn and receive recognition for their learning. However the concerns raised about the Accreditation of Prior Experience and Learning in Chapter ten, and the issues highlighted in the discussion of literacy work in Chapter twelve, sound a note of caution. Experience which adults have gained through life is often limited by economic or social disadvantage and may not match educational expectations. AP(E)L can only accredit experience which adults have gained. We must not assume that the recognition of prior learning is going to offer educational equality in an unequal society. As Judy Wallis discusses in Chapter twelve, literacy development which has also featured in the development of work-based learning schemes should not only focus on instrumental English learning. For many adults an ability to have their own speech and writing valued is the first step to developing their language skills. New ideas and new educational practices will not automatically create access and could even place new barriers to learning.

Adults who are involved in formal learning have a wide variety of experience and bring with them contradictory and competing identities. Educators and the discourse of education may wish to label learners as particular 'types' of students, but if we allow ourselves to work with these labels we will re-create exclusive forms of education. The government wants to create a 'learning society'. The Economic and Social Research Council is currently offering grants to explore what a learning society could be. If we are to create a culture of learning amongst the population, it is important to work in partnership with adult learners, and for learning to be a dialogue between facilitators and group members engaged in the learning process. I do not only mean the adult education notion of negotiating the curriculum or drawing on individual adults' experience in our teaching. I mean something far more radical. I mean learning as a genuine partnership. In the final section of this chapter I will discuss possible ways of enabling this dialogue which are both critical and democratic.

Ways Forward? Democracy in Learning

There is a multiplicity of identities involved in the education process: complex individual identities; groups which are shaped and changed by the variety of participating individuals; communities constructed within the context of a socio-historical frame; and institutions whose meaning will be mediated by structures and individual professionals. These complex overlays of personal identity, social structures and power make the idea of democratic learning more difficult to implement, yet a genuine recognition of difference between individuals and groups provides the groundwork for a more equal learning environment.

In Sweden, where over 80 per cent of workers are unionised, the trade union movement, in partnership with university adult education, has developed a specific style of learning which offers the possibility for mutual respect and status between learners and facilitators. Unlike much trade union education in Britain, which consists of limited day release programmes, the Swedish education movement operates on a more flexible request basis. Groups will meet in work time in the workplace when they have defined a problem which to wish to investigate. These groups are called 'research circles' (Harnsten, 1994). Each group works together to investigate a shared concern, with the support of a trained researcher. Central to the ethos of these circles is the idea that each participant brings with them particular knowledges which will be valuable to the research being undertaken. The agenda is set by the trade unionists, and the researcher, like any researcher who is contracted to conduct research, works within the confines of this agenda. The framework which the Swedes have constructed is very different from that of most adult education teaching. It establishes a different set of identities for the participants in a circle. Each member knows that their knowledge is necessary to the development of the research. The idea of research circles was developed by Karl-Axel Nilsson while working with union representatives in 1977. He emphasises: 'The researchers were not to function as teachers, but rather participants of the circle' (Nilsson, 1990).

Many of the principles of research circles could be readily applied to our adult education structures. It is an accepted principle of adult learning that all adults bring with them knowledge which will be useful in further study (Rogers, 1986). Good practice in community education will focus on requests from communities rather than offers of education coming from institutions (Brookfield, 1986). Research techniques are often an appropriate way of examining subject material. The principle of a mutual investigation of a topic, with all participants bringing specific skills to the investigation, could readily be applied to all forms of adult learning, including assessed work.

By creating a different framework in a group and replacing 'learning' with 'investigation', the group power relations are altered and all participants receive esteem and respect for what they can bring to the study. Using these principles with adults whose experience is different from conventional knowledge within the education discourse could be particularly rewarding as many topics could be examined from diverse cultural and social perspectives which would offer new and different interpretations of knowledge. The key to this power shift is a different attitude to knowledge. The discourse of teaching and learning, no matter how liberatory, is framed by a notion of an established body of knowledge which needs to be imparted. A research discourse emphasises new contributions to that body of knowledge. In other words a research discourse has potentially more space for difference and can recognise that it is necessary to build on and challenge the accepted body of knowledge.

Of course research is also fraught with inequalities of power. Research ethics are a major concern of research methodology (Benmayor, 1991; Gluck, 1991). However if the basis of the relationship between participants is rooted in a group investigation, it avoids some of the inequalities which the social roles of tutor and student suggest. Unlike an education discourse which identifies the tutor as 'knowledgeable' and the students as requiring knowledge, the research discourse suggests that all the participants have to discover and investigate the chosen topic. Working with these principles does go some way to redefining what adult learning could be.

Although many recent developments in education have caused frustrations and difficulties for adult educators, it is still possible to find spaces to develop radical and innovatory education such as the research circle approach. For example, there is a growing emphasis on group work in education. The principles of the research circle are ideally suited to this style of education and the research circle methods establishing tasks and investigative activities for the group would create a greater depth of understanding in the group activities.

Another current emphasis in adult, further and higher education is monitoring and evaluation. Any research project requires rigorous monitoring and evaluation. Quality assessment through monitoring and feedback systems could be creatively adapted to the particular needs of the research group. The information about students required in adult and further education could be seen as an intrinsic part of the circle. Each research circle begins with an assessment of skills available to the group and this assessment could be used by participants to assess their own and the project's development. This information could be used for quality assurance purposes. Clearly there are issues of what monitoring and assessment is for. However, it is possible to redefine quality assurance to enable a more participatory education with monitoring and evaluation which is sparked by participants in relation to the needs of the investigation.

I do not suggest that research circles are the solution to education's difficulty in working with those groups who have been marginalised in learning, but I do think that their approach could offer a more democratic and useful learning environment for many 'others' who come into adult education. It is an approach which could address some of the concerns highlighted in the projects described in this book. Looking to the future, several of us working in the NOW programme are discussing the idea of research circles with the groups and people we work with, in the hope that we can develop a framework for learning which is reciprocal and equal. This is of course a research circle in itself. Perhaps we will monitor and evaluate it and write it up for next time!

References

Benmayor, R. (1991) 'Testimony, Action Research and Empowerment. Puerto Rican Women and Popular Education', in Gluck, S. B. and Patai, D. (1991) *Women's Words: The Feminist Practice of Oral History*, London: Routledge.

Brookfield, S. (1986) *Adult Learners, Adult Education and the Community*, Milton Keynes: Open University Press.

Cross, G. (1990) *A Social History of Leisure Since 1600*, State College, PA: Venture Publishing.

Freud, S. (1930) *Civilisation and its Discontents*, London: Penguin.

Gluck, S. B. (1991) 'Advocacy Oral History: Palestinian Women in Resistance', in Gluck, S. B. and Patai, D. *op. cit.*

Goffman, E. (1961) *Asylum: Essays on the Social Situation of Mental Patients and Other Inmates*, New York: Doubleday.

Harnsten, G. (1994) *The Research Circle – Building Knowledge on Equal Terms*, Stockholm: The Swedish Trade Union Confederation.

Howard, U. (1994) 'Writing and Literacy in Nineteenth Century England: some uses and meanings', University of Sussex, unpublished D. Phil. thesis.

Mass Observation Education Directive Responses (1991) Mass Observation Archive, University of Sussex.

McNair, S. (1994) *An Adult Higher Education*, Leicester: NIACE.

Mead, G. H. (1934) *Mind, Self and Society*, Chicago: University of Chicago Press.

Nilsson, K. A. (1990) Quoted in Harnsten, G. (1994) *op. cit.*

Plummer, K. (1983) *Documents of Life: An Introduction to the Problems and Literature of the Humanist Method*, London: George, Allen and Unwin.

Rogers, A. (1986) *Teaching Adults*, Milton Keynes: Open University Press.

Scheff, T. (1990) *Micro Sociology: discourse, emotion and social structure*, Chicago: University of Chicago Press.

Notes on Contributors

Freda Ansdell, Nan McCubbin and *Sonia Plato* are adult basic education tutors at Hastings College of Arts and Technology. They convene Shorelink Writing Group.

Sahar Awar comes from Lebanon and has lived in the UK for 11 years. She works as a Bilingual Assistant in English for Speakers of Other Languages classes in Brighton and Hove.

Anne Bellis is a teacher of English for Speakers of Other Languages in the Brighton area.

Kim Clancy had worked in cultural media for a number of years. She is currently living in Devon and works part-time in adult education. She is completing a PhD examining representations of women in the 1960s.

Pam Coare has worked for many years in both adult basic education and adult education, and at present is employed at the Centre for Continuing Education (CCE) at the University of Sussex to organise courses for disadvantaged groups, in partnership with community organisations.

Jennie Fontana is a freelance writer and part-time lecturer for the University of Sussex and the Open College of the Arts, and author of the poetry collection published by Stride, *Lost Stations*.

Gus Garside is a professional musician with extensive experience of working in a wide variety of settings with people with learning difficulties and people with mental health problems. He also works part-time as the West Sussex Arts Development Officer for Artability.

Gerry Holloway teaches women's history on the Access to Higher Education Women's Studies course and the certificate in Women's Studies as well as various undergraduate courses at the University of Sussex. She has also recently published a report on accreditation as a challenge to liberal adult education.

David Longman is a lecturer in education at the University of Sussex Institute of Education, where he has taught a variety of IT courses for many years.

Jill Masouri recently completed an Access course and a Certificate in Women's Studies at CCE, where she is planning to complete a part-time degree.

Nick Osmond was born in 1933 and with many of his generation rejected the middle-class Tory ideology which he inherited. In his fifties, after early retirement, he became active in adult literacy work and community publishing, part of a lifelong quest for fuller communication and an alternative community.

Kathy Smith is a tutor in special needs with many years' experience in this field. She is currently working at CCE.

Mary Stuart came into adult education during the 1970s anti-schools campaigns in South Africa and has worked with a wide range of adults both in South Africa and in London and the south-east of England. She is currently responsible for educational guidance and learner support within CCE.

Alistair Thomson is an editor of *Oral History* and teaches courses about life history work and adult learning and education for CCE, where he is responsible for continuing education research and development.

Judy Wallis was co-ordinator of the East Sussex Adult Basic Education and Writing project from 1991 to 1993. She is currently working on a project for adults returning to education at Lewes Tertiary College.

Index

Afterword

As this book was going to press, the Higher Education Funding Council for England announced the result of a major allocation of funds for 'widening provision' in higher education. The widening provision funds were largely allocated to institutions interested in developing educational guidance and learning support for individuals and groups marginalised in education. In the Centre for Continuing Education at the University of Sussex our increasing interest in this field in recent years contributed to the comparative success of our bid.

For the most part, bids which focused on provision of community courses for disadvantaged groups were unsuccessful, by contrast with the previous round of funding for this work four years ago which had supported such provision. A number of significant programmes, for example units with an excellent track record in provision of courses for people with disabilities, have lost their funding. New Opportunities Work at CCE will no longer have core HEFCE funding for provision of courses described in this book, and will need either to accredit the provision or find alternative funding, for example from Europe. This dramatic change in the funding and prospects for New Opportunities Work highlights the insecurity of work with educationally marginalised groups. This is not only a problem in higher education but is part of a wider set of issues in adult education. In effect, non-accredited community provision which does not have direct vocational outcomes is increasingly difficult to finance and support. The redirection of adult and continuing education towards accreditation is explored in this book. We point out some of the dangers of this development.

There are, however, opportunities as well as risks in using guidance and learning support as the basis for widening higher education provision. The University of Sussex and other institutions will now be able to offer more extensive and appropriate support for people who have been failed by and excluded from the education system. As one adult educator commented on the recent changes: 'Perhaps we have been too precious. There are people from communities who can succeed in HE if we offer them support and we must enable them.' The new pot of widening provision money can help us achieve this aim.

What is clear is that university adult education with radical 'social purpose' aspirations can no longer operate through a model of community-based provision for educationally disadvantaged groups. It must now be embedded within individual institutions and the HE sector, as it has been for many years in the polytechnic/new university sector. The struggle for the future will be to ensure that this embedding process makes HE more accessible for a wider range of people while at the same time challenging and changing the practices and curricula of HE. If we are not careful the social purpose aspirations of radical university adult educators will be swallowed up and lost.

Also Published by NIACE

Learning from Experience: Empowerment or Incorporation?

Wilma Fraser (WEA Tutor Organiser, South Eastern District)

APL/APEL is now a well-established practice in all forms of adult, further and higher education, offering a bridge between past experiences and future learning goals. But who gets to say which experiences, and whose, will count towards accredited qualifications? What is gained, and what is lost, in the translation of private experiences into the public sphere? This challenging and critical examination of current trends in learning from experience is based on a wide-ranging 'Making Experience Count' project and looks at experiential learning in relation to courses:

- at Ford Motor Company
- within outreach provision for marginalised groups
- with women
- with long-term unemployed
- in higher education
- with ethnic minority groups.

Offering both theoretical insights and unique practical wisdom, this book will be essential reading for all practitioners and managers in post-compulsory and professional education who really want to make experience count.

Wilma Fraser is tutor-organiser, WEA South Eastern District and honorary research fellow, School of Continuing Education, University of Kent.

ISBN 1 872941 60 5
paperback; 224 pages, incl. bibliography
£12.00

Adult Learning, Critical Intelligence and Social Change

edited by Marjorie Mayo and Jane L. Thompson (Ruskin College, Oxford)

What lies behind the current pre-occupation with education and its relationship to economic growth? Has the idea of community engagement in the mixed economy of welfare through a radical, critical form of participative learning disappeared, or is it re-emerging in a different form?

Adult Learning, Critical Intelligence and Social Change offers a wide range of perspectives on these and other issues which have emerged since the 1980s. In the last 15 years, adult education has been subject to restructuring around the promotion of market forces, moving away from the agenda of education for transformation towards a narrower agenda of meeting vocational needs. In the process, it has become demonstrably less neutral and more overtly controversial, more vital than ever in providing essential skills and knowledge and in developing alternative visions for democratic social change. This book reviews the context of these developments and focuses on contemporary debates in workplace- and community-based adult education and the impact of NVQs, competence-based approaches and APL on women and ethnic minority communities.

The book opens with a critical review of the context for these changes and of the theoretical debates which attempt to analyse and explain them. The chapters which follow offer specific challenges to postmodernism in relation to adult learning, and focus more generally on critical debates around culture and theory. Developments in trade union education, women's education and vocational education are considered in depth.

Both as an expert overview of developments since 1980 and as a source of inspiration for a more progressive agenda, this collection will appeal to students and practitioners in all forms of adult education.

Marjorie Mayo is a tutor at Ruskin College, Oxford. Jane L. Thompson is Director of the Women's Studies Programme at Ruskin College.

ISBN 1 872941 61 3
paperback; 300 pages, incl. bibliographies
£12.00

About NIACE

NIACE: The National Organisation for Adult Learning is an independent advisory and development body promoting the interests of adult learners. NIACE works with national and local government, education providers, employers and the voluntary sector, and is active in research and development, publishing and conference organisation.

For further information, including a full list of current publications, please contact NIACE at:

21 De Montfort Street, Leicester LE1 7GE; tel 0116 255 1451.

00021912